Anti-Oppressive Practice in Health and Social Care

Anti-Oppressive Practice in Health and Social Care

Viola Nzira and Paul Williams

Los Angeles • London • New Delhi • Singapore • Washington DC

First published 2009

SAGE Publications Ltd
1 Oliver's Yard
55 City Road
London EC1Y 1SP

SAGE Publications Inc.
2455 Teller Road
Thousand Oaks, California 91320

SAGE Publications India Pvt Ltd
B 1/I 1 Mohan Cooperative Industrial Area
Mathura Road
New Delhi 110 044

SAGE Publications Asia-Pacific Pte Ltd
33 Pekin Street #02-01
Far East Square
Singapore 048763

Library of Congress Control Number: 20089203910

British Library Cataloguing in Publication data

A catalogue record for this book is available from the
British Library

ISBN 978-1-4129-2267-8
ISBN 978-1-4129-2268-5 (pbk)

Typeset by Cepha Imaging Pvt. Ltd, Bangalore, India
Printed in Great Britain by The Cromwell Press Ltd,
Trowbridge, Wiltshire
Printed on paper from sustainable resources

Contents

Preface

This book is intended for students training for qualifications for professions in health or social care, for example nurses, social workers, therapists or medical personnel. It is also likely to be useful for existing practitioners in these fields. It seeks to provide a foundation for knowledge and practice that is anti-oppressive. We hope that after reading this book, and perhaps engaging in further study relevant to their particular role and circumstances, readers will be able to develop a strategy that constitutes a holistic and comprehensive approach to preventing and tackling discrimination and oppression, in their personal relationships, within the organisations in which they learn or practise, and in the communities in which they live or work or have other activities.

While covering academic issues that need to be understood if anti-oppression is to be effective, this book is essentially practical in that we hope the reader will gain information and ideas to develop a strategy that will maximise their ability to prevent and tackle discrimination and oppression in all circumstances in which they may be encountered. This is particularly important in the health and social care field, where people come to us with difficulties that can only be made worse if negative discrimination or oppression is also experienced.

Structure of the book

The book is divided into four parts:

- **Part I** Concepts: Chapters 1 and 2
  useful concepts for anti-oppression
- **Part II** Organisations: Chapters 3, 4, 5 and 6
  implications for organisations, with emphasis on health and social care services
- **Part III** Individuals: Chapters 7, 8, 9 and 10
  development of anti-oppression by individuals, with emphasis on students in health and social care
- **Part IV** Reflection: Chapters 11 and 12
  developing continuous learning through reflection

Part I Concepts

Part I outlines concepts that are useful to understand in order to effectively pursue anti-oppression. An overview of discrimination and oppression is provided in Chapter 1, taking into account some significant historical world events that have shaped current thinking on issues of discrimination and oppression. The prevalence of oppression is highlighted, with examples from African, African-American and Jewish experiences. How such groups responded to acts of oppression, through direct challenges against the oppressors and a determination to be survivors and not victims, is recounted. It is suggested that we can learn from how oppressed people themselves have successfully challenged discrimination and overcome oppression. This chapter also introduces concepts of identity, social devaluation and power and their association with oppression, which are discussed in more detail in later chapters. Frameworks for tackling social devaluation are described as guides for the development of anti-oppressive practice. Exercises are provided within this and subsequent chapters to support individual learning and begin the process of reflective practice, a theme that runs through this book.

The exposition of the nature of discrimination and oppression is followed in Chapter 2 by a consideration of some concepts in common use in this field, in order to aid understanding, development and maintenance of anti-oppressive practice. The concepts are covered under the headings:

- community and culture
- power and empowerment
- equality and anti-oppression
- identity and relationships

Under each heading key concepts are used to provide a focus, and explanations are given as to how an understanding of meaning can support anti-oppressive practice. Some of the concepts from this chapter are developed further in subsequent chapters.

Part II Organisations

Anti-oppression can be developed and pursued at the political, social and cultural level, at the level of organisations, and at a personal individual level. Part II covers the political and ideological background and its implications for a commitment to anti-oppressive practice within organisations, particularly health and social care provision.

Chapter 3 examines the concept of equality from ideological and political perspectives to highlight possible influences on strategic developments. The influence of these ideological and political perspectives on professional practice is discussed. Drawing on the findings of the MacPherson Inquiry (1999) and the subsequent interpretation of institutional racism, a race equality paradigm is used to illustrate some of the difficulties that can be encountered when attempts are made to implement anti-oppressive practices within health and social care organisations, due to the different interpretations attached to race, racial identity, racial group and ethnicity. Reference to legislation is made with regard to how court rulings have influenced the creation of a working definition of a racial group. Examples are included to show how individual and institutional racism can operate. Interpretations of stereotypes and ethnicity are included to show the connections with racism. The importance of being knowledgeable about these areas is highlighted, so that practitioners can assess the impact of actions at individual or organisational levels and decide on remedial action so as to promote anti-oppressive practice. Exercises are given to encourage creativity in approaching equality issues.

Chapter 4 discusses in more detail ideas about equal opportunities. The arguments for equality are contrasted against natural tendencies towards inequality. An analysis of the distinction between liberal and radical conceptions of equal opportunities provides the reader with a basis from which to contextualise their own organisation. Some of the moral and legal reasons for equal opportunities are stated and summaries of current UK anti-discrimination laws are included within this chapter because they provide the framework for equal opportunities policy development. It is acknowledged that there has been some progress in adopting and implementing equal opportunities policies in health and social care, but the pace of change has remained slow. Health and social care practitioners can use the law to challenge discrimination as part of a package of measures to promote anti-oppressive practice. Commitment to implement their organisation's equal opportunities policy as part of their duty of care is emphasised within this chapter.

Chapter 5 discusses the importance of respecting and fostering diversity while recognising the complexities involved. A historical and chronological account of changes in terminologies used in relation to equal opportunities from the 1960s to the present day is provided to show the evolutionary nature of the process. Current emphasis is on work organisations being expected to create the conditions conducive to the management of a diverse workforce with diverse needs. Valuing diversity starts from the position that people's differences are an asset rather a burden to be tolerated, particularly in health and social care where the recipients of care come from diverse backgrounds. The business case for diversity management is stated. However, it is recognised that the change in management styles required to effect change could result in negative and destructive conflict. Lack of careful planning and incremental implementation could cause disruption. It is suggested that those practitioners who are ready to embrace the principles of anti-oppressive practice can become diversity champions and offer support to their colleagues.

In Chapter 6, the discussion focuses on minimalism in terms of meeting just the anti-discrimination minimum legal requirement, and the contrasting approaches in terms of taking an active stance to eliminate discrimination. With minimalism, the criticism is that the impact has been limited because the laws are not easy to enforce. People have to complain before action can be taken, and even then success rates remain low. What the legal framework offers is the opportunity for innovative employers to take proactive steps through specified action to redress identified imbalances. Explanations of positive action and positive discrimination are provided to ensure that the differences and the legal usage are understood. The more recent requirement of a statutory duty for public authorities to have in place equality schemes is explained, leading to consideration of the concept of mainstreaming equality. An integrated mainstreaming equalities approach would ensure that equality ideas become part of everyday practice. To get to that stage a practical incremental model – MPEM – is included for consideration and critique. Practical examples, exercises and discrimination case examples are also included in this chapter.

Part III   Individuals

Part III presents some frameworks and strategies for the development of a personal anti-oppressive stance by individuals, with examples largely taken from work with students on professional courses in health and social care. Chapter 7 discusses the wide variety of aspects that make up a person's identity as seen by themselves and by others. It is argued that building up a knowledge base about different identities can assist avoidance of stereotypes and engender respect. Researching accounts relating to a particular service user group and culture illustrates the positive characteristics, interests, skills and practices of that group. The importance of appreciating different languages and belief systems is highlighted. Additional knowledge of particular significance is that of understanding how individuals or groups have survived oppression as well as an appreciation of their contribution to society. Readers are encouraged not to be daunted by what they need to know so as to be anti-oppressive. Knowledge will always be limited, but developing and using specific information can be part of preparation ahead of meeting recipients of care, and it can lead to generalisable skills of anti-oppression.

The chapter describes a framework for anti-oppressive action that can be applied to any groups or individuals at risk of oppression – the WISE principles. The elements are:

- **W** = **W**elcome
- **I** = **I**mage
- **S** = **S**upport
- **E** = **E**mpowerment

The framework is intended to help students or practitioners to take a holistic approach in considering how to work in an anti-oppressive way during interaction with service users and colleagues. A systematic explanation is provided under each of the four elements that make up the framework to enable students to assess and appreciate possible implications for practice. It is recognised that, as with any model, there will be limitations. However, recognition of limitations is helpful as it enables students to begin to think of alternatives or additions to the framework.

Chapters 8 and 10 provide curriculum and assignment ideas to support students in developing their anti-oppressive knowledge base. Examples of students' research and assessed assignments have been included to illustrate the level of engagement over two years of a three-year social work degree programme. Students share their research findings with their peers as well as creating an evidence-based individual action plan for anti-oppressive practice. Students' work highlights the value of a holistic approach to anti-oppressive practice.

Application of theoretical knowledge is tested when students go out on practice placements. Fieldwork experience using social work practice placements as the main focus is discussed in Chapter 9. Specific areas covered include:

- assessment of suitability of the placement
- student preparation prior to going out on placement
- supervision while on placement
- monitoring and evaluation of the placement.

The process followed should enable the student to learn about anti-oppression before, during and after the placement and to put into effect knowledge gained and skills developed. Students are assessed on their ability to practise in an anti-oppressive way by skilled practice teachers, using guidelines from professional bodies such as the General Social Care Council. Included in the chapter are case examples of some of the complexities that can arise. Implementation of equal opportunities policy among placement agencies is discussed in order to illuminate further the gaps between equality theories and practice, as well as raising questions about suitability of placements to support students to practise in an anti-oppressive way. It is concluded that recognition by students of the gaps between equality theory and practice is invaluable, because it provides a basis for work with service users to identify ways of tackling organisational structural limitations.

Part IV   Reflection

Promoting anti-oppression at the cultural and structural levels as well as through personal interaction can be supported by continuous assessment and evaluation. This is the main focus of Chapter 11. Through a series of questions readers are encouraged to check and assess their own actions and the state of affairs within work organisations. The assessment and evaluation process can assist the discussion and understanding of essential aspects of knowledge and actions that can be taken within organisations, communities and society as a whole. Assessing anti-oppression within organisations is included as well as ideas about ways to be involved and be informed about communities. Cultural acceptability issues are also featured. Action at different levels and through a variety of agencies to promote anti-oppression is strongly recommended. Full recognition is made of the dangers inherent in fighting oppression.

Finally, Chapter 12 revisits some of the political and ideological issues that complicate the process of developing anti-oppressive practice. Approaches to resolving these issues are suggested, through reflection, involvement of and partnership with service users, and an incremental approach to change. Anti-oppressive practice is presented as a political task based on respect for the wide diversity of identities.

A brief note about terminology

We have adopted the convention, sometimes seen as controversial, of referring to 'Black people' with a capital 'B' while using a small 'w' to refer to 'white people'. Our rationale for this is that:

- it acknowledges the phenomenon of 'white privilege' discussed in Chapter 2
- it acts as a counter to the relatively negative connotations of 'black' compared with 'white' in the English language
- it recognises the social and political construction of the concept of 'Black people' in the context of both oppression and liberation
- in the context of the holistic approach to anti-oppression that we advocate and our wish to avoid any suggestion of a 'hierarchy' of oppressions, it nevertheless expresses our particular solidarity with people who are at risk of oppression based on skin colour or ethnic origin.

Main aim

The main message we aim to put across throughout this book is that anti-oppressive practice in health and social care is possible, despite the many perceived barriers at individual and organisational levels. Our intention is to assist and inspire students and practitioners to become creative in developing an anti-oppressive stance in work and life, with enjoyment and enthusiasm and without embarrassment or denial.

Viola Nzira
Paul Williams

Acknowledgements

This book emerges from almost twenty years of teaching modules on social justice and inclusion and social policy. Our style and approach to writing this book has been guided by what students taking these modules have found useful as well as their suggestions for improvement. We thank them for their feedback.

The book has also been informed by our personal experiences and our own learning. We see ourselves as on a journey towards anti-oppressive practice – a journey that never ends. We acknowledge all the help and support we received from a wide variety of sources along the way.

We would like to thank June Jackson, Manager of the Centre for Ethnic Minority Studies (CEMS) at Royal Holloway, University of London, for her ideas, support, directed reading and access to CEMS equalities research reports.

We would like to acknowledge the learning we have gained from colleagues at the University of Reading who have contributed to our understanding and teaching of social justice and anti-oppression, particularly Horace Lashley, Phil Mignot, Doug Badger, Nick Ashwell and Alison Cocks.

We are very grateful to the students who kindly gave their permission for the inclusion of extracts from their assignments (Chapters 8 and 10): Myrleene Beckford, Francesca Booth, Paul Brewster, Nalene Edwards, Kathryn Holman, Natasha Hutchings, Daniel Jones, Jane Lynch, Alison Miller, Matt Neads, Nikki Osborne, Laura Pitman, Louisa Stock and Maddie Willens.

We also thank Robert Elsie for his kind permission to reproduce the Albanian poem in Chapter 8, and Peggy McIntosh, Catherine Jones and the University of Reading for extracts from their publications.

Finally, our thanks are due to the reviewers and editors at SAGE for their encouragement and valuable advice.

Part I
Concepts

1

Introduction to Oppression and Anti-oppression

Aim

- To present a picture of the general nature of discrimination and oppression.
- To illustrate their seriousness and pervasiveness, throughout the world and throughout history.
- To present examples and frameworks for understanding oppression.
- To signpost positive thinking as an approach to anti-oppression.

Human societies all over the world, and at all times in history, have been very sensitive to differences – differences of gender, skin colour, size, strength, ability, place of origin, language, religion, political allegiance and so on. This has combined with a strong sense of 'belongingness' – defining Self and Other – and the possession of power, giving control over 'The Other'. The result has been stratification both within and between societies, with subjugation of the weak by the powerful, often by violent means. Philosophy, religion, art, science and wealth (what we might call 'civilisation') have served to some extent to culturalise and socialise people into more peaceful and tolerant lifestyles, yet this has been accompanied by ever more sophisticated means of exerting power over others. Human divisions are today as prevalent and powerful as ever. The gap between rich and poor in the world is ever widening. Wars and genocides are as frequent as ever.

Discrimination and oppression

The experience of those against whom power is exercised is often one of being discriminated against and oppressed. In this book we draw a distinction between discrimination and oppression. Discrimination relates to inequality and unfairness. Power is exerted over those who are seen as different in such a way that fewer opportunities, fewer resources, less protection and fewer rights are available to them than to more powerful or higher-status groups. Oppression goes even beyond this, to involve a lower evaluation of the worth of individuals or groups, a rejection of them, exclusion from valued social roles, and even a denial of their existence or right to exist.

Discrimination and oppression are associated with a number of traits of human beings towards those they perceive as different. There may be prejudice – negative beliefs about people, often based on stereotypes and myths, and certainly based on lack of understanding and empathy. There may be devaluation – beliefs and actions that reflect a lower valuation of an individual or group: a valuation as of less worth, less significance, less importance, of people to whom all sorts of things can be done that would not be acceptable to oneself. There may be neglect – deliberate or unintended – resulting in negative experiences and risk of harm to health, welfare and even life. There may be ignorance – through lack of interest, lack of effort, or simply lack of information – resulting in damaging or upsetting behaviour towards others, however unintended. And there may be perpetuation of inequality – due to self-interest, lack of motivation for justice, or feelings of powerlessness. Such human traits as these are likely to operate in combination, making the tackling of discrimination and oppression a very difficult task.

Ignorance and prejudice

An example of a combination of prejudice, devaluation and ignorance is illustrated by this quotation from the 1908 edition of *Chambers Encyclopaedia*, under the heading of 'Negroes':

> The disposition of the Negro is usually pacific and cheerful. He is not easily depressed by poverty or thoughts of the future. Content that his immediate wants are provided for, he rarely prepares for a distant contingency. Eminently gregarious in his instincts, he is usually to be found in certain streets and quarters of the town exclusively occupied by members of his own race. His interest in the past is weak, and few or no reminiscences of his ancestral languages, traditions, superstitions or usages have been retained. His religion is emotional and exerts but a moderate influence on his morality . . .
>
> Story-telling, singing and music are favourite diversions of the coloured population . . . They produce music of pleasant though not artistic character. No Negro composer . . . has attained celebrity. Their songs are . . . generally defective in prosody and without merit, being often little more than words strung together to carry an air . . .

> The Negro is . . . unwilling to make the necessary mental effort to obtain [education] . . . [After puberty] there supervenes a visible ascendancy of the appetites and emotions over the intellect, and an increasing indisposition to mental labour . . . It is a rare exception for one of them to undertake the studies requisite for a profession; and when one does, he is content with what is barely sufficient for its remunerative practice . . .
>
> Many thoughtful and learned men see in the increasing coloured population a standing menace to the institutions and culture of their country.

Given the same level of prejudice, devaluation and ignorance in relation to women (reflected, for example, in the male-oriented language in the above quotation), we can appreciate the struggle to overcome discrimination and oppression of someone like Condoleezza Rice, currently US Secretary of State, and her ancestors.

Condoleezza Rice was born into a 'negro' (it would now be called 'African-American') family in Birmingham, Alabama, in 1954. Her father, and her grandfather before him, were Presbyterian Church ministers. They lived in a middle-class, though predominantly Black, area of town. Condoleezza attended a segregated school for Black children only. She had plenty of experience of discrimination and oppression. In 1963 one of her closest friends was killed when white racists bombed a Baptist Church Sunday School for Black children. Her parents were strong believers in the value of education, and Condoleezza was brought up under their belief that white supremacy could only be overcome by Black people being 'twice as good'. Condoleezza excelled at languages and music. Her family moved to Denver, Colorado, in 1967 and Condoleezza attended a Catholic girl's school. At age 15 she enrolled in a music college with a view to becoming a concert pianist (she still gives occasional piano concerts). Not believing she was good enough to earn a living through music, she attended Denver University to study political science. She proved academically extremely able, obtaining her Bachelor's degree at age 19, her Master's degree at age 20, and a PhD at age 26. She specialised in international affairs and became fluent in Russian, as well as being able to communicate well in German, French and Spanish. She was appointed to an academic post at Stanford University, rising to Professor of Political Science and Provost (senior academic officer) of the University. In 1990 she was appointed principal adviser on the Soviet Union to President George Bush Senior. In 2000, she was appointed National Security Adviser by President George W. Bush, and in 2005 became US Secretary of State. (Biographical information from www.answers.com/topic/condoleezza-rice.)

Bias in history

One phenomenon that perpetuates prejudice and ignorance is the writing and teaching of history from a particular perspective. History is likely to be written and taught from the perspective of the dominant culture of the writer or teacher. Thus, for example, European history recounts the world explorations of Europeans: Cook, Columbus, Cabot, Marco Polo. This perspective is often called Eurocentric; it sees Europe as the central, dominant culture in the world. Unlikely in European historical accounts, at least until recent attempts to present global perspectives, are descriptions of world explorations by Africans (Karenga, 1993) or the Chinese (Menzies, 2002), for example. The tendency of different cultures to see themselves as the most important is reflected in geographical names: the term 'Mediterranean' means 'centre of the world', as does the word 'China' ('Zhonghua' in Chinese, meaning 'central country').

The telling of history from a particular dominant cultural perspective renders the contribution of people from other cultures invisible. We will give two examples of this, both involving the relegation of Black people to a lesser role than they deserve in accounts from a Eurocentric perspective.

Mary Seacole

Many British accounts of the early development of modern nursing practices derived from experience in the Crimean War place emphasis, usually sole emphasis, on the role of Florence Nightingale. Often omitted from mention is the equally valuable contribution in that context of a Black woman nurse, Mary Seacole.

Mary was born in Jamaica in 1805. Her mother ran a boarding house for injured soldiers, and taught Mary her basic nursing skills. Mary travelled widely to complement this knowledge, including visits to Britain. On one of these visits, in 1854, she asked the War Office if she could be sent as an army nurse to the Crimea so that she could work with wounded soldiers. This request was refused, but Mary financed her own travel to the Crimea where she established a 'British Hotel' providing accommodation for injured officers. From this base she would travel to the battlefield to tend to individual wounded soldiers on the spot. Amongst the fighting men she became as well known and respected as Florence Nightingale. Her reputation followed her on her return to Britain, and in 1857 a festival was held in her honour at which thousands of people contributed to a fund to support her. (Information from www.bbc.co.uk/history/historic_figures/seacole_mary.shtml. See also Robinson, 2005.)

Mary wrote an account of her life, recently re-published by Penguin (Seacole, 2005), though she still does not achieve the prominence of Florence Nightingale in accounts of nursing in the Crimean War. However, there is a Mary Seacole Centre for Nursing Practice at Thames Valley University, founded in 1998 by Professor Elizabeth Anionwu. She named it after Mary Seacole 'as so few people seemed to have heard about this amazing Jamaican woman and her enormous contributions to nursing soldiers in the Crimean war' (www.maryseacole.com).

The focus of the Centre is 'to enable the integration of a multi-ethnic philosophy into the process of nursing and midwifery recruitment, education, practice, management and research'.

Exercise

Have you ever heard of Mary Seacole? Find out about her life and contribution through the Internet, libraries or other sources.

The British slave trade

In 2007 Britain celebrated the 200th anniversary of the passing in Parliament of a Bill to end the British slave trade. William Wilberforce had given a speech in the House of Commons in 1789 which lasted four hours, passionately arguing the case for the abolition of the slave trade. It took him another 18 years to gain enough support for the Bill to be passed. There is no doubt that Wilberforce was the leader of the movement to achieve this, and that his actions were the most powerful and effective. He is certainly appreciated amongst Black people. There is a Wilberforce University for Black students in America, and a Wilberforce Institute for the Study of Slavery and Emancipation, based in Hull, whose patron is Archbishop Desmond Tutu from South Africa. However, the story is often told as if Black people, whether free or slaves or ex-slaves, played no significant role. Melvyn Bragg, for example, draws attention only to white British contributors to the anti-slavery movement:

> Elizabeth I had said that the slave trade would 'call down the vengeance of heaven', and there was a strain in English life and thought which was opposed to the slave trade from Elizabeth up to contemporaries of Wilberforce. William Paley, for instance, rejected slavery in his book *Principles of Moral and Political Philosophy*. Adam Smith, in *The Wealth of Nations*, condemned slavery for rather different reasons, as an inefficient system of production, as slaves had no prospect of owning property and were promised no incentive to work. (Bragg, 2006: 158)

Krise (1999) assembled an anthology of literature from the West Indies written between 1657 and 1777. This includes several anti-slavery pieces by Black writers, for example *A Speech Made by a Black of Guadeloupe* (1700) and *The Speech of Moses Bon Saam* (1735). Carretta (1996) similarly edited a collection of writings by Black authors in the eighteenth century. These include: *Narrative on the Uncommon Sufferings and Surprising Deliverance of*

Briton Hammon, a Negro Man; Thoughts and Sentiments on the Evil and Wicked Traffic of the Slavery and Commerce of the Human Species, Humbly Submitted to the Inhabitants of Great Britain by Ottabah Cugoano, a Native of Africa; and *The Interesting Narrative of the Life of Olaudah Equiano, the African, Written by Himself.* Thus we can see that behind the movement to abolish the British slave trade were many contributions by Black people.

Wilberforce was the spokesperson in Parliament for the Society for the Abolition of the Slave Trade, founded in 1787. A prominent member of this Society was a Black ex-slave, Olaudah Equiano, whose book *The Interesting Narrative* was published in 1789, the same year as Wilberforce's speech. The book is re-published by Penguin (Equiano, 2003). Equiano was kidnapped from Nigeria at age 11 and taken as a slave to Barbados. He was allowed by one of his various owners to trade and earn money, and he eventually saved enough to buy his freedom. He became a merchant seaman, based in London. He was active in the movement to abolish the slave trade, and after his book was published he travelled all over Britain talking about his experiences as a slave. His book was re-issued in nine editions between 1789 and 1794 and sold so many copies that it made Equiano a wealthy man. It had a major influence on the eventual abolition of the slave trade, but this is seldom mentioned in accounts of that achievement. For a biography of Equiano see Carretta (2007). There is an Equiano Society, formed in London in 1996, which aims to publicise and celebrate the achievements of Equiano and his other Black contemporaries.

Equiano particularly argued an economic case for the abolition of slavery, believing that the opening up of direct trade in manufactured goods with Africa would be much more lucrative than the subsidised plantations utilising slave labour in the Caribbean. He wrote:

The abolition of slavery would be in reality a universal good . . . Tortures, murder and every other imaginable barbarity and iniquity are practised upon the poor slaves with impunity. I hope the slave-trade will be abolished. I pray it may be an event at hand. The great body of manufacturers, uniting in the cause, will considerably facilitate and expedite it; and, as I have already stated, it is most substantially their interest and advantage, and as such the nation's at large (except those persons concerned in the manufacturing of neck-yokes, collars, chains, handcuffs, leg-bolts, drags, thumb screws, iron-muzzles, coffins, cats, scourges and other instruments of torture used in the slave trade). In a short time one sentiment alone will prevail, from motives of interest as well as justice and humanity. (Equiano, 2003: 234)

A rather different kind of influence on the abolition of the slave trade was rebellion by slaves themselves. Slaves were not all passive and resigned to their fate. Many rebelled against individual slave owners, and many escaped, resulting in some organised rebellions against slavery. Escaped slaves in the Caribbean were known as 'Maroons'. They set up several communities in places where discovery and attack were difficult. One such community was known as 'Nanny Town', situated in the Blue Mountains in Jamaica.

Its name derives from the fact that its leader was a woman, known as 'Nanny Maroon'. After escaping from slavery on a sugar plantation with her five brothers, Nanny organised the Blue Mountains community of Maroons. In the 1720s and 1730s, she led raids to free more slaves, and is said to have helped over 800 slaves to escape. Nanny Town was constantly attacked by British troops, but because of its location and the skill of the Maroons in resistance, the community survived, eventually being granted the right to their land and their freedom. Nanny acted as spiritual leader to the community and used an extensive knowledge of herbs to maintain the community's health. It is said that she organised the community along the lines of an Ashanti tribe in Africa. She was killed in a British attack on the community in the 1730s. Today, Nanny Maroon is regarded as a heroine of the struggle against slavery; her portrait is on the 500 Jamaican dollar bill (Gottlieb, 2000; see also http://en.wikipedia.org/wiki/Nanny_Maroon).

The fact of slave rebellions and the difficulty of destroying Maroon communities such as Nanny Town were additional factors in convincing Britain to abolish the slave trade.

Of course, in celebrating particular acts of abolition of slave trading, we should not be complacent in thinking that slavery has been abolished altogether. Baroness Caroline Cox in Britain has been an outspoken leader of campaigns against slavery in the present day. Her recent book *This Immoral Trade* contains detailed studies of slavery in Sudan, Uganda and Burma. The introduction to the book states:

> Slavery remains rampant worldwide, despite the celebrations surrounding the bicentenary of its abolition in Britain. At least 27 million men, women and children are enslaved today, ranging from prostitutes in London to indentured workers in Burma. (Cox and Marks, 2006: 1)

Exercise

Through the Internet, libraries or other resources, find out more about the lives and achievements of Olaudah Equiano and Nanny Maroon.

Oppression throughout history

One of the longest-standing historical (and current) examples of oppression through prejudice is that of Jewish people. Jews form less than 1 per cent of British society (fewer than half a million people), but discrimination and oppression against them is common, despite the major contribution they make to British business, social and cultural life. Indeed, it is so common that much of it goes unreported in the news media.

The *London Evening Standard* for 21 June 2004 reported that in the previous four years over 100 synagogues in Britain had been desecrated by vandals. Typical were these incidents:

In June 2004 a window of the South Tottenham Synagogue in London was smashed and burning rags were thrown inside. A large number of books were destroyed, including prayer books over 100 years old that had been smuggled out of Nazi Germany in the 1930s. Rabbi Michael Biberfeld said that some of the books were priceless, having been out of print since the war. He said: 'The people who saved them from the Nazis in 1938 risked their lives. For them to be destroyed is a tragic end.' Among the burnt books was a signed copy of a six-volume set of the Mishna Berura, a code of Jewish law written over 100 years ago. 'It was a very important devotional piece,' said Rabbi Biberfeld.

The following day, there was another arson attack on the UK headquarters of the Jewish educational body Aish Ha Torah in Hendon, London. The synagogue and offices were destroyed, causing £250,000 of damage. Again, many books and manuscripts were lost, including the life's work of several scholars and Rabbis based at the centre. Two handwritten scrolls of the Torah were ripped and desecrated. Rabbi Naftali Schiff, director of the Hendon centre, said: 'The desecration of Kristallnacht in 1938 is imprinted on the Jewish psyche of my generation, and seeing scrolls of the law torn and lying on the floor of my own synagogue in London is devastating. This mindless act of hatred and destruction rings yet another warning bell across the country to men and women of reason, tolerance and mutual respect to join together to ensure the flames of extremism and intolerance are not allowed to engulf these shores.'

(Information from Hopkirk, 2004)

'Kristallnacht', or the Night of Broken Glass, refers to events on the night of 9 November 1938. Rampaging mobs throughout Germany and the newly acquired territories of Austria and Sudetenland freely attacked Jews in the street, in their homes and at their places of work and worship. At least 96 Jews were killed and hundreds more injured, more than 1,000 synagogues were burned (and possibly as many as 2,000), almost 7,500 Jewish businesses were destroyed, cemeteries and schools were vandalised, and 30,000 Jews were arrested and sent to concentration camps. Immediately afterwards the Nazi government passed a law confiscating all insurance monies due for the damage caused. (Information from http://www.jewishvirtuallibrary.org/jsource/Holocaust/kristallnacht.html.)

Six million Jews were murdered by the Nazis during the Second World War, in labour camps such as Auschwitz, in special death camps such as Sobibor and Treblinka, and in their homes by special army battalions called Einsatzgruppen. Prior to this mass killing, Jews had been herded into huge ghettos: the Warsaw ghetto held almost half a million Jews, the Lodz ghetto 200,000. In a trial in Germany in 1970, Franz Stangl, Commandant of the Treblinka death camp in 1942 and 1943, was convicted of overseeing the deaths of 900,000 people.

Reading the history of the Jewish people, however, shows that nothing Hitler did had not been done before (Johnson, 1987; Ausubel, 1984). During the early part of their 3,000-year history, the Jews were a close-knit people who largely kept themselves to themselves, giving rise to the first expressions by others of anti-semitism. There is a record by a Greek writer around 300 BC (non-Christians may prefer the terms BCE – Before the Common Era – and CE – Common Era – rather than BC and AD) describing Jews as 'inhospitable and anti-human'. In 133 BC, another declared that Jews should be annihilated because they were the only people on earth who refused to associate with the rest of humanity. In 63 BC the Romans captured Jerusalem and Jews lived under Roman rule for the next century. In AD 19, the Roman Emperor Tiberius expelled all Jews from Rome. In AD 66 there was an uprising of Jews in Jerusalem against the repression of the Romans. The Romans completely destroyed Jerusalem. The Roman historian Tacitus recorded that 600,000 Jews were killed and over 500,000 captured and taken to Rome as slaves.

In AD 130, Emperor Hadrian decreed the banning of circumcision and the teaching of the Jewish holy text, the Torah. This led to a further rebellion of Jews, resulting in a four-year civil war in which 580,000 Jews were killed. One historical account talks of 'the blood of murdered women and children flowing for a mile like a turgid stream into the nearby sea' (quoted by Ausubel, 1984: 90).

Such events increased the process of dispersal of Jews to other parts of the world but, as Christianity spread, the Jews often became scapegoats for the ills of the societies in which they settled. For example, despite the major contribution of Jews to the establishment of the Moorish occupation of Spain between 800 and 1400 AD as one of the most advanced civilisations in the world, the defeat of the Moors and the ensuing inquisition led to widespread massacre of Jews and their expulsion from Spain (Perez, 2004). Even earlier, the 16,000 Jews living in England were expelled by Edward I in 1290 AD, and they were not allowed back until the time of Cromwell, 1656. Jews were banned from England for over 350 years.

In Germany, Jews were blamed for the Black Death in 1348 and almost all Jews in Germany were killed or fled east to Poland. They gradually returned but were subject to great prejudice. In 1543, Martin Luther published a pamphlet called 'On the Jews and Their Lies' in which he urged: 'their synagogues should be set on fire, and whatever is left should be buried in dirt so that no one may ever be able to see a stone or cinder of it' (quoted by Johnson, 1987: 242). He described Jews as 'poisonous envenomed worms'. In 1573 the Lutherans finally got their way, and Jews were banned from Germany altogether.

In 1516 in Italy it was decreed, not that Jews would be expelled from the country, but that they must live on an island off the coast in a Jews-only community, known as a 'ghetto'. Within it, there were very poor living conditions, massive overcrowding, poor employment opportunities, exploitation and slavery, and curfews preventing movement both inside and outside the ghetto. The basic idea was much older. Probably the first ghetto was established in Poland in 1266, where it was decreed that:

> lest the Christian people be infected with the superstition and depraved morals of the Jews living among them, we command that the Jews live apart in houses next to one another in a sequestered part of the city, separated from the dwellings of Christians by a hedge, wall or ditch. (quoted by Ausubel, 1984: 134)

Jews who had returned to Germany by the early 1700s were made to wear yellow badges to identify themselves. In many European countries, Jews were subject to special taxes, to restrictions on employment and education, and to bans on them writing or speaking in Hebrew. In Austria in 1787, Jews were compelled to change their Hebrew-sounding names and to buy new names. Names that were cheap were Weiss, Schwarz, Gross, Klein. More expensive were names of flowers or precious stones: Lilienthal, Edelstein, Diamant. Very poor Jews had offensive names given to them: Eselkopf (donkey-head), Schmalz (greasy), Borgenicht (thief).

By the mid-nineteenth century there was a large population of Jews in Russia, suffering widespread persecution. In 1881, Tzar Alexander III pushed through a government order encouraging the active killing of Jews – an activity that became known as a 'pogrom'.

So we can see that before the advent of Nazi Germany, there were well-established historical precedents for:

- Making Jews wear badges to identify them.
- Herding Jews into ghettos.
- Using Jews as slaves.
- Active government-sponsored pogroms to kill Jews.
- Expulsion of Jews from their communities.
- Mass ikilling of Jews thought to be a threat.
- Destruction of synagogues.
- Banning of expression of Jewish culture and language.

The Jews, however, are survivors rather than victims. The diaspora of Jews in all the major societies of the world continues to make a considerable contribution to the wealth, culture and social life of those countries (Ausubel, 1984).

Exercise

There are a large number of books about the Holocaust, as the murder, torture and enslavement of Jewish people in Nazi Germany is called. Try to find and read some first-hand accounts by people who survived or people who died but left records of their experience. Two collections of such accounts are Robertson (2000) and Joseph (2003), but there are many more.

The prevalence of oppression

The Jews are but one example of oppression in operation. Indeed, the Holocaust was but one of many genocides pursued in the twentieth century:

- *Turks against Armenians:* Between 1915 and 1923 over a million Armenians were killed by actions of the Ottoman government in Turkey (Dadrian, 1995).
- *Stalin against Ukrainians:* In 1932, 7 million people died in the Ukraine as a result of a famine deliberately created by the Stalin government (Mace, 1997).
- *Pakistan against Bengalis in Bangladesh:* At least 1 million people were killed by the Pakistan army in Bangladesh in 1971 after a popular uprising claiming independence; Bangladesh was formerly East Pakistan (Bhattacharyya, 1988).
- *The Khmer Rouge against Cambodians:* Over 2 million people were killed in Cambodia in 1975 by the Khmer Rouge under Pol Pot (Kiernan, 1996).
- *Hutus against Tutsis in Rwanda:* Up to 1 million people were killed in just ten weeks in Rwanda in 1994 (Des Forges, 1999).

and many more continuing up to the present day. And in Nazi Germany, the Jews were not the only, nor indeed the first, group to be targeted for elimination. The gas chambers were first invented to kill large numbers of people with learning difficulties, before the technology was developed for the mass killing of Jews (Williams, 2006).

The first gas chambers were developed by doctors, nurses and technicians within institutions for people with learning difficulties in Germany and Austria. Because of their experience, some of the nurses and administrators from these hospitals were later sent to design and supervise the setting up of the gas chambers in the death camps in Eastern Poland for exterminating the Jews. For example, Michael Hermann, formerly Chief Male Nurse at Hartheim Castle, an institution for people with learning difficulties in Austria, was sent to establish and run the gas chambers at Sobibor, one of the death camps for killing Jews in German-occupied Poland.

A statistical record found after the end of the war showed that over 70,000 people with learning difficulties or neurological conditions were killed. The gas chambers, situated inside former hospitals and asylums for disabled people, were disguised as shower rooms. A perforated gas pipe, fixed at a height of about a metre, went through the room. The pipe was connected with gas containers in the room next door. Carbon monoxide entered the room through the holes in the pipe. Up to 60 people were crowded into the 14-square-metre room which was locked by steel doors. Through a control window in the wall, the doctors and administrators watched the people die. It took several minutes before they were all dead. Afterwards, a fan extracted the gas from the gas chamber.

Death certificates were issued for the families, but the data on them about cause, time and place of death were false. (Information from www.chgs.umn.edu, website of the Center for Holocaust and Genocide Studies at the University of Minnesota, USA.)

It is chilling to recognise that the killings were administered by doctors and nurses who had previously cared for and treated the people. Other professionals, such as social workers, actively colluded in these events or at the least made little protest about what was happening (Kunstreich, 2003).

Contribution, survival and positive self-perception

In this book we stress the importance of studying the authentic first-hand experience of people themselves who have encountered oppression or are at risk of oppression. This is for several reasons.

First, we need to be appreciative of the efforts of people themselves to resist and overcome oppression. This helps us to see people not as helpless and needing pity, but as deserving of respect and admiration. It also avoids us giving sole credit for anti-oppressive reforms to 'rescuers' from more dominant groups, as in the example above of the abolition of the British slave trade.

As an example of self-contribution to anti-oppression, we can quote the achievements of women in the face of oppression in male-dominated societies. In ancient history there are many examples of women leaders, such as Boadicea and Cleopatra. Examples in the Middle Ages would include Hildegard of Bingen and Joan of Arc. Some more recent examples of achievement include (Jackson, 2007):

In 1883, Jane Stewart was the first woman to join the British Army (to lead a training school for army nurses).
In 1869, Elizabeth Blackwell became the first registered woman doctor in the UK.
In 1903, Marie Curie became the first woman recipient of the Nobel Prize.
In 1918, the suffragette movement achieved votes for women, though still only if they were over age 30.
In 1919, Lady Astor became the first woman MP.
In 1928, women achieved equal voting rights with men.
In 1929, Margaret Bondfield became the first woman government cabinet minister.
In 1953, Vijaya Pandit became the first woman President of the UN General Assembly.
In 1955, Barbara Mandell became the first woman news reader on television.
In 1958, Hilda Harding became the first woman bank manager in the UK.
In 1960, Sirimawo Bandaranaike became the world's first woman Prime Minister, in Sri Lanka.
In 1963, Valentina Tereshkova became the first woman in space.
In 1970, Annie Nightingale became the first woman radio DJ in Britain.
In 1972, women were admitted to the London Stock Exchange and were able to become professional jockeys.
In 1976, Mary Langdon became Britain's first woman firefighter.
In 1979, Margaret Thatcher became Britain's first woman Prime Minister.
In 1981, Baroness Young became the first woman leader of the House of Lords.
In 1988, Elizabeth Butler-Sloss became the first woman Appeal Court Judge.

In 1992, Betty Boothroyd became the first woman Speaker of the House of Commons.

In 1994, the first woman priests were ordained in the Church of England.

In 2007, Moira Cameron became the first woman Beefeater, guarding the Tower of London.

It seems intensely patronising to list these achievements of women, as if they should surprise or amaze us! Nevertheless, each one of those listed was achieved by the efforts of women themselves in the face of male-dominated conventions and much opposition by men in power.

Second, people who have experienced oppression directly often have a more positive and helpful perception of themselves than those whose views derive from the culture that has perpetuated the oppression. We can see an example in the Black American singer and actor Paul Robeson, born in 1898. One of his most famous songs, sung in his rich deep voice, is 'Old Man River'. This song was originally written by Jerome Kern and Oscar Hammerstein as part of the musical *Show Boat*, first produced in 1927. The original lyrics depicted Black Americans as down-trodden, pathetic people:

> There's an old man called the Mississippi,
> That's the old man that I'd like to be.
> What does he care if the world's got troubles?
> What does he care if the land ain't free?
>
> You and me, we sweat and strain,
> Body all aching and racked with pain.
> 'Tote that barge! Lift that bale!'
> Get a little drunk and you land in jail.
>
> I get weary and sick of trying,
> I'm tired of living and scared of dying,
> But Old Man River,
> He just keeps rolling along.

Robeson, however, changed the lyrics when he sang the song. The entry under 'Old Man River' in the Internet encyclopaedia Wikipedia (http://en.wikipedia.org) states:

The changes in Robeson's concert renditions of the song shift the portrayal of Joe away from a resigned and sad character who is susceptible to the forces of his world, to one who is timelessly empowered and able to persevere through even the most trying circumstances.

Here is Robeson's version of the verses above:

> There's an old man called the Mississippi,
> That's the old man I *don't* like to be.

What does he care if the world's got troubles?
What does he care if the land ain't free?

You and me, we sweat and strain,
Body all aching and racked with pain.
'Tote that barge! Lift that bale!'
You show a little grit and you land in jail.

But I keep laughing instead of crying,
I must keep fighting until I'm a-dying,
And Old Man River,
He'll just keep rolling along.

Exercise

Through the Internet, libraries or other resources, find out more about the life and achievements of Paul Robeson. If it interests you, find and listen to a recording of his singing. How do you think his singing related to his anti-oppressive beliefs?

There are examples amongst disabled people of this same process of replacing negative perceptions held by the dominant oppressive culture with positive imagery reflecting the positive characteristics and contribution of the people themselves. Judith Snow, a person with severe physical impairments, has written a paper called 'Giftedness versus Disability', contrasting her own life and needs with that of an Olympic athlete. She argues that her contribution to community can be as great, and that if she were seen as gifted instead of disabled the same level of support and resources might be provided. She concludes:

> The community is denied the talents, gifts, contributions and opportunities of all the people who are excluded. The answer is simple – see me as gifted, not as disabled. Throw away the concept of disability. Welcome the concept of giftedness. (Snow, 2007)

Ronald Davis wrote a book called *The Gift of Dyslexia* in which, as a person with dyslexia himself, he argues that people with dyslexia have special talents – in thinking non-verbally, in intuition and awareness, in multi-dimensional thought processes, in creativity, in curiosity, and in special mastery of skills that are learned (Davis, 1997).

Resisting the perception of you by the dominant culture is not easy, and it takes assertiveness and courage to proclaim your different valuation of yourself. Caiseal Mor (2007) writes about his autism under the title *A Blessing and a Curse*. His own view, however, is made clear:

In my humble opinion autism is a wondrous gift – a blessing of sorts. As far as I'm concerned, autistic benefits far outstrip any drawbacks you can imagine. But it's taken me a lifetime of self-examination and inquiry to arrive at that conclusion. (Mor, 2007: 9)

The relativity (or 'social construction') of perceptions of disability as necessarily negative is well brought out by Vic Finkelstein (1981). He wrote a story about a community of disabled people who used wheelchairs. Their houses had low ceilings and doors. Able-bodied people who visited or came to live there often bumped their heads and suffered with painful backache because they always had to stoop. They were prescribed helmets and body-braces by the community's doctors. They had problems gaining employment or appearing on television because they looked odd doubled-up and they had difficulty making eye contact. Charities were set up to raise money for them. Eventually they started a pressure group to improve conditions for themselves, whereupon they were said to have a chip on their shoulder and to be unable to accept and come to terms with their condition!

A third product we can derive from authentic first-hand accounts is a perception of people as survivors rather than victims. This helps us in health and social care services to see ourselves as working in partnership with people to meet their needs in an empowering and anti-oppressive way. There are many accounts of the survival of people through often extreme oppressive circumstances. Some examples are:

- Anonymous (2005) *A Woman in Berlin*
  The diary of a German woman in Berlin after its liberation by the Russian Army in 1945. Subject to great cruelty and oppression, including repeated rape, she describes her survival strategy, achieved through great courage and resilience.

- Jean-Dominique Bauby (1998) *The Diving Bell and the Butterfly*
  This is an account by a disabled person severely impaired following a stroke. His body felt like a diving-bell but his mind was still like a butterfly. He dictated this book over several years by indicating words and letters by blinking one eye.

- Quentin Crisp (1996) *The Naked Civil Servant*
  The autobiography of a gay man, telling of his survival strategies during a time when he wished to proclaim his sexual orientation but when homosexual behaviour between men was illegal. He had a job as a model in an art college. The college was supported by the government and he often had to pose nude: hence he described himself as 'a naked civil servant'.

- Nelson Mandela (1994) *Long Walk to Freedom*
  The autobiography of the African National Congress leader who survived racist oppression and a long term of imprisonment to emerge as head of the post-Apartheid South African government and a highly respected international statesman.

- Bob Turney (1997) *I'm Still Standing*
  The remarkable story of a man who survived almost twenty years in prison, and dyslexia, to qualify as a social worker, write a book, and become a family man and an advocate for young people at risk of offending.

- Donna Williams (1998) *Nobody Nowhere*
  One of the first autobiographies of a person with autism or Asperger's syndrome, in which she describes her experiences as well as gives advice on understanding autistic people. There have since been several other autobiographies published by people with autism, including that by Mor (2007) mentioned above.

Exercise

Find one of these books, or a similar autobiography by a person who has experienced oppression. Try to find time to read it. As you do so, make notes on what you learn about the author's strategies for survival. What can you learn about strategies for yourself to apply anti-oppressive practice?

Levels of oppression and discrimination

Neil Thompson (1993) has provided a model of the operation of forces of discrimination and oppression at three levels. The model is known as PCS. **P** stands for the personal or psychological level. It refers to the personal interactions of people, the thoughts, beliefs and actions of individuals, and the values, stereotypes and prejudices that individuals hold about others. **C** is the cultural level, the pattern of communal values and behaviours resulting from consensus and conformity within a particular society or culture. **S** is the structural level, the way in which power and resources are used in society to maintain or tackle divisions. The **P**, **C** and **S** levels interact to maintain and influence each other.

Critiques of Thompson's model (for example Payne, 2005) have questioned the links implied by Thompson between personal actions, culture and structure. Nevertheless, it is helpful to consider oppression operating at these three levels. It can be argued that the direction of influence between the personal, cultural and structural can differ in different situations.

For example, we can examine the influence of these factors in Rwanda, leading up to the terrible genocide of people identified as Tutsi by those seeking to retain the power of those identified as Hutu (Des Forges, 1999; African Rights, 1995). There was a very tight structure of communication and command between government and people. This structure was used to distribute weapons to local Hutu militia groups. Propaganda by the Hutu-dominated government had begun to portray Tutsi people as a danger to Rwandan society. This was reinforced by the media, with radio broadcasts and news-papers describing Tutsis as 'cockroaches' and 'snakes'. Thus, a culture was built up of hatred and suspicion of Tutsis. The trigger for the genocide was the appar-ent assassination of the Rwandan president, a Hutu. Despite Hutus and Tutsis having led peaceful lives as neighbours in villages without much personal animosity, structure and culture came together to influence ordinary Hutu people to turn on their Tutsi neighbours and join in government-sponsored attacks. Almost a million people were killed in just ten weeks.

We can see here the influence of structure and culture on personal actions, but there are situations in which it might be argued that the influ-ence is in the other direction. Initial government action to combat HIV/AIDS in Britain was to circulate every household with an alarmist leaflet warning of danger. Meanwhile there were few or no specialist struc-tures for the prevention or treatment of HIV/AIDS. The media presented HIV/AIDS as primarily associated with gay sex. Thus, both structure and culture contained elements likely to be experienced as oppressive by people in need. It was friends and families of people with HIV/AIDS, organisations representing the gay community where HIV/AIDS was initially most preva-lent, and individual advocates for people with HIV/AIDS such as Princess Diana, who took a more responsible and responsive stance and pressed for the development of specialist facilities and an end to negative and discrim-inatory perceptions of people with HIV/AIDS. (See the website of the Terence Higgins Trust, www.tht.org.uk; for an account of a similar process in South Africa, see Walker, 2007.) Today we have a much more balanced and helpful perception of people with HIV/AIDS and their needs, and although discrimination and oppression are still found, they are much reduced. Specialist diagnostic, treatment and care services are more devel-oped, and research into prevention is supported. It can be argued here that personal actions influenced culture and structure.

The useful point represented by Thompson's model is that oppression operates at different levels, and hence anti-oppression must also operate at those different levels to be effective. Anti-oppressive action at the personal level is likely to be easier to achieve than action at a wider cultural or struc-tural level. Many strategies for anti-oppressive practice have concentrated on the personal level, as indeed does much of this book. However, some writers have been very critical of this approach. For example, Ashrif says of the strategy of 'raising awareness':

Racism was divorced from structures and procedures and instead was confined to the white psyche. Race Awareness Training distorted the language and analyses of the Black movement such that racism was severed from its exploitative nature and rendered classless. Racism had been viewed as a psychological problem suffered by white people. (Ashrif, 2002)

Ashrif presents an alternative 'activist' approach, involving challenging power structures, oppressive institutions and gender and class inequalities.

We hope in this book to present some strategies for both a personal and a wider cultural and structural activist approach.

Summary

- Discrimination relates primarily to unfairness, inequality and injustice.
- Oppression may go further and involve a low valuation of a person's worth that may put them in danger of rejection, harm or even death.
- There are many examples of oppression throughout history and throughout the world.
- Authentic accounts of people who have experienced or are at risk of oppression can engender respect and indicate components of effective anti-oppression.
- Positive thinking helps the development of anti-oppression.
- Oppression operates at different levels, so anti-oppression must too.

2

Useful Concepts in Anti-oppression

Aim

- To introduce a number of concepts, understanding of which can help the development and maintenance of anti-oppressive practice.
- To discuss briefly each topic, under the headings Community and culture, Power and empowerment, Equality and anti-oppression, and Identity and relationships.

Community and culture

Under this heading we will present commentary on these topics: Diversity, Culture, Cultural competence, Multi-culturalism, Competent community, Inclusion and exclusion, Integration, Participation, and Community action.

Diversity

Diversity refers to the presence of a wide variety of identity characteristics amongst the people in a particular community: old and young, big and small, from a wide variety of ethnic groups, representing different religions, from all classes, disabled and non-disabled, with a wide range of lifestyles and political beliefs, of different sexual orientations, and in a range of parental and family roles. Diverse communities offer opportunities for a wide range of experiences and relationships amongst members, fostering understanding and removing stereotypes and prejudice. Sometimes, however, they are seen as diluting the 'culture' of particular groups, and this may be viewed as undesirable by some community members.

The opposite of a diverse community is a closed community, where the community is built around one identity within a category, to the exclusion of other identities within that category: for example, older people only, disabled people only, rich people only, Jews only. Communities may be closed by choice, as with some communities for older people in America; or they may be forced on people, as with ghettos for Jews or institutions for disabled people.

Closed communities may preserve and strengthen a particular 'culture', but they reduce the experiences available to members, and they may be very vulnerable to misunderstanding, prejudice, oppression and even attack from those outside. Miller and Gwyne (1972) describe the effect of institutional care for disabled people as their 'social death'.

Culture

Culture refers to the traditions, beliefs, patterns of behaviour and creative productions of a particular identity group, particularly those that are considered important by that group. A concept of 'culture' can be developed for any identity group, not just those relating to ethnicity, nationality or religion. By researching the beliefs, behaviours and creations of any group that are important to that group, we can gain a picture of what can be called the 'culture' of that group (for a light-hearted example see Fox, 2004). A good way to explore this is to find an organisation, self-help group or internet website that represents an identity group. The actions of the group, or the content of the website, will provide useful leads into the 'culture' of the group. This can be done for groups representing different ages, different life experiences (for example, ex-offenders or survivors of domestic violence), different disability or health status groups, different genders, different life conditions (for example poor, homeless, refugees, asylum seekers), different lifestyles (for example travellers, students), of different economic and social classes, people of different parental status (for example fathers, lone parents), different political ideologies, different ethnic groups, different religions, different sexual orientations or identities, different sizes (exceptionally large, tall or short).

Cultural competence

This refers to the ability of an individual or an organisation to acquire sufficient knowledge of the culture of diverse groups to increase tolerance, understanding and acceptance and to reduce stereotypes, misunderstandings and prejudice (Pope-Davis et al., 2003). In a health and social care context, where the aim is not just to accept people but also to help and support them, such knowledge can have the additional function of ensuring that support is provided in a culturally sensitive and respectful way. For example, attention can be paid to provision of appropriate food, appropriate care of hair and skin, use of appropriate modes of greeting, arrangements for practice of religion, welcoming of traditional modes of dress, and so on (O'Hagan, 2001; Asamoah, 1996).

Multi-culturalism

At one level, multi-culturalism merely refers to the co-existence of different cultures in a particular community or society. However, an important additional element that is often striven for is equality of acceptance and respect. In many societies, though, there is a historically and traditionally dominant culture. Some members of that culture may feel that multi-culturalism risks dilution or even loss of important elements of that traditional culture. This in turn may lead to attempts to impose elements of the dominant culture on members of other groups, who may feel oppressed as a result and may become isolated from mainstream society.

In recent years the apparent effects of multi-culturalism in Britain have been heavily criticised. Even Trevor Phillips, at the time Chair of the Commission for Racial Equality, gave a speech in 2004 advocating dropping use of the term 'multi-culturalism' and replacing it with discourses about integration and a unified national culture. This view is argued in detail by West, who says: 'Far from promoting integration and inclusion, multi-culturalism has done nothing except encourage separatism and strife' (2005: 45).

However, a more balanced view, emphasising the benefits of a multi-cultural approach within a framework of national values, is presented by Madood (2007).

Competent community

The concept of a competent community refers to one that is able to include and cater for all the needs of a wide variety of identity groups – ideally all identity groups (Iscoe, 1974). The concept was particularly developed in relation to avoiding the exclusion from local communities of disabled people, because of a failure of communities to establish the means of meeting their needs, for example for care, education, leisure, work or social life. The principle underlying the notion of the competent community is that education, health, social, economic and support services should be available locally so that the needs of all people can be met within the local area

(Kretzmann and McKnight, 1993). In the context of anti-oppressive practice, this principle can be extended to include the ability to provide all
these things for people of all identities – old and young, big and small,
from all ethnic groups and religions, of both genders and all sexual orientations, of all economic and social classes, disabled and non-disabled, and
so on.

A related concept is that of 'social capital' (Field, 2002) in which the
strengthening of networks and relationships within communities is linked
to increased competence and achievement of that community.

Inclusion and exclusion

The essence of oppression is enforced exclusion from desirable opportunities and experiences. Correspondingly, the essence of anti-oppression is
inclusion. We have to include the proviso of enforcement in exclusion for
it to constitute oppression, since some people or groups may wish to
exclude themselves, with all the risks that that may entail. Voluntary
exclusion is not necessarily a good idea, but it does not constitute oppression. However, involuntary exclusion can happen in a variety of ways.
There need not be any explicit rules or pressures that exclude people,
though those may certainly operate, as can be seen in the history of the
Jews recounted in Chapter 1. There may be much more subtle influences
that keep people out of opportunities or certain social relationships or
economic settings. An example is the 'glass ceiling' experienced by women,
disabled people or working-class people in work settings, where overt
policy may purport to encourage equality in seeking promotion to senior
posts, but in practice there are limits to the progress that is actually made
by members of those groups (Cabinet Office Strategy Unit, 2003; Women
and Work Commission, 2007; for an international perspective
see Society for Human Resource Management, 2007). Another example
would be the relatively low representation of ethnic minorities in financial
institutions in the City, in parliament, in the police and in academia
(Tackey et al., 2001).

Genuine inclusion requires awareness and positive action by those with
the power to influence situations, and commitment to attitude change
amongst those with privileged status in relation to inclusion.

Integration

This refers to a situation where not only is there inclusion of different identity groups through policies of equal opportunities, but there are supportive contacts and good relationships between different groups in practice –
in housing, in work, in education, in health facilities, in leisure and social
settings.

Participation

This concept takes anti-oppression even further by expecting not just integration in the sense of physical presence, but actual participation in equal proportions and with equal effect. Thus we would expect people from ethnic minorities, disabled people, gay people, people of all classes, men and women, young and old, in numbers equal to their proportion in the community, to be using local facilities, to be voting in elections, to be achieving academic or professional qualifications, to be benefiting from education and health resources, to be using leisure facilities, and so on. If members of particular identity groups are not participating as we would expect, the reasons need to be explored and the situation remedied. This may require better information, active policies of inclusion and welcome and support, and avoidance of any subtle or not-so-subtle forces of exclusion.

Community action

Communities operate through networks of relationships, usually including many special-interest groups of community members. These groups may facilitate interests and 'culture' through catering for particular identity groups. Other groups may be concerned with more general issues. Community groups may operate in ways that exacerbate social divisions, or they may greatly help anti-oppression by encouraging inclusion and participation. Each such network or group needs to ensure that it is not, intentionally or unintentionally, excluding people on irrelevant criteria. This does not mean that every group has to accept everyone. It is quite right that, for example, a women's group would not accept male members, or a Christian fellowship would not accept members who are not committed Christians. However, one would hope to see in each group an acceptable proportion of ethnic minority members, or gay members, or working-class members, or disabled members, and so on. When community groups develop cultural competence, the way is open to the achievement of a competent community.

Power and empowerment

In this section we will cover the concepts of Power, Empowerment, Choice and freedom, 'Political correctness', and Advocacy.

Power

Power is a rather elusive concept. Often it is easier to see power when it is directed, or potentially directed, against you than it is when you possess it.

For example, as lecturers we do not, unless we wish to be particularly conscious of the issue, see ourselves as exerting power over our students. Rather we see ourselves as facilitators of learning and as imparting our knowledge in order to help them for their future. Students, however, often see lecturers as wielders of great power – power to determine what is learned, power of selection, power of assessment, power of discipline, power in giving references, and so on.

We all have power in some aspects of our lives (Haugaard, 2002). The first step in anti-oppression is to recognise the areas of power that we have, and commit ourselves to use it for the benefit of people and not to oppress them. Oppression is often the result of powerful people or social forces exerting power over the weak. Sometimes it is the majority exerting power over a minority, using the power of numbers. Sometimes minorities gain power over much larger majorities, as for example in the era of apartheid in South Africa.

Human beings love power, and any threats to their power may result in violent actions to retain it. Many genocides, including the Holocaust of the Jews in World War II, have resulted from a belief that a group constitutes a threat to those in power.

It cannot be suggested that we do not need power. Anti-oppression requires power to enforce positive anti-oppressive policies. Power is the engine that drives both oppression and anti-oppression (Adams, 2003; Thompson, 2006). However, in seeking anti-oppression, we are perhaps more likely to deliberately decide not to use our power, than if we think others deserve to be oppressed, or if we are unconscious of the issue.

Empowerment

Empowerment involves addressing the imbalance of power between groups in society. In order to achieve a true balance, it is necessary not only for a relatively powerless group to be given more influence, but for those in a position of power to give up some of that power. The latter goes against human nature and so is inherently unlikely to happen, though there are some mechanisms to encourage it that have been developed by those with higher ideals, for example democracy and the establishment of human and legal rights.

The usual route to empowerment is through disempowered groups, through their own actions, demanding and securing empowerment. Women have become more empowered through the suffragette movement and later the feminist movement. Disabled people have become more empowered through the disability rights movement. Black people have become more empowered through the struggle for civil rights and anti-discrimination legislation.

Even when weaker groups in society achieve a certain degree of empowerment, the extent is often still controlled by a more powerful social group, and credit for the 'gift' of empowerment is claimed by those in power. As we saw in Chapter 1, the emancipation of Black slaves is historically claimed by white activists rather than being credited to the efforts of Black people themselves. Disability rights legislation, race relations legislation, and even equal opportunities legislation to give women more rights, were enacted by the gracious permission of non-disabled, mainly male, almost entirely white legislators, after long and painful protest by the recipients themselves.

Choice and freedom

A major consequence of others having power over you is a loss of choice and freedom. Correspondingly, a major element in anti-oppression is ensuring that people have choice and freedom. Personal autonomy is nowadays taken as the highest human value in much of Western philo- sophical ethics, with major implications for health and social care services (Brazier, 1991; Gillon, 1986).

However, a number of qualifying points can be made about choice and freedom. First, the way they are exercised is likely to be strongly influenced by past experience. If people's lives have been very restricted and their experience of choice very limited, the knowledge basis of their choices may be inadequate. In other words, their choices may not be in their best inter- ests. It is, of course, an arrogant assumption for one person to claim they know better than the person themselves what is in their interests. Nevertheless, it may be true – particularly in the case of children, vulnera- ble adults, or people who exhibit anti-social behaviour.

Second, loss of choice and freedom is not the only component of oppres- sion, and for some people remedying other components may have greater priority. Enforced exclusion, enforced denial of access to education, health or relationships, being de-skilled, or being treated in a demeaning and disrespectful way, are other components of oppression. Remedying them for particular individuals or groups in certain circumstances may justify some coercion to achieve 'best interests'.

'Political correctness'

The term 'political correctness' is now used almost always in a negative, mocking way to describe some event that the speaker considers bizarre or excessive as a remedy for an alleged wrong or injustice. (See for example Browne, 2006 and Philpot, 2000.) Indeed, in researching for this book, we could not find a single reference presenting political correctness in positive terms.

However, it is worth considering the origins of the term. The word 'polit- ical' refers to struggles to gain power and influence. 'Political correctness' was originally an attempt to give greater power and influence to disadvantaged or relatively powerless groups to determine their experiences. Thus, for example, the language used to refer to a group might have been solely determined by others, and might not convey respect for the group. Those who wish to avoid oppression of the group would do well to ask members of the group what language they would be happier with, and to adopt that language themselves. This principle, of asking the people themselves what they prefer and acting on the reply, can be extended into many other areas, of rights, relationships, housing, work, education, health, social care, and so on. True 'political correctness' redresses the imbalance of power and influence between groups in society. A good example would be the design of environments to ensure accessibility for disabled people, especially as a result of involving disabled people themselves in that design.

As an example of an attempt to find a 'middle way' between the excesses of political correctness and a total rejection of it, here is the statement on language that has been included in student handbooks on social work courses at Reading University:

POLICY STATEMENT ON ANTI-DISCRIMINATORY LANGUAGE

It is expected that everyone concerned with the programme – tutors, practice teachers and students – will be engaged in a creative search for language that helps to reduce discrimination and oppression. Students will be expected to show evidence throughout their involvement in the programme that they are engaged in this search. At the very least, there will be avoidance of language that is clearly abusive, insensitive or well known to be discriminatory and unacceptable.

Over and above this, there should be an active process of considering the appropriateness of the language we use. As well as their dictionary meaning, words may have positive or negative image connotations inherent in their meaning or origin, or acquired through common or historical usage. Also, the people to whom a particular word refers may have expressed dislike of it, or may have actively adopted it as a group for political purposes.

Decisions about the appropriateness or acceptability of words will depend on the relative importance given to communicating with others through the accepted meaning of the word, avoidance of the negative connotations or imagery associated with the word, and following the wishes of the people to whom the word refers. Often, the wish to support the empowerment of people who have had little control over what happens to them in society, will lead to prominence being given to the expressed preferences of those people. However, this may sometimes hamper accurate communication, or the people themselves may not have expressed a view, may not have a consistent or agreed position, or may be unaware themselves of some of the connotations of words.

The words we use should not simply reflect personal opinion or preference. We should strive to be able to justify the words we use by arguments that reflect our thinking about the above considerations. Within this context, and with the recognition that some words will always be unacceptable because of their widely recognised offensiveness, the requirement of the programme is for evidence of the process of thinking about the development of personal and institutional language, rather than adherence to a prescribed list of particular words considered 'acceptable' or 'correct'.

However, we should recognise that others are further ahead on the journey than we are, and their thoughts and conclusions are worthy of study and possibly emulation. The programme therefore undertakes to provide students, practice teachers and tutors with papers to aid discussion and decisions about language.

Advocacy

Advocacy is the representation of a need or an idea, either by a person or group on behalf of themselves, or by someone or an organisation on behalf of another person or group. Advocacy is allied to political action, since it usually involves seeking greater influence in decision-taking. However, it can involve other actions, such as helping people to integrate and participate in community life. Self-advocacy by disadvantaged groups, and advocacy on their behalf by others, can be vehicles through which injustices can become better recognised, people can become more involved, respected and included, and remedies found for oppression suffered.

There are many different kinds of advocacy, and any of them can be useful in particular circumstances. It is often best if different forms of advocacy can work together. Each form of advocacy has its strengths and limitations, as indicated in Table 2.1.

The role of human service professionals is likely to involve an element of advocacy on behalf of those they support (Coulshed and Orme, 2006; Payne, 1997; Bateman, 2000; Brandon and Brandon, 2001; Brandon, 1995; Gray and Jackson, 2002).

Equality and anti-oppression

This section covers the concepts of Equality, Social justice, Discrimination, Restoration, Privilege, Social devaluation, Oppression, and Rights.

Equality

It is remarkable that, despite the centrality of the notion of equality in anti-discrimination and anti-oppression, very few people believe in it or practise it. Human beings are naturally competitive, always striving to be unequal. Hierarchical structures abound, in society as a whole, in nearly all organisations, in local communities, and even in families.

Table 2.1 Advocacy

Type of advocacy	Example	Strengths	Limitations
Paid advocacy	Solicitor	Expertise, especially on legal rights; powerful representation.	Costly; often an unnecessarily 'heavy' response.
Advocacy as part of a professional role	Social worker; nurse	Influence within services; time allocated as part of job; experience and knowledge of needs.	Usually working with more than one person, so attention limited that can be given to individuals; bound by conditions of employment; possible conflict of interest, e.g. if a person needs help to complain about colleagues or employers.
Advocacy by an organisation on behalf of a group	Mencap; Royal National Institute for the Deaf; Age Concern	Expertise; power deriving from membership; influence on national policy.	Usually concerned with general rather than individual issues.
'Formal' problem-oriented advocacy	Ombudsman; Citizens' Advice Bureau; local councillor; MP; patient advice (PALS)	Formal or legal basis; independence; authority by virtue of role.	Often oriented towards complaints or specific problems.
'Informal' single issue unpaid advocacy	Crisis or instrumental, outcome-oriented Citizen Advocacy	Flexible; informal; expression of citizenship and social capital; minimises conflict of interest since unpaid and voluntary.	Concerned with single issues rather than long-term needs.
'Informal' long-term unpaid advocacy	Relationship-based Citizen Advocacy partnerships; advocacy by family and friends	Same as informal single issue unpaid advocacy, plus: long-term; relationship-based; protective as well as empowering.	Great trust required that the relationship will pursue the person's best interests.
Self-advocacy by individuals on their own behalf	Creative arts; taking part in own reviews; expressing wishes; involvement in person-centred planning	Empowering; ensures relevance; participatory; enhances self-esteem.	Lacks power; depends on adequate support.
Self-advocacy by a group on behalf of its members	People First; National Pensioners Convention; British Council of Disabled People	Gives a voice to the otherwise unheard; expression of basic rights; supportive to members.	Likely to be concerned with general rather than individual issues; depends on financial and advisory support for success.
Advocacy by individuals on behalf of a group	Elected representatives; Partnership Board; Advisory panels	Contribution of relevant views; expression of democratic participation and rights.	Individuals may not be representative; views expressed may not be those of the group as a whole.

Source: Williams, 2006

In economics, we may have a concept of 'equal pay for equal work', but what constitutes 'equal work' is riddled with assumptions about the worth of people that rest entirely on acceptance of inequality. John Cole, former BBC correspondent, pointed out in a recent radio broadcast that chief executives of companies can earn up to 120 times the salary of their employees. And the concept of 'equal pay' only applies within a particular society. While the average wage in Britain is around £25,000 a year, that in Bangladesh is around £400 a year, and that in some African countries even less. These gaps are getting larger, not smaller. If we believed in and sought economic equality in the world, then we would accept that, unless we use up the world's resources at an even greater rate than at present, North America, Europe and Japan would have to become much poorer, and China and India would have to curb their current growth, in order to allow Africa and South America to catch up. Without this, the slogan 'make poverty history' is tokenistic. Yet voluntarily becoming poorer is not on the agenda of any government, think-tank, organisation or academic institution anywhere in the Western world (Barry, 2005).

Without equality of resources, it is difficult for people to achieve equality in other aspects of life. Nevertheless, some attempts to achieve equality in narrower fields outside the issue of global economics can be approached through the other concepts considered here (Thompson, 2003b). We devote the next chapters of this book to analysis of concepts of equality and their implications in health and social care.

Social justice

Justice in a legal context is concerned with 'just deserts' – what people deserve according to their observation of, or transgression against, agreed laws and constraints in society. Contained within this notion of justice is the idea of fairness, for example that the punishment should fit the crime, and that legal processes should be followed impartially (Rawls, 2005). The concept of 'social justice' extends this commitment to fairness into other aspects of social life – education, health care, social care, access to benefits, and so on (Hurley, 2005). Fairness means that no one should be excluded from access to or benefiting from an available resource for reasons that are irrelevant to the purpose of that resource. At least debate and negotiation, and in many cases political action, has to take place to determine what is 'irrelevant' in particular circumstances. Skin colour, gender, disability, sexual orientation, age, social class, have all been considered relevant in all sorts of human endeavours and social structures, until political action – nearly always by groups representing people with the excluded characteristics – has determined that they are not (Pearce and Paxton, 2005; Wilkinson, 2005).

Discrimination

Negative stereotyped beliefs about people with certain characteristics in the categories just mentioned – skin colour, gender and so on – constitute prejudice. Where prejudice occurs in those with power to exclude, negative discrimination is likely to occur. Discrimination will be characterised by experiences of unfairness by individuals, by denial of opportunities, and by under-representation of people with particular characteristics. Anti-discrimination legislation establishes structures to allow individuals to have the fairness of their experiences, opportunities and representation judged against criteria of relevance, and for appropriate remedies to be available.

Discrimination can also arise through ignorance. For example, an organisation may be unaware of aids available to support disabled people, or how to provide information that will reach and be appropriate for ethnic minorities.

The MacPherson Report (1999) into the killing of Stephen Lawrence gave recognition to the phenomenon of 'institutional discrimination'. This is where a whole organisation operates in such a way as to discriminate against certain people or groups, because of inbuilt organisational structures and assumptions. This phenomenon can still exist, even where most or all of the individuals in the organisation are committed to anti-discrimination. In the case of Stephen Lawrence, the cause of blunders was not so much racism by individual officers as an assumption by the whole Metropolitan Police Force that Black people were more likely than white people to commit crime. This led to the initial arrest of Stephen's Black friend at the scene, while the gang of white killers got away. (See also Law et al., 2004.)

Institutional discrimination can be seen in many education, health and social care agencies, leading to less good treatment of disabled people and poor people, for example – even if this is completely unintended by any one individual in the whole agency.

Restoration

Within the legal concept of 'justice' there is the idea of 'restoration', whereby the balance of harm and benefit between offender and victim is addressed by making the offender compensate the victim in some way (Johnstone, 2003). This can be extended within the idea of 'social justice' to refer to a restoration of fairness where it is demonstrated that discrimination has taken place. As described elsewhere in this book, effective restoration requires positive policies and positive action to ensure that discrimination is eliminated and genuine fairness is accorded to all those whose characteristics are irrelevant to the task in hand. This may well involve not just 'treating everyone the same', but identifying active ways of compensating for risks of discrimination faced by certain groups. Examples would be providing appropriate aids to performance for disabled people, or having active policies for recruitment of women or members of ethnic minority groups.

Privilege

A useful concept for understanding discrimination is that of 'privilege'. Rather than saying that certain social groups are at risk of discrimination, we can view the issue as one of particular identities carrying with them 'privilege'. This refers to the fact that certain groups are automatically accepted as worthy of inclusion, good treatment, respect and support. White, middle-class, male, heterosexual, British, mature but not old, Christian, home-owning people are likely to be such a privileged group in the UK. It can be argued that only when privileged people recognise their privilege and consciously work to curb its operation in situations of diversity, can discrimination be eliminated.

One of the first people to draw attention to this way of thinking was Peggy McIntosh in the USA. She wrote a seminal paper entitled 'White privilege and male privilege: a personal account of coming to see correspondences through work in Women's Studies' (McIntosh, 1988; see also Lipsitz, 2006). McIntosh compared her circumstances to those of African-American female colleagues in her building and line of work. She wrote an autobiographical list of unearned advantages that she experienced by virtue of having 'white' skin and Anglo-European facial features. Some examples from her list of 46 elements of unearned racial advantage include:

- I can if I wish arrange to be in the company of people of my race most of the time.
- I can turn on the television or open to the front page of the paper and see people of my race widely represented.
- I can be sure that my children will be given curricular materials that testify to the existence of their race.
- I can swear, or dress in second-hand clothes, or not answer letters, without having people attribute these choices to the bad morals, the poverty or the illiteracy of my race.
- I can do well in a challenging situation without being called a credit to my race.
- I can be pretty sure that if I ask to talk to the 'person in charge', I will be facing a person of my race.
- I can easily buy posters, post-cards, picture books, greeting cards, dolls, toys and children's magazines featuring people of my race.
- I am not made acutely aware that my shape, bearing or body odour will be taken as a reflection on my race.
- I can worry about racism without being seen as self-interested or self-seeking.
- If my day, week or year is going badly, I need not ask of each negative episode or situation whether it has racial overtones.

- I can be sure that if I need legal or medical help, my race will not work against me.
- I can arrange my activities so that I will never have to experience feelings of rejection owing to my race.

Social devaluation

Our identity, which we will discuss in Chapter 7, is defined not only by ourselves but by others. When our identity is defined negatively by those in power, oppressive experiences are highly likely to result. The social process involved has been called 'social devaluation'. It involves the casting of a person into negative social roles, for example of menace, object of ridicule, burden, sick, eternal child, subhuman creature (Wolfensberger, 1969, 1992, 1998; Race, 1999, 2003).

The idea is similar to that of 'stigma', described by Goffman in an influential book in the 1960s: *Stigma: Notes on the Management of Spoilt Identity* (Goffman, 1963). The concept of stigma is also discussed by Burke and Parker (2006), Mason et al. (2001) and Green (forthcoming).

The resulting social processes constituting devaluation, and the consequent oppressive experiences for the people who are devalued, are outlined in Table 2.2.

The oppressive experiences of people resulting from social devaluation have been called their 'wounds', a term originally coined by Jean Vanier (Wolfensberger, 1992; Williams, 2001). Vanier's solution to the problem of social devaluation and the consequent 'wounds' was to advocate 'life-sharing' between privileged people and those at risk of devaluation, in a spirit of equality (Vanier, 1979). Wolfensberger (1998) has developed a framework for tackling devaluation which he calls 'social role valorisation'. It involves systematic, empirically based measures to avoid the casting of people in negative social roles and to assist perceptions of them as being in socially valued roles, through avoidance and reversal of the devaluing social processes outlined in the Table 2.2. He especially applies this framework to the operation of human services (Race, 2003).

Oppression

At the beginning of Chapter 1 we gave our definitions of discrimination and oppression: the former involving inequality and unfairness, the latter adding the element of social evaluation as of low worth, leading to unwelcomeness, exclusion and even death. Here we will mention some other concepts and definitions of oppression and discrimination.

In a feminist context, Alison Jaggar defined oppression as 'unjust, humanly imposed restrictions on people's freedom' (Jaggar, 1983: 5).

Table 2.2 Social devaluation

Social process	Experience of the person or group
Denial or restriction of opportunity or support for development or functioning	Impairment, loss of opportunity, experience and competence
Relegation to low status	Being looked down on, treated as second class
Systematic rejection by social agencies or from social networks	Rejection, being unwanted
'Symbolic marking', or surrounding people with negative, degrading and damaging imagery	Pervasive negative interpretation of one's nature and identity to others
Scapegoating as the cause of social problems	Constant risk of unjust accusation, punishment or ill-treatment
Distantiation, segregation	Enforced separation from valued people and valued social relationships and experiences
Assumption of a high degree of power over particular groups	Loss of control, loss of decision-making about one's own life
Physical discontinuity, moving people about without their control	Loss of history, belongingness, possessions, sense of physical continuity, relationships
Relationship discontinuity, treating relationships as unimportant	Frequent sudden disappearance of people in one's life without own control or knowledge, loss of relationships, fragility of relationships, betrayal
Lack of freely given relationships, discouragement or denial of the importance of natural relationships	Relationships are unnatural, artificial and very fragile; allegiance is to others, not oneself; people are discouraged from relating to one
Deindividualisation, regimentation, mass treatment	Being regimented, denial of choice, being regarded as a number or just one of a group rather than a unique individual
Poverty-making	Poverty, few possessions, insecure possessions, few resources, inability to improve one's social condition
Restriction of experience, denial of participation in social events or opportunities	Restricted or narrow experience, boredom, a wasted life, loss of knowledge and competence, few relationships
Cutting off from religious participation, treating spiritual life as unimportant	Spiritual needs unmet and spiritual life undeveloped
Life-wasting through low intensity, quality or relevance of service or support	One's time being wasted, lack of support, boredom, poverty of experience
Brutalisation and even death-making	High risk of assault, impairment, denial of life-saving treatment, or even being killed

Source: Williams, 2001

In a legal context, the Court of Appeal decided in 1987 that oppression should be defined by the Oxford Dictionary entry:

Exercise of authority or power in a burdensome, harsh or wrongful manner; unjust or cruel treatment of subjects, inferiors, etc.; the imposition of unreasonable or unjust burdens.

Marilyn Frye has given the definition:

> A systematic, invisible, group-specific and exploitative social structure, meant to keep one group in an inferior or submissive position. (Frye, 1998: 49)

Dalrymple and Burke (2006) emphasise powerlessness, suggesting that this can lead to negative self-image, negative experience, lack of opportunity, insecurity, stress, exclusion, rejection, being treated as inferior, and feelings of inadequacy, helplessness and dependence. They stress the role of the law in tackling discrimination and oppression. They also stress the need for oppression to be defined by those who experience it, echoing the need to study authentic first-hand accounts. Morris also talks of 'disabled people's struggle to take over ownership of the definition of oppression, of the translation of their subjective reality' (1992: 160).

Thompson describes discrimination as a process that results in oppression. He defines oppression as 'the hardship and injustice brought about by the dominance of one group by another; the negative and demeaning exercise of power' (2003a: 34). He suggests eight processes that make up discrimination: stereotyping, marginalisation, invisibilisation, infantilisation, welfarism, medicalisation, dehumanisation and trivialisation. We can see a similarity here with Wolfensberger's concept of social devaluation through being cast into negative social roles: for example, menace, eternal child, sick person, subhuman, object of ridicule (Wolfensberger, 1969, 1998).

To reiterate the distinction we use in this book: oppression goes rather further than discrimination in giving people bad experiences. Whereas the essence of discrimination is injustice or unfairness, the essence of oppression is being disliked and unwelcome, and you being made aware of that. One way of putting this is to say that oppression involves being cast into a negative social role, for example as a threat or a nuisance, an excessive consumer of resources, sick or non-human. If you are seen in this way, negative experiences are highly likely for you.

Exercise

See if you can find other definitions of discrimination and oppression. Have a go at writing your own definitions, based on the understanding you have gained of their meanings in practice.

Rights

One approach to avoidance of oppressive experiences is to establish civil or legal rights, through constitutions or the law. This strategy gives people protection against harm, even if they are cast into a negative social role. Many groups at risk of oppression consider this is the best strategy: 'I don't care what people think about me, as long as I am protected from bad experiences.'

However, it can be argued that being valued is actually a greater safeguard. Rights can be taken away, but if others value you they may protect you and advocate for you even in the absence of rights. All rights were taken away from Jews in Nazi Germany, but a few survived because they were hidden or enabled to escape abroad by non-Jewish friends or benefactors. The moral task of seeing people as valuable and seeking and supporting valued social roles for them is an important strategy alongside the establishment of rights and protective legislation.

Identity and relationships

In the final section of this chapter we will cover a few topics that help to map out the task of seeing people as valuable and seeking valued social roles. Those topics are Identity, Deconstruction, Survivorhood versus victimhood, and Relationships.

Identity

As covered in Chapter 7, we need to be aware of how people define their own identity, how others see their identity, and the importance each attributes to different aspects of identity. Respecting and valuing identity, and developing the ability to convey that respect and valuing through knowledge of what particular identities entail, is an important part of being anti-oppressive (for example Owusu, 2000; Spencer, 2006).

Deconstruction

One source of difference between people themselves and others about identity, and a major source of stereotyping, is the fact that many concepts of identity are socially constructed rather than having a fixed identifiable basis in real experiences. The concept of being an 'older person', for example, is socially constructed. 'Older people' may not feel any different from younger people, may not be less fit or less able to work, or less able to do anything. Our physical sexual characteristics are biologically determined, but our gender identity is heavily influenced by conventional concepts of gender roles and gender behaviour (Elam, 1994). Disability is at least partly a social construction: if the world were designed for wheelchairs, we might all possess a wheelchair for convenience, and being a wheelchair user would not necessarily be related to having an impairment and so would not immediately conjure up the identity of 'disabled person'. Ethnic identity can be defined by certain criteria, but supposed differences between ethnic groups may be merely assumptions with little basis in fact. The example was given in Chapter 1 of an early-twentieth-century encyclopaedia entry about African-American people.

Being clear about which beliefs about identity are socially constructed rather than real – the process of 'deconstruction' of conventional ideas about identity – helps us to avoid stereotypes and to appreciate and welcome diversity.

Survivorhood versus victimhood

Being regarded as a victim may entail being cast into a negative social role, as a pathetic person who must be pitied and be an object of charity. This can in itself bring experiences of oppression. In general, people do not like being thought of as victims – it places them in an inferior position relative to others. Much better to foster is the concept of 'survivorhood'. We can then look for, respect and learn from the strategies that people themselves adopt to overcome oppression. We can work in equal partnership with them against oppression, rather than having a relationship based on power imbalance.

Relationships

The easiest context within which to pursue anti-oppression is the personal one – that is, in our personal relationships with people of different identities that we encounter. A strategy that can be used at any of the levels delineated by Thompson (Personal, Cultural and Structural – see Chapter 1) is outlined in Chapter 7. Even if we feel we cannot have great influence over cultural or structural forces, we can strive to be personally anti-oppressive towards those we meet. An anti-oppressive stance is not just a question of treating everyone the same. Just as institutional or organisational policies need to be proactive and not just reactive, so our personal anti-oppressive practice needs to be active, thoughtful, knowledgeable and evaluated. We need to have an informed sense of the identity of the other person, what aspects of identity are important to them, and the need to avoid stereotyping. Within that, we can equip ourselves with at least some knowledge of culture, language, beliefs and likely experiences of the person that will help us to put them at ease, respect them, and adopt, if necessary, an advocacy or support role based on partnership and mutual learning.

The task of anti-oppression

If we wish to be anti-oppressive, the concepts, examples and frameworks so far discussed can help us to see the requirements. We need to:

- respect and welcome diversity
- rid ourselves, as far as possible, of stereotypes and prejudices through gaining accurate knowledge of people or groups that differ from us in some aspect of identity
- use any power and privilege we have to benefit people and not 'wound' them through social devaluation
- work for communality, sharing and equality
- be aware of negative aspects of the culture and structures of the society in which we live, and try to counteract them and change them
- recognise the pervasiveness and seriousness of oppression in the world, and commit ourselves to positive action to remedy and prevent it
- study first-hand accounts by those who experience oppression, to understand its reality, nature and prevalence, and to gain authentic knowledge for tackling it.

In later chapters we will outline various approaches to these tasks.

In the academic context of professional training, we also believe it is important to have a critical analysis of important concepts (Dominelli, 2002a, 2002b; Thompson, 2003a), and we begin this process with further analysis of the concepts of equality, diversity, equal opportunities and anti-discrimination in the following chapters, especially as they relate to organisational issues and practice.

Summary

- A wide variety of concepts is relevant to anti-oppressive practice.
- Understanding these concepts can help progress towards anti-oppression.
- Critical analysis of concepts is important.
- The concepts generate action tasks that can be adopted.

Part II

Organisations

3
Equality

Aim

- To present ideological and political ideas that have influenced interpretations of the term 'equality'.
- To encourage students and practitioners to reflect on how these ideas may have informed their own interpretation of equality.
- To explore the example of racism, and particularly institutional racism, in relation to equality.
- To discuss some implications for health and social care services and personnel.

Equality, along with liberty and fraternity, was one of the three watchwords of the French Revolution, and ever since the drive for equality has been behind movements for national, racial, sexual and class liberation (CEMS, 2006). The study of equality is complex because individuals, groups and communities have different interpretations, and so practical applications of the idea are likely to differ among those people and groups. Interpreters of the concept include those who argue *against* equality (Lucas, 1971; Cavanagh, 2002). It seems therefore important to explore differing theoretical propositions associated with equality as a way of encouraging debate among health and social care practitioners. Such debate can lead to the creation of new ideas appropriate to current social issues requiring intervention as part and parcel of everyday practice.

According to Hatch, 'A theory is an explanation, that is, it is an attempt to explain a segment of experience in the world' (1997: 9).

The segment of experience considered here – equality – is particularly important because it impacts on political thought and shapes social demands, even though there is lack of clarity on its meaning. Theory building is needed in the areas of equality and inequality in health and social care to support analysis of complex behaviours, as well as to underpin practice (Thompson, 2003b). This chapter will attempt to explain concepts of equality. We will consider a number of dimensions of political, philosophical and social influence that continue to stimulate debates at national and local levels.

Political theories

Political theories of liberalism, neo-liberalism, socialism and 'New Labour' will be explored here because of their importance to discussions about health and social care provision as segments of the welfare state. This exploration of welfare theories will highlight some of the factors that inform health and social care practice, and some of the complexities that require attention. From such a process of analysis, it may be possible to discover effective means of dealing with complicated and sometimes very sensitive issues, as well as stimulating critical thought and creativity among practitioners. Anti-oppressive practice in health and social care is about taking appropriate professional action that will make a positive difference in vulnerable people's lives. Reflective, critical and creative thinking can aid the development of these strategies for action (Ferguson et al., 2002). Equality theories ought to inform the way the army of workers servicing the welfare state work, and offer alternative ways of thinking about the approaches they might use to challenge discriminatory processes, procedures and infrastructure.

Since health and social care provision forms a significant part of the welfare state and is likely to do so for the foreseeable future, political theories of equality are particularly relevant to policy and practice in this area.

Liberalism

We can begin by considering liberalism. Liberalism is concerned with retaining individual freedom in the context of political developments. It can be viewed as a collection of related philosophies about roles and functions of our institutions in shaping group and individual social life (Gray, 1989). Liberalism has made a significant contribution to contemporary social thought and political action (O'Brien and Penna, 1998). It has remained dominant for decades in debates around equality, fairness and justice. Practitioners in health and social care who implement social policies are bound to have been strongly influenced by political liberalism. However, it has been suggested that:

> Liberalism has never attempted, in any respect, to secure substantive equality. That is, it has never promoted the goal of enabling the development of a truly 'free and

equal' society where everyone has access to equal resources for participation in the society's communal and institutional networks. (O'Brien and Penna, 1998: 39)

Thus, the dominance of liberalism over decades may have dictated a slow pace of change, and limited progress towards the substantive equality sought by those who favour re-distribution of goods and services through state intervention.

Liberalism champions the maintenance of individual freedom and advocates minimal institutional state interference in order to allow individuals to develop their own talents. The idea of individuals meeting their welfare needs through free and independent action somewhat contradicts the right to equality. However, embedded in liberalism is the theory of justice that informs and supports the reduction of inequality.

Among health and social care practitioners who believe that the UK is a liberal society, their commitment and amount of effort exerted to pursue the achievement of justice and fairness are likely to depend on their assessment of the problem. Tensions can arise between those who advocate state intervention to bring about justice and fairness in the way health and social care services are provided and delivered, and those who oppose too much interference and state control. Those who favour a radical approach to promoting equality would find limitations in liberalism because the well-being of vulnerable health and social care service users requires a combination of self-help and external intervention. The need for external intervention is echoed in the Equalities Review, within their definition of an equal society:

An equal society protects and promotes equal, real freedom and substantive opportunity to live in the ways people value and would choose, so that everyone can flourish. An equal society recognises people's different needs, situations and goals and removes the barriers that limit what people can do. (2007: 16)

This Equalities Review's interpretation of equality includes within it some aspects of liberalism in relation to freedom. However, the changes suggested would require significant institutional interference to bring about a more equal society, a position not favoured by liberalism. 'In theory, liberalism promotes an equality of opportunity that is rooted in an inequality of outcome' (O'Brien and Penna, 1998: 44).

Neo-liberalism

Neo-liberalism places emphasis on the duty and responsibility of individual citizens to help themselves and each other. The notion of equality in neo-liberalism centres around equality of freedom from coercion from the state, and equality of all citizens before the law. Neo-liberalism argues against the idea of substantive equality in material terms, because of its encroachment on individual liberty. Minimalist state intervention in providing for the population's welfare is desired and individuals are expected to take on most of the responsibility for welfare provision. Thatcherism is considered by some to be the political system closest to neo-liberal ideas (see Harvey, 2007).

However, health and social care provision post-Second World War has been the responsibility of the state, and the services have been collectively paid for through taxation, suggesting that the idea of minimalist state intervention within this segment of welfare has not been accepted. Successive governments have adopted a strongly interventionist policy, and the electorate have come to expect free health care at the point of use and to expect that most of the personal social care provision for vulnerable children and adults will continue to fall within the umbrella of state provision.

While equality before the law is thought to be compatible with freedom, neo-liberalism may raise concerns about demands for social justice. The particular concern is that such demands will result in laws that will curtail individual freedom when systems are put into place to ensure compliance, suggesting a very invasive state (Blakemore, 2003). Equalities legislation would probably fall within that range of laws perceived to curtail individual freedom. However, again, in the UK, systems have been put in place to ensure compliance with social justice legislation, including, currently, the amalgamation of existing equalities commissions to form the Equality and Human Rights Commission.

Overall, neo-liberalism opposes egalitarianism as an expression of equality in its purest form because it is thought that striving for such a utopian ideal would entail a corresponding decline in individual responsibility, resulting in increased state welfare dependency. 'In place of the "right" to benefit, neo-liberalism substitutes the "duty" to support, and in place of the desire for "equality" it substitutes the value of "freedom"' (O'Brien and Penna, 1998: 104).

However, it can be argued that implicit within the idea of freedom is the right to resist oppression. Thus, even in terms of neo-liberal thinking, professional practitioners in health and social care need to be conversant with rights, statutes and entitlements leading to justice and fairness.

Rawls' theory of justice

Justice as fairness is associated with equality, and Rawls' (1971) publication on a theory of justice continues to influence current debates on the subject. He points out that equality is an aspect of the concept of justice and as such advocates the 'elimination of arbitrary distinctions and the establishment, within the structure of a practice, of a proper balance between competing claims' (1971: 77).

The competing claims can be assessed to establish a just distinction on the basis of achieving equality in terms of accepted tangibles such as benefits or burdens. Rawls' theory suggests that inequality of treatment can be justified and allowed if every party will gain from the inequality. Therefore the allowable inequality would not be arbitrary, but well considered. The thinking behind this assessment of allowable inequality seems to be that taking corrective and remedial action in favour of the least advantaged may be acceptable, because justice will be seen to be done. This line of thought is revisited in Chapter 6 under the subjects of positive action and positive discrimination. Rawls' theory can be seen as bridging the gap in liberalism between equal opportunities and equality of outcome.

Socialism and social democracy

Socialism advocates state involvement to create, promote and protect the rights of citizens. The interventions are thought to be necessary so as to offset the inequalities brought about by capitalism and free markets. Social democratic principles support socialist thinking because they are based on the belief that government action can be used to alter distribution of resources for economic and social ends, thereby tackling inequality so as to move towards fairness and justice (Alcock, 2003). Included in the notion of social democracy is that individuals will be willing to give up some of their freedoms to the state, for the benefit of the citizens as a whole. Those who subscribe to the notion of state intervention may do so on the basis that excessive inequality can bring about destructive conflict, because those affected may perceive a denial of their natural rights, thereby denying them social justice. According to Blakemore (2003), social democratic principles have traditionally informed health and welfare services. It can be expected that social democratic ideas about equality form the basis of much everyday practice in this field.

New Labour and the 'Third Way'

In considering further the concept of equality as a political term (Thompson, 2003b), we can review the approach of the current UK government to the removal of disadvantage in accessing the range of health and social care goods and services. Politically, New Labour's ideology, generally documented as the 'Third Way', can be viewed as a critique of socialism (Old Labour) and neo-liberalism. The emphasis has been on modernisation

in response to global, cultural and political changes, highlighting responsibility and obligation as well as government's commitment to tackling
social exclusion and poverty. It is argued that the 'Third Way' ideology
of the New Labour government has paved the way for a renewed emphasis
on cooperation and collaboration, reducing inequality through increased
social cohesion (Powell, 1999).

Socialist critics of New Labour have seen the 'Third Way' as a continuation of neo-liberal Thatcherism. For example, this is how Rojek (2003)
describes the views of Hall (1998):

> In cultural policy, Hall declares that New Labour promotes self-reliance, family
> values, competitiveness and entrepreneurial dynamism. He berates Blair for
> 'ruthlessly emasculating' the Labour Party and replacing real debate with the
> carefully controlled blandishments of the Millbank public relations machine. (Rojek,
> 2003: 153)

The 'Third Way' emphasis on equality of opportunity through tackling
causes of inequality and social exclusion can be considered as a carefully
thought-out move away from the earlier socialist debates on equality of
outcome through redistribution of wealth and resources. For a detailed
discussion on equality of opportunity see Chapter 4.

The 'Third Way' ideas associated with equality of opportunity emerged
from the debates about rights and obligations during Labour's first term in
office in the late 1990s, culminating in a Green Paper: 'At the heart of the
modern welfare state will be a new contract between the Citizen and
Government, based on responsibilities (duties) and rights' (Department for
Education and Employment, 1998).

The thinking behind the duty of government and the duty of the
individual seemed to be about helping people to help themselves. There
would be fewer people dependent on welfare state benefits when more
individuals became economically independent through paid work.
Equality here involves employment and economic independence for all
those able to achieve it, while in turn the government accepts a duty to
support those unable to work so that they too can live a life of security
and dignity.

Again, Hall (1998) expresses dissatisfaction with this strategy as a means
of achieving equality, because of the links he sees with neo-liberalism.
The strategy includes deregulation of the market and the reconstruction of
the public sector through a new managerialism. Hall favours more state
management of the economy and systematic public investment to redress
inequalities, whereas New Labour is in favour of self-reliance, competitive-
ness and entrepreneurial dynamism. Such opposites serve to illustrate the
difficulties in achieving an agreed political philosophy to underlie the
pursuit of equality.

Exercise

Consider the influence of liberalism, neo-liberalism, Rawls' theory, socialism and the 'Third Way' on a health or social care service familiar to you.

What do you think each theory would say about priorities in provision of health and social care, and the possible rationing of provision?

What is your view of the way equality should be interpreted and pursued in health and social care services?

The influence of theory on practice

Liberalism, neo-liberalism, Rawls' theory, socialism and the 'Third Way' have all influenced health and social care provision within the framework of the welfare state. We have seen that equality means different things to different people and groups, and within different frameworks of political and social philosophy. There is, however, a consensus about the importance of fairness and justice for all. Differences emerge in respect of mechanisms that can be adopted for achieving fairness and justice. These differences impact on the meaning of equality and how to achieve such a goal. This is a particularly important issue in health and social care, where those who consume what is on offer do so from a position of vulnerability.

The Equalities Review developed a definition of equality that encompasses 'equality of process and worth, but is richer in its scope. It takes a fuller account of variations in need and the diversity of people's values and preferences than a definition based purely on equality of outcomes' (2007: 15). This definition includes four concepts: equality of process, which relates to equality of opportunity; equality of worth, which relates to the according of equal value to every human being; equality of meeting need, which relates to equality of outcome; and equality of choice, based on respecting individual values. While this definition can be a helpful starting point, the practicalities of achieving equality will need concerted and incremental effort from all who are committed to the principles and values of a fair and just society. Most health and social care practitioners are likely to want to make a significant contribution towards that goal of a more equal society.

The example of race equality

Issues in the achievement of equality can be illustrated by considering the rise of international migration bringing together people originating from diverse societies. A key focus in the debate about equality has been on 'race'. The topic of race equality often causes considerable discomfort amongst practitioners in the health and social care sector. For this reason, and because of its inherent importance, we will explore in this chapter how discrimination on the grounds of race can perpetuate inequalities.

In focusing on the single paradigm of race equality, we are aware of the difficulties associated with discussing equality issues in this way. Questions are likely to be raised, such as: Why single out race equality? Is there a hierarchy among oppressions? Our rationale is that race affects everyone and cuts across all the other paradigms covered by legislation, such as gender, sexual orientation, disability and religion. In addition to this, race discrimination is a highly contentious topic which often causes discomfort, suggesting that if this hard nut is cracked it might become easier to make measurable progress towards equality in other areas.

The health and social care sector seems well placed to theorise, analyse and clarify approaches that can be considered in the quest to achieve equality. As a segment of the welfare state, health and social care services attract those who wish to make a difference in other people's lives through caring. So challenging identified inequalities across this sector can be expected to be an integral part of caring. External support along this journey is available, for example through the new single Equality and Human Rights Commission. The Commission has responsibility for working with all organisations, including health and social care organisations, to implement equality policies within the framework of new managerialism. This can be particularly illustrated through consideration of race discrimination and consequent inequality. Beneficial changes in health and social care services can be identified, which can be generalised to other areas of discrimination and oppression.

The terms 'race' and 'racism' tend to generate considerable emotion. These concepts, although generally understood simplistically, in reality incorporate a complex body of ideas which have evolved over time. Studying the development of such ideas within a historical context can be illuminative. The meaning of the term 'race' has shifted over time both within and between popular and scientific contexts. The word 'race' has been used to refer to groups of all sizes ranging from a single family, through those sharing a local and regional culture, to nations and nationalities and even to the whole of humanity – 'the human race'.

Race was not initially associated with skin colour, but skin colour came to be seen as a distinguishing feature of major national 'races' of people, and the crude descriptive dichotomy of 'black' and 'white' became established. In fact, of course, what we call 'black' and 'white' skin colour each include a very wide range of mixed colours. The terms are just crude generalisations for 'tendency to be darker in skin tone' and 'tendency to be lighter in skin tone'. Unfortunately, given the negative associations in the English language of the term 'black', and the positive associations of 'white', this terminology fed into negative stereotypes and prejudice against 'black' people. This linking of black with negativity persists as part of the heritage within the English language.

Exercise

Write down all the phrases you can think of which include the word 'black', and all the phrases you can think of which include the word 'white'. Then mark each as having negative connotations, having positive connotations, or being neutral.

Are there more negative and fewer positive connotations in your 'black' list than your 'white' list?

If yes, do you think that this may influence, however unconsciously, beliefs and perceptions about 'black' people?

The origins of racism

In the seventeenth and eighteenth centuries, the term 'race' conveyed ideas of shared ancestral descent. With the rise of nineteenth-century 'scientific racism', scientists and other scholars began to provide allegedly more scientific arguments for a lower valuation of certain people as human beings, particularly to justify colonialism, by categorising humanity into races:

> Scientific racism refers to scientific theories of the 19th century, which drew on physical anthropology, anthropometry, craniometry, phrenology, physiognomy and other now discredited disciplines, in order to provide a typology of different races, based on a biological conception of the race. Such theories, which have been now discredited as pseudo-science or proto-science, provided ideological justification for racism, slavery and colonialism during the New Imperialism period of the second half of the 19th century. (Entry in www.wikipedia.org)

A misinterpretation of Darwinism was also deployed to give further credibility to the idea that races had evolved hierarchically, with Europeans at the top and Africans at the bottom, though there is nothing in Darwin's work that suggests his support for this theory (Hawkins, 1997). Racial classification continued to be used by some scientists during the 20th century and provided justification for political ideologies such as Nazism and Apartheid. More recently, empirical research to argue for the existence of a racial hierarchy in physical and intellectual capacity has kept debate alive. These arguments have been put forward at a time when geneticists have shown that there is no basis in human genetic make-up for distinguishing races and that there is far more variation between individuals within a population group than between groups. However, 'any suggestion of systematic biological differences between groups of people from different parts of the world – beyond the superficially obvious ones of skin colour and anatomy – is almost certain to raise hackles' (*Economist*, 2006).

The 'superficially obvious' aspect, that of skin colour, remains one of the most influential factors governing societies' attitudes to members of minority groups (Coker, 2001). As members of society, those who work in the care sector are likely to hold some of those generic attitudes about those who belong to racial minority groups. Such attitudes could be either negative or positive.

The widespread propagation of the historical pseudo-scientific accounts within British society led to people's attitudes to race being influenced by those accounts. It is likely that some of the attitudes projected by some white people towards Black people in Britain have also been shaped by traditions of slavery, colonial rule and the empire, when British people were imbued with the idea that they were born to rule the world. The reverse could be suggested also in terms of the attitudes towards white people of those whose ancestral origins are linked to former British colonies, given their experience of being enslaved and colonised.

Defining 'race'

The way the word 'race' has been used reflects changes in popular understanding of the causes of physical and cultural differences. Legal rulings have moved the debate forward, forcing the creation of a working definition of a racial group, hopefully to enable individuals to engage with the demands of a modern UK society and to assist people's understanding of equality.

According to the House of Lords (*Mandla* v. *Dowell Lee* [1983] AC 548 HL), a racial group is characterised by:

- a long shared history of which the group is conscious as distinguishing it from other groups, and the memory of which it keeps alive
- a cultural tradition of its own, including family and social customs and manners, often but not necessarily associated with religious observance.

Other relevant characteristics include:

- a common geographical origin or descent from a small number of common ancestors
- a common language, not necessarily peculiar to the group
- a common literature peculiar to the group
- a common religion differing from that of neighbouring groups or from the general community surrounding it
- being a minority, or being an oppressed group, within a larger community.

In the pursuit of equality within health and social care services, it would be expected that practitioners would afford any group defined as a racial group on these criteria equal status in the planning and delivery of care.

However, it is necessary to acknowledge that while definitions provide a starting point when considering a given subject, they have limitations, especially in studying emotive subjects like those of race equality and racism, because of differences in interpretation. Whose definition would be considered to be credible? In terms of anti-racist legislation, some groups have had to fight for inclusion, such as Irish people, Jews and gypsies. Whatever a group's view of itself, official recognition as a racial group can be dependent on rulings by the courts.

Institutional racism

The House of Lords definition of a racial group came about as result of cases of racial discrimination in the workplace. In such cases racism was considered to be the root cause of such forms of unlawful discrimination. While most court cases of racial discrimination have been about employment, institutional discrimination in relation to the provision and the delivery of health and social care has received considerable attention, particularly in the area of mental health, when investigations have brought to the attention of the public the nature of institutional racism and its consequences. For example, institutional racism was found in the case of David Bennett, a 38-year-old African-Caribbean patient, who died on 30 October 1998 in a medium secure psychiatric unit in Norwich after being restrained by staff for a period of about 25 minutes (NSCSHA, 2003).

Fernando highlights the importance of anti-oppressive practice issues remaining on the agenda of health and social care services. He states:

> Cultural psychiatry research and theory is now extensive, but as a body it is politically weak and has very little impact on training of professionals who by and large run the mainline mental health services in the UK . . . The picture in the UK at present is of a few interested and committed individuals struggling at the grass roots (usually in the voluntary sector) to bring into being services that are responsive to and appropriate for a multicultural society. (2005: 433)

Racism can be defined as a combination of prejudice and power that intentionally or unintentionally discriminates against and suppresses a person or a group of persons on the grounds of colour and race. This simple definition

$$\text{colour prejudice} + \text{power} = \text{racism}$$

has been around for quite a while and has a part to play in getting people to think about the potential abuse of power within the care sector.

More recent developments following the MacPherson Inquiry (1999) have moved the debate forward by producing a working definition of institutional racism, with a view to promoting equality between races. The definition of institutional racism is considered by many to be a more helpful one when dealing with problems arising within organisations, such as those providing health and social care:

> The term institutional racism should be understood to refer to the way institutions may systematically treat or tend to people differently in respect of race. The addition of the word 'institutional' therefore identifies the source of the differential treatment; this lies in some sense within the organisation rather than simply with the individuals who represent it. The production of differential treatment is institutionalised in the way the organisation operates. (MacPherson Report, 1999: 1–2)

Institutional racism is also later defined as:

> The collective failure of an organisation to provide an appropriate and professional service to people because of their colour, culture or ethnic origin. It can be seen or detected in processes, attitudes and behaviour which amount to discrimination through unwitting prejudice, ignorance, thoughtlessness and racist stereotyping which disadvantage minority ethnic people. (MacPherson, 1999: 34)

The MacPherson Inquiry focused on the service afforded by an organisation (the Metropolitan Police) to Stephen Lawrence. This model of inquiry allows those working within health and social care provision not only to examine their own attitudes, but also to check out the institutional practices and procedure for potential discrimination that could cause real harm to those partaking in services. According to Denman (2001), the concept of 'institutional' racism is important precisely because it is to be contrasted with more traditional concepts of racism. The traditional 'rotten apples' analysis identified racism within an organisation with a small number of prejudiced individuals. Institutional racism, by contrast, is about the effects of practices, conditions and norms which do not reside in particular individuals, but rather are located within the organisation itself.

The MacPherson definition provides a clearer focus on organisational processes and outcomes, regardless of whether the element of racism is overt or covert, and without the source of such outcomes being solely attributable to the actions of individuals. A further benefit is that the definition is written in general terms so that it is potentially applicable to any kind of organisation and across all forms of discrimination that need to be tackled so as to achieve equality. It thus takes a holistic approach towards mainstreaming equality. It is written and explained in everyday rather than obscure or academic language, making it accessible to professionals and members of the public. Its acceptance and adoption by many parts of the public sector as a basis for action illustrate that it is usable.

Exercise

Do you think that some of the terminology emphasised by MacPherson, such as 'institutional racism' and 'collective failure', might be interpreted as removing responsibility entirely from individual staff?

How do you think organisational responsibility can be combined with individual responsibility to ensure the elimination of racism at both levels?

Relevance to health and social care

To consider further the question in the above exercise, we can look at how responsibilities are allocated in an organisation. We will focus particularly on health and social care services.

On the one hand, individuals have a responsibility for their own actions on behalf of the organisation, and managers have a responsibility for those working alongside them. From a health and social care corporate perspective, all personnel arguably share a collective responsibility for the conduct of social care business affairs. This includes helping to promote appropriate standards of practice and taking appropriate remedial steps when conduct appears to be wrong. In the case of race discrimination it is unlawful, and is therefore unacceptable. Behaviours observed to be contributing to discrimination could be appropriately challenged on the basis of their negative impact on the proper conduct of health and social care business.

More importantly, the application of the principles of duty of care, professional ethics and standards of conduct all point to elements of responsibility lying with all staff. That said, it cannot be ignored that even among individuals who strive to be unquestionably fair in their attitudes and treatment of others, prejudice and discrimination in relation to race or other characteristics may remain possible. Childhood socialisation within a particular cultural context lays foundations of which most people remain unaware, and adult socialisation into other specific cultural contexts such as education and occupations extends this. So vigilance on the part of the individual practitioner is important in terms of self-check and self-assessment and the production of evidence to demonstrate compliance with professional codes of practice.

Behavioural change in these areas remains problematic and a real challenge to the caring professions. With particular attention to the NHS, research evidence identifying the nature and extent of inequality and discrimination continues to be published, for example: Commission for Racial Equality (1983), Rowden (1990), Cassidy (1995), Sawley (2001), Coker (2001) and Harrison (2004). In some instances, nurses have been struck off the Nursing and Midwifery Council register for racist behaviour at work. Staines (2006) cites examples of the use of offensive language by some white nurses towards their Black and minority ethnic (BME) colleagues. Examples of the language used included terms such as 'darkies', 'wogs', 'chinkies', 'slanty-eyes' and 'black bastards'.

It seems particularly worrying that some individuals who care for vulnerable people can hold such negative attitudes towards people who are different from them. This illustrates how the now discredited scientific racism has had an impact on some people who consider themselves to be caring and therefore worthy of remaining on the professional register of a caring profession. It is worrying because it is very likely that the quality of service to BME patients offered and delivered by an individual who addresses her colleagues in such derogatory terms will be questionable.

Fortunately, reported cases about the use of such language appear to be comparatively rare. However, racial harassment and bullying are reported to be on the increase and BME nurses have indicated that the problem is far more deep-rooted than a few racist individuals with antiquated views: 'Discrimination is often covert and manifests itself in lack of career progression' (Staines, 2006: 13). Failure to act when concerns about racism are raised would fall within the realm of institutional racism.

Towards an action plan

Those in the know seem to be acknowledging that the NHS still has a long way to go towards achieving race equality. Anionwu (2005), cited by Staines (2006), in her capacity as head of the Seacole Centre for Nursing Practice, has raised concerns about limited career progression for BME nurses. The main criticism she makes concerns a lack of a high profile and priority for stamping out discrimination.

A radical approach to a public investment programme for equality, as advocated by Hall (1997), leading to equality of outcomes that are measurable, might satisfy those on the receiving end of racism and discrimination within health and social care, either as workers or recipients of care. One of the main drawbacks at present is a lack of credible, objective organisational equality measurement tools. The new capabilities framework under consideration could offer a way forward at the level of the organisation (Equalities Review, 2006). At the level of personal interaction between service user and worker in health and social care, measuring equality ought to be just as important. If the importance of this is accepted, what is meant by equality needs to be made explicit so that all parties know what to look for. Creating equality measurement protocols would have to be developed to help individuals measure their performance. However, personal reflection on the use of stereotypes and exploration of potential dangers is uncomplicated and can be carried out on an individual basis by all caring professionals in a self-directed way. The results of such an exploration can inform equality measurement protocols.

Reflecting on one's stereotypes can be a useful starting point for individuals working in the care sector. This might seem rather basic and simplistic, but the use of derogatory language by some professionals, as cited in NMC misconduct hearings, would suggest that for some individuals there is still a need to start at a very basic level to recognise their own prejudices and the injustice of discrimination. Among those who have moved on, way beyond this basic level, there are opportunities to assist the creation of appropriate and usable equality protocols, to pilot them and to report the results.

Self-assessment is important because at the present time the problems are compounded by the fact that assessment of suitability to practise does not include evidence to demonstrate that practitioners will not be oppressive in their dealings with service users and colleagues. Gaining the appropriate professional qualification and registration are prerequisites for being allowed to practise, and professional codes of conduct do make specific references to issues of avoiding bias and discrimination. For example, doctors are expected to 'avoid bias on the grounds of sex, race, disability, lifestyle, culture, beliefs, colour, gender, sexuality or age' (GMC, 2003). Likewise, social care workers are expected to 'promote equal opportunities for service users and carers', and 'to respect diversity and different cultures and values' (GSCC, 2002). However, monitoring to ensure that such codes are adhered to remains problematic because of differences in interpretation of what constitutes appropriate behaviour in relation to equality.

In addition to these differences in interpretation, the systems-led nature of health and social care means that vulnerable service users must fit into the existing power structures. Such arrangements are not conducive to the promotion of equality because of the power differentials. When considering racism, it has been argued that at the individual level the deep-rootedness of the problem goes back to childhood socialisation. It can therefore be engrained and rather difficult to dislodge. Hence the focus on institutional practices as referred to earlier rather than just the individual. Gaine (1995) showed that even in primary schools where children appeared to their teachers to be working and playing amicably and respectfully together, hidden tape recorders picked up racist remarks. Until every individual working in the care sector has had the opportunity to reflect and acknowledge that racism tends to exist in most situations where people from different racial backgrounds live and work together, equality outcomes will probably remain aspirational. According to Anionwu (2005): 'Things will not change unless stamping out discrimination and promoting equality and diversity are as high on the Department of Health's agenda as saving money' (cited by Staines, 2006: 13).

The task ahead

In discussing the issue of denial, Taylor makes the point that 'in many communities and institutions the leaders would deny the existence of racism because they believe they have countered it successfully' (2003: 52).

Because of the basic level from which some people might need to begin the process of exploration, it may be relevant on a practical level for individuals to go back to basics and explore the concept of stereotypes and how they use such stereotypes, so that when the long-awaited high profile, which Anionwu suggests is needed, does arrive, individuals will be more likely to be receptive to the expected changes.

Stereotypes as codes give a quick, common understanding of a person or a group of people. These codes relate to, for example, social class, age, gender, occupation, race or religion. It is generally accepted that stereotyping is part of human nature, and that everyone has and uses stereotypes. They are to some extent essential, to enable individuals to compare, predict, judge and evaluate the world around them and also to deal with routine or unusual situations (CEMS, 2006). Additionally, according to Thompson: 'A stereotype is not simply a personal prejudice – it is part of the culture that is "transmitted" from one generation to the next, thereby proving instrumental in maintaining existing power relations' (2003a: 84).

Professional practitioners need to find a way of guarding against the oppressive use of stereotypes through their normal cycle of reflection in action.

Exercise

Think about the stereotypes you hold yourself in relation to groups of people categorised by social class, gender, age, occupation, race or religion. For each group identify your likes and dislikes about members of the group, and what you see as good or bad characteristics of the group.

Try to analyse where your beliefs come from. Consider sources of your beliefs in your upbringing, especially family influences.

Consider how your beliefs might influence interactions with people whose characteristics or background are different from your own.

The concerns about stereotypes are that they reduce a wide range of differences among people to simple generalisations and transform assumptions about particular groups of people into reality. Stereotypes can perpetuate social prejudices that can inform behaviours that contribute to inequality. Being clear about the dangers of stereotyping enables a deeper understanding of how prejudice and discrimination can occur in unconscious and unwitting ways. This in turn enables individuals to decide for themselves the changes in behaviour they need to make to help them with their professional practice, so that those on the receiving end of their care benefit from appropriate quality care.

Quality and equality

According to Rohan Collier, 'Equality is about the quality of service; indeed there cannot be high-quality services without equality' (1998: 19).

The use of racially abusive language cited by Staines (2006), and the presence of stereotyped views, both impact negatively on the individual on the receiving end of such interactions. Stopping such behaviours can be tackled through education and political action.

Political commitment on equality issues can be evidenced through support for initiatives such as the creation of the Social Exclusion Unit (set up in 1997), the NHS 'Positively Diverse' programme (launched as a pilot project in Bradford in 1995 and broadened out to the whole NHS in 1998; see NHS Confederation, 2005), the 'Vital Connection' equalities framework published by the NHS Executive (2000) and more recently the Equalities Review (see Equalities Review, 2007). These initiatives imply that there is a great deal more to be accomplished in terms of policies, procedures and practices aimed at eliminating discrimination and creating a just and fair society.

In social work, the General Social Care Council has provided a framework for curriculum issues in social work education. The curriculum content is informed by the core values that should inform practice. These values are powerful and provide a framework for non-discriminatory practice for each practitioner. For example, one of these core values is that 'social workers should identify, analyse and take action to counter discrimination, racism, disadvantage, inequality and injustice, using strategies appropriate to role and context' (quoted in University of Reading, 2007: 81).

During training, social work students are required to produce evidence to demonstrate their ability to interact with service users in an anti-oppressive manner, and are formally assessed. It is expected that a process of reflection and self-assessment will continue after graduation, so that equality issues remain embedded in daily practice.

However, practitioners also need usable protocols to aid reflection and self-assessment on anti-oppressive practice.

Leadership

What is needed is consistent organisational leadership about what equality means within health and social care provision and how to move the organisations towards mainstreaming equality, so that the thinking and the actions become embedded in everyday practice. A transformational type of leadership is probably what is required. A transformational leader is one who takes risks to bring about desired change. Such a leader would have a vision of the future and the ability to get other people to be excited about the benefits of equality. For desired change to become a reality, this transformational leader needs to continue to sell the vision, maintain heightened awareness and interest among organisational members, and increase their confidence in implementing change (Martin and Henderson, 2001; Kumar and Kumar, 2002).

Because transformational leadership is value-centred, all parties should share the vision, and have mutual trust and respect, in order for the change to be accepted. To tease out how transformational leadership can make a difference towards achieving equality in health and social care organisations, an exploration of the subject of equal opportunities to combat unlawful discrimination is necessary. Chapter 4 considers in more detail issues of equality of opportunity.

Tapping into the political commitment evidenced by the plethora of government reports on equality could support the invigoration of tired policies or the creation of new ones. But more importantly, when the courts have ruled in favour of the complainants in cases of discrimination, organisations have been advised to have policies and procedures in place to demonstrate non-discriminatory practices. Anti-discriminatory legislation will inform and direct the discussion in the next chapter.

Summary

- Political theories provide a basis for different interpretations of the meaning of equality.
- Health and social care practitioners are likely to have different views of equality, based on the influence of different theories.
- Issues in working towards equality can be illustrated by considering racism.
- The concept of 'institutional racism' is particularly important.
- Strategies for avoiding and tackling racism can be developed in health and social care services.
- Leadership is needed in this task.
- Individuals can be aware of their own contribution to equality, alongside organisational strategies.

4
Equal Opportunities

Aim

- To explain the distinction between equality and equality of opportunity.
- To show how that distinction has influenced the development of equal opportunities policies.

Following on from the discussion in the previous chapter on equality, this chapter considers a sub-section of equality in terms of equality of opportunity. The theoretical distinctions associated with liberalism, neo-liberalism and socialism which have shaped the conceptualisation of equal opportunities are discussed. The role of legislation in influencing equal opportunities policies and strategies for action is included. Pointers are offered from which practitioners in health and social care can evaluate fairness and justice within the context of service provision and the delivery of care in an anti-oppressive way.

Liberalism

The liberal conception of equality is associated with the notions of fairness and justice as highlighted in Chapter 3. These notions inform the detailed rules and regulations of the formal policies that are designed to ensure that unfair and unlawful discrimination is avoided. According to Jewson and Mason (1986), this liberal conception suggests that equality of opportunity exists when individuals are afforded space to compete for social rewards on an equal basis. The notion of competition brings to the fore ideas about gains and losses in employment chances and in access to health and social care services.

Ideally, liberalism implies that the rules of competition would be fairly enforced by practitioners to ensure that discrimination does not occur. In this regard, the principles of fairness and justice are embodied in the for-mulation of equal opportunity policies. In promoting equality through appropriate policies, government ministers have gone on record stating a commitment to stamping out discrimination:

> The government is working to transform Britain into a society which is inclusive and prosperous. Eliminating unjustified discrimination wherever it exists and making equality of opportunity a reality for all is at the heart of the Government agenda. Equality of opportunity is not only inherently right, it is also essential for Britain's future economic and social success . . . We will continue to act to stamp out discrimination, remove barriers and improve the position of groups facing dis-advantage and discrimination in employment, public life and public service delivery. (Mo Mowlam, 1999)

This statement can be viewed as an intention by government to intervene and regulate in line with liberal thinking that advocates some degree of state regulation of society in order to attain acceptable levels of freedom and liberty for all (Arblaster, 1984).

The acceptable levels of freedom and liberty for all would not be achieved, it is argued, unless there is government intervention through regulation to eliminate discrimination. Otherwise, those who are disadvantaged by dis-crimination would not enjoy liberty and freedom.

According to the liberal view, discrimination can be tackled by ensuring that talent and ability are paramount; therefore the removal of procedural barriers makes it possible for the best person to win on merit. However, the extent to which these notions of liberalism and merit can inform the policies that can be implemented so as to tackle inequalities in health and social care remains questionable. In the *Vital Connection* document about equalities in the NHS, one of the stated aims is 'to recruit, develop and retain a workforce that is able to deliver high quality services that are fair, accessible, appropriate and responsive to the diverse needs of different groups and individuals' (NHS Executive, 2000: 12).

The aim is couched in terms of diversity of the client group, but recruitment is couched in terms of merit. At first sight this may seem appropriate. However, the problem with the notion of merit is that it can sometimes be used as a catch-all word to encompass a range of characteristics: talents, skills, abilities, who you know, your 'old school tie' connections, your accent, dress and so on (CEMS, 2006). Social components can become a relevant part of a person's qualities for the job in question because of the value given to such qualities. The winners would be those individuals socialised along similar lines to the decision-makers. Those from different backgrounds categorised by social class, gender, disability, age, religion, sexual orientation and ethnicity may be found wanting in such qualities and therefore deemed unsuitable for undertaking particular jobs (CEMS, 2000).

Similar to other businesses, merit in social enterprises like health and social care is likely to be considered the thing that gets the job done best. However the problem might be that efficacy of common culture and like-mindedness in getting the job done favours a particular group of people at the exclusion of others who display different characteristics from decision-makers. As possible examples, working-class people, disabled people and people from Black and minority ethnic communities are likely as groups to display different characteristics from decision-makers external to these groups, and are more likely to be excluded unless diversity is valued as functionally relevant to job performance and optimisation of service delivery. Liberalism and meritocratic ideas appear not to give attention to the social and structural sources of inequality, because of the emphasis on the procedural mechanics created for the removal of barriers to competition.

Jewson and Mason (1986: 315) assert that the aim of liberal equal opportunities policies is the removal of unfair distortions to the operation of the labour market by means of institutionalising fair procedures in every aspect of work and employment. The removal of identified unfair distortions would lead to equal treatment of individuals as employees or recipients of services. However, the equal treatment cannot guarantee equal outcomes even if that is what is intended, suggesting the need to go beyond equal treatment should identified need warrant it.

Radical liberalism

As stated earlier in Chapter 3, O'Brien and Penna (1998) suggest that liberalism promotes ideas of equality of opportunity that are rooted in an inequality of outcomes.

This paradox might offer a partial explanation for the limited commitment to challenging the unacceptability of disadvantage and discrimination because people are accustomed to seeing and accepting different outcomes for certain groups. In pushing for progress on equal opportunities, a radical-liberal approach that takes into account measurable outcomes has had some support. This approach is viewed as different because it goes beyond equal treatment and meritocratic implementation of fair procedures. The radical approach puts the emphasis on direct intervention in order to achieve a fair distribution of rewards among recipients. Radicals are much more interested in measurable outcomes and less so on the rules of the contest. The absence of a fair distribution of rewards among disadvantaged groups is accepted as evidence of unfair discrimination that requires state intervention to put things right. However, it has been noted that Jewson and Mason's (1986) distinction between liberal and radical-liberal approaches to equal opportunities is not that marked, because procedural and structural changes advocated by the two approaches do not challenge in any significant way existing institutions that have contributed to the existence and continuation of discrimination (O'Brien and Penna, 1998).

Among health and social care practitioners who subscribe to the radical-liberal approach, equality data are essential to demonstrate fairness. Therefore, 'equal opportunities cannot be said to exist until the representation of Black people and women in the divisions of the labour force reflects their presence in society as a whole' (Jewson and Mason, 1986: 315).

The representation issue is important among those who subscribe to the radical view, particularly in health and social care, because of the links to service quality as stated in some government publications. For example:

> Securing and developing a workforce that reflects and understands the diversity of the population is fundamental to serving the needs of all, and such diversity helps to reassure users that they will be more likely to get the service they need. (NHS Executive, 2000: 9)

The radicals challenge the liberal notions of talent and ability because of the implicit values among those in positions of power that inform the choice of what are acceptable behaviours, knowledge and skills. This criticism implies that the radicals would propose different means to achieve equality within work organisations from those advocated by liberals. Politicisation of the decision-making process would be a radical approach, enabling those on the receiving end of discrimination to make demands for change to achieve fair measurable outcomes, whereas the liberals would emphasise the importance of fair procedures that would be rigorously implemented to produce fair outcomes. In any case, rigorous implementation of such procedures has remained by and large aspirational, as evidenced by the findings of the Equalities Review (2007).

Neo-liberalism

Radicals argue that their approach to equal opportunities is more likely to produce better results than the approach of liberals. But neo-liberals would suggest not. Neo-liberalism offers a counter argument to liberalism from the angle of personal freedom and justice. Hayek (1982) suggests that the legal system must treat all citizens alike without regard to differences and inequalities in individuals. The ideas about social justice, and the support of those ideas through legislation in an attempt to redress inequalities, are viewed as unhelpful. The state is expected not to intervene to redress substantive social and material inequalities, because manipulation of outcomes through the legal framework as a result of demands for social justice is thought to lead to corruption of the legal system. Such corruption would impact negatively on individual freedom.

Neo-liberalism advocates minimal state involvement in people's everyday lives, including welfare provision. Neo-liberals favour competitive market values. The economy is seen as having a self-balancing, trickle-down effect. Market mechanisms are expected to ensure protection for all, supported by other forms of non-state help, while protecting individual freedom. In place of the 'right' to benefit, neo-liberalism substitutes the 'duty' to support, and in place of the desire for 'quality' it substitutes the value of 'freedom' (O'Brien and Penna, 1998: 104). However, both Conservative and Labour governments have enacted anti-discrimination laws leading to the creation of institutions charged with responsibility for enforcing policy implementation. The existence of Equality Commissions is clear illustration of significant state intervention in an attempt to stamp out discrimination. The effectiveness of government intervention strategies has been variable during the period that anti-discrimination laws have been in place: 'Britain is in many ways a fairer and more equal society than at any time in living memory' (Equalities Review, 2007: 12).

Perhaps the variations in terms of measurable progress are due in part to different party political interpretations of what is an unacceptable level of persistent discrimination and inequality in society. How best to use public resources in order to achieve fairness and justice in the way public services such as health and social care are made available and delivered is also still undecided.

Implication for health and social care

Liberalism, neo-liberalism and the Third Way have all contributed to the debate and all appear to subscribe to a core value of universalistic equality before the law. This core value ought to make ongoing development of the promotion of equal opportunities readily acceptable within caring professions.

While the differing views we have outlined have each contributed to the debate and influenced some progress on the equality front, significant change as measured by those on the receiving end of discrimination has remained an issue of concern (Equalities Review, 2007). Lack of clarity about the best way forward has possibly contributed to a slow pace of change. Those who service the welfare state, particularly those in the caring professions that espouse caring values, would be expected to challenge discrimination as part and parcel of their normal way of working. However, research evidence suggests that health and social care professionals do not challenge discrimination as a matter of course, and at times collude with discriminatory practices (Staines, 2006; Fernando, 2005; Coker, 2001; Collier, 1998). Personal values, political ideologies, interests and commitment, all influence what individual practitioners consider to be of importance to their careers and how to take on board issues like equal opportunities.

When it comes to considering ideas about mainstreaming equality, so as to avoid discrimination by incorporating equality principles in everyday practice, progress has been slow, which has led to a perceived need for new anti-discrimination legislation in the twenty-first century. Lack of consensus on the meaning of equality in the field of health and social care has probably contributed to inaction:

> Evidence shows that there is still a lack of awareness and understanding about what equality means, how it relates to what organisations do, what is required (or permitted) under the law in practice and who is responsible for delivering on this. (Equalities Review, 2007: 93)

Cavanagh (2002), whose philosophical position against equality of opportunity offers something provocatively different, is worthy of note in relation to the possible direction of the debate about equal opportunities and discrimination. His ideas could be considered as offering a partial explanation for the continuation of some of the discriminatory practices in health and social care:

> By keeping the idea of non-discrimination conceptually separate from the idea of meritocracy, it enables us to maintain our conviction that discrimination is wrong because it wrongs those who are discriminated against. (2002: 81)

He has argued that the language of equality is confusing, clumsy and fails to address directly the concern that people's chances should not be affected by other people's prejudices. He proposes that people's prejudices should be tackled directly. Health and social care practitioners, who have a duty of care and are funded from the public purse, have a responsibility to put right the wrongs brought about by prejudice-based discrimination, provided they accept that it is wrong to discriminate. If so, it ought to be possible to incorporate the idea of challenging prejudices through reflective practice.

Cavanagh (2002) is critical of the liberal approach in terms of the mixture of the principles of meritocracy, equality and anti-discrimination. The abhorrent nature of discrimination means that the subject remains topical and the state is expected by its citizens to facilitate change. So far the state has responded through anti-discrimination and equality legislation, thereby mandating health and social care organisations to demonstrate that there is fairness and justice within their sphere of responsibility. Equal opportunity policies have thus resulted from a minimum-standard legal-compliance expectation.

Exercise

So far, liberalism and meritocracy have been the major frameworks influencing equal opportunity policies. Given the criticisms of these ideas, and the view of Cavanagh (2002) that current approaches to challenging prejudice and discrimination are clumsy, bureaucratic, complicated and expensive, try to brainstorm some alternative approaches to ensuring that discrimination is eliminated at institutional and individual levels within the care sector.

Towards a plan of action

Both liberal and radical-liberal conceptions imply that the concept of equal opportunities:

- is about social justice
- recognises that disadvantage and discrimination exists in society
- seeks to remove disadvantage and discrimination by action.

In acknowledging these three themes, an equal opportunities policy within a health and social care organisation would be expected to indicate how the formulated procedures and employee behaviour would support equality goal attainment.

Anti-discrimination legislation informs specific areas for attention, such as disability, gender, religion, sexual orientation and ethnicity. For example, if workplaces are not accessible to potential employees with a disability, this will affect the likelihood of a disabled person applying, and the likelihood of a disabled person being appointed. Conscious awareness of this is important because work environments have traditionally been created for the benefit of able-bodied people to the exclusion of disabled people. Putting in place measures to stop the potential discrimination against disabled people would satisfy fairness and justice. So, equality of opportunity processes should be a means to ensure that identified kinds of inequality are checked and corrected, so that measurable outcomes can be confirmed as an integral part of health and social care business outcomes.

However, there needs to be some recognition that allocating equal shares can be potentially risky if variations in need and preferences are ignored. This aspect is significant in health and social care delivery where the uniqueness of the individual should be respected, but where it is expected that everyone should benefit equally and unprejudicially from available services. The general thinking is that those who present themselves for employment or care can expect identical treatment, but it need not necessarily mean equal treatment. In practice, asking someone in a wheelchair to use the stairs because that is what everyone does is not equal treatment (Equalities Review, 2006: 71).

With regard to service users, it may be that they are not able to access a particular service because of inappropriate facilities or lack of knowledge about the services. The required action would be to ensure that adequate facilities are available to a knowledgeable service-user community.

Exercise

Within health or social care services familiar to you, how adequate do you think the facilities are for all potential user groups?

How knowledgeable about your service are the communities representing potential user groups likely to be?

Do your answers to these questions highlight gaps that require attention if there is a commitment to make a difference?

Drawing on liberal and social democratic principles in order to provide equal opportunities, those who work in health and social care organisations can give consideration to:

- ensuring that equality issues are embedded within personnel selection criteria
- creating appropriate procedures for recruiters to follow when appointing staff
- informing potential employees that their application will receive fair treatment
- ensuring that policies do not directly or indirectly discriminate against particular groups of people
- providing accurate and accessible information about the service on offer
- ensuring that action is taken when service users or staff raise concerns of discrimination
- involving service users in monitoring service quality
- assessing and measuring the impact of anti-discrimination procedures and publicising outcomes.

A creative approach is also likely to be helpful, and creativity and initiative need to be supported, encouraged and rewarded within organisations. For example, a Sikh patient was using the occupational therapy service offered by a Primary Health Care Trust to help him find employment. He was interested in teaching religion. The standard suggestions for mainstream teaching were not suitable for him, and he did not feel he had the right skills to go into the line of work that was on offer. One of the occupational therapy workers put him in touch with a Sikh priest, who invited the patient to the local temple (Gurdwara). This resulted in him finding an opportunity to train as a teacher through the Gurdwara where he felt comfortable as he fulfilled the entry requirement skills. Having found this opportunity, the worker said that this patient's demeanour changed, and he started to improve. This positive outcome was a result of the worker taking the initiative to go outside the confines of the standard provision within the Trust and seek to address the individual's needs, thus providing him with equal opportunities.

Such examples of workers taking the initiative to go outside the confines of the standard provision of service within the Trust could be considered as additional and troublesome work. Organisational support for workers would be important, in recognition of therapeutic innovation and creativity.

The moral case

The current position with regard to legal compliance is that all public sector organisations, including health and social care organisations, are required to have policies in place to ensure equality of opportunity in employment and in the services provided.

Exercise

For the organisation for which you work, or in which you are a student, find and read the organisation's equal opportunities policy, if you are not already familiar with it.

What principles and values is it based on?

How adequate do you think it is?

The argument behind equal opportunities policies is that by becoming genuinely inclusive and making better and appropriate use of all employees, the care sector can become more effective and improve the quality of service delivery (Collier, 1998). Implicit in this argument is that discrimination is not only wrong but is also bad for health and social care business because of the potential to under-utilise talent both within the existing groups of employees and through exclusion at the point of entry. As public sector organisations such as health and social care enterprises operate on a non-profit basis, they have a moral obligation to put to good use financial resources provided from taxation. To further enhance an understanding of the complex subject of discrimination and the potential damage that might be caused, we will discuss some moral reasons in support of equal opportunities. Morality underlies the legal principles which set minimum standards of conduct in public and social life.

Morality or ethics tells us what is right and what is wrong. Tackling discrimination has been informed by legislation which assumes that most people disapprove of what is seen as unjust inequality. The discourse of 'fair play' and 'social justice' encourages engagement with the moral case for equality. The philosophical basis for this has been debated for centuries.

Plato's *Republic* tackles the issue; some examples of modern treatments are Williams (1993) and Oderberg (2000a, 2000b). The School of Health and Social Care at Reading University was fortunate in the 1990s in having a full-time lecturer in moral philosophy. He was able to teach nursing and social work students systematic consideration of ethical issues (see Cain, 1995, 1997, 1998, 1999a, 1999b, 2002). In relation to the discussion here, these would include such questions as:

- Should people have the same opportunities regardless of different physical features, characteristics, wealth or reputation?
- Should consideration, advancement and reward be based only on merit, that is, an ability to do a certain job and meet specified criteria?
- Why is it important to behave ethically?

According to Saunders (2000), meritocracy is regarded by some as an important moral principle. The association with fairness and justice encourages people to give meritocracy serious consideration within the realm of equal opportunities.

However, some critics (for example Bagilhole, 1997) have expressed some concerns about its application. Interpretations of 'merit' in relation to taking decisions about the best person for the job have been challenged for ignoring other important characteristics such as gender or socio-economic status. When these characteristics are ignored or are not acknowledged, the recruitment outcome might involve a perpetuation of the status quo, suggesting inherent inequalities in the merit principle itself. The assumptions have been that as long as people are treated on merit they will get their just rewards, and that if discrimination is removed then over time the deserving will rise to the top: 'The mountain tops are within reach. All that is needed is the ability and he will start climbing' (Saunders, 2000: 91).

However, there are limitations inherent in these lines of thought because powerful elites are likely to be the ones deciding who qualifies as deserving. As part and parcel of developing an understanding of how discrimination occurs within health and social care organisations, it is important to continue to expose the limitations of the ideas in current usage. Continual exposition can be beneficial in pinpointing where problems lie so that they can be addressed. Thompson supports and cites the importance of continual self-assessment of one's knowledge base in the field of inequality:

> The field of inequality is a constantly changing one, with new challenges arising all the time. What is needed, then, is a degree of humility, a recognition that, however skilled, experienced or well informed we are, there is always a margin of error, and always scope for learning – an important principle on which to base all attempts to promote equality. (2003a: 7)

The reference to humility and acceptance of possible margins of error are poignant in health and social care because practitioners work with vulnerable people.

The legal and political case

Legal and political reasons for the development of equal opportunity policies can be linked back to social history over the last two centuries. Changes caused by such events as the industrial revolutions and migration to cities, migration from Europe to the new worlds of the Americas, Africa and Australasia, and later migration into the industrialised cities of the Northern Hemisphere have stimulated political changes. New and greater numbers of different groups have forced political changes on governments so that basic laws now try to reflect the interests not just of the ruling political elite but also, in theory, the whole of society. Equal opportunities thinking has been transformed by some basic laws in the UK, particularly regarding gender, race and disability. More recently, due to the influence of the European Union, further laws and regulations on human rights, sexual orientation, religion and age have been introduced. This transformation is reflected in surveys on public attitudes to equality, in that people are much more willing to discuss equality issues and show support for the aim of achieving greater equality of opportunity within a modern liberal democracy (Equalities Review, 2006). The review findings seem to suggest a perceived decline in the levels of gender and disability discrimination but not in relation to race, sexual orientation or religion. Education and legislation were cited as helpful levers in tackling discrimination-induced inequality.

Legislation indicates minimum standards and provides a clear statement of social disapproval of discrimination. The extensive legislation listed below offers people protection from discrimination and can support social institutions in tackling underlying structural problems interfering with progress towards achieving social justice and inclusion.

Anti-discrimination legislative framework

Employment Equality (Age) Regulations 2006
The European Commission Employment Directive requested Member States to prohibit age discrimination by 2006. The UK regulations came into force on 1st October.
Employment Equality (Religion or Belief) Regulations 2003
Outlaws discrimination (direct and indirect), harassment and victimisation on the grounds of religion, religious belief or similar philosophical belief.

Employment Equality (Sexual Orientation) Regulations 2003
Outlaws discrimination (direct and indirect), harassment and victimisation on the grounds of sexual orientation.
Race Relations Act 1976 and Race Relations Amendment Act 2000
Prohibits discrimination on the grounds of race or ethnic origin. The Act generally applies to the fields of employment, planning, housing, the exercise of public functions and the provision of goods, facilities and services. The Amendment Act specifies a legal duty to promote good relations between people of different racial groups and to have in place an equality scheme that is monitored for impact.
Sex Discrimination (Gender Reassignment) Regulations 1999
A measure to prevent discrimination against transsexual people, on the grounds of sex, in pay and treatment in employment.
Human Rights Act 1998
Makes it unlawful for a public authority to breach the Convention of Human Rights. It states that all UK legislation must be given a meaning that fits with the Convention Rights if that is possible.
Disability Discrimination Act 1995 and 2005
Prohibits discrimination against disabled people in employment, provision of goods, services, facilities and premises. Under the 2005 Act public bodies have a duty to promote good relations between disabled persons and other persons and have in place an equality scheme that is monitored for impact.
Sex Discrimination Act 1975
Prohibits sex discrimination against individuals in employment, education, and the provision of goods, facilities and services. It also prohibits discrimination in employment against married people and, since the Civil Partnership Act 2004 came into force, the same protection is afforded to those in civil partnerships as to those who are married.
Equal Pay Act 1970
Gives an individual a right to the same contractual pay and benefits as a person of the opposite sex doing the same job.

In using the legal framework above, discrimination would be judged to have occurred when one person has been treated less favourably than another because of their disability, marital status or race, for example. With disability discrimination the focus is on disadvantage because of the way society is organised. Therefore, it is society that needs to change and become inclusive by removing the barriers stopping disabled people's full participation in all aspects of societal endeavour. Within equal opportunities, discrimination refers to the different and usually more negative experiences people from certain groups encounter because of being different from the majority.

Anti-discrimination legislation provides a framework for tackling discrimination by setting minimum standards for conducting employment and service delivery. The existence of these laws would suggest that there more work still to be done even though progress has been made (Equalities Review, 2007).

Barriers to equality of opportunity

It seems fair to say that discrimination is not as blatant as it was in the past. For example, research into the experiences of minority students and staff in architecture and the built environment found that this group was well represented among students and most of them completed their studies successfully. However, within the same study, students viewed the curriculum as Euro-Anglo-centric with a particular cultural loading, and that academic staff had a colour-blind approach at the teaching stage but not at the assessment stage. Because of these experiences, the attitude of minority students was one of enduring the course, finishing and leaving to go and practise architecture of their choice (CEMS, 2005).

This example shows progress made as well as areas for further development. Some of the issues raised within this study are applicable across the care sector. The attitude of students to endure, finish and leave has implications for the continuation of under-representation of minority academic staff. One feeds into the other, since experiences of discrimination can sap the incentive to continue with research and an academic career. Research into the experiences of Black and minority ethnic (BME) staff in two NHS trusts found that many of them linger at lower or middle grades and are often reluctant to pursue complaints about racial discrimination because of the fear of repercussions. Past experience of less favourable treatment and exclusion saps the incentive to try for promotion (CEMS, 2002).

Barriers to achieving equal opportunities may be at an individual or organisational level. Barriers at the individual level may include:

- assuming that everyone is the same with similar values and needs
- denial and lack of recognition that there are inequalities
- being uncomfortable with someone who is distinctively different to oneself
- lack of confidence to deal with discriminatory situations
- fear of losing power
- internalisation of oppression
- lack of interest and energy
- comfortable and content with the status quo
- belief in the superiority of one's group
- lack of knowledge and skills.

Examples of organisational barriers to equal opportunities include:

- lack of leadership and commitment to effect change
- inappropriate work structures and organisational culture
- inappropriate policies and procedures

- lack of designated resources
- exclusionary work environment
- burdensome workloads
- ignoring evidence of the extent of discrimination.

Exercise

Within a health, social care or educational organisation that you are familiar with, review whether you think any of the above individual and organisational barriers are present. Think of some strategies that could be tried to effect positive change, using anti-discrimination legislation or other means.

The barriers listed above can be tackled if there is a willingness to do so. Political and managerial leadership have a pivotal role to play. Research can be carried out to confirm or refute the existence of barriers, followed by education for staff in areas that would benefit from such an approach. It would be expected that health and social care students would be exposed to professional training curricula that take into account equality issues. The knowledge gained from research and instruction can help individuals to locate problem areas within their own organisations or the ones they come into contact with in the course of business.

Other strategies for anti-discrimination

In their role as advocates for those they support, health and social care practitioners should challenge discrimination and, as professionals, their personal practice should not stigmatise service users. A persistent push for change also needs to be sustained by those on the receiving end of discrimination.

One of the main criticisms of the current anti-discrimination legislation is that it is cumbersome and yet fragmented in an attempt to address particular areas of discrimination, as the list of anti-discrimination laws included in this chapter confirms. According to Equalities Review (2007), plans are under way to produce a coherent and integrated package through a single law on equality because it has been recognised that the complexity of the current anti-discrimination legal framework means that challenging discrimination through the courts is difficult for many people, so they do not complain. People on the receiving end of discrimination are vulnerable. They are often just trying to make ends meet, or are negotiating their way through complicated societal systems in order to have a sense of belonging. Reliance on litigation runs the danger that much unlawful discrimination is not addressed, because people are scared to come forward. However, the desirable position would be one in which health and social care workers, because of their commitment to anti-oppressive practice, can assess any potential detrimental impact of policies and engage in the development of measures designed to promote equality, as well as advocating for those who are marginalised. This would be in line with the thinking behind professional values, for example the stated core social work value, 'take action to counter discrimination'.

The duty of care accepted by all who choose a career in health and social care, plus the existence of anti-discrimination legislation, places a responsibility upon these professionals to challenge discrimination. It is also morally right and just to do so. The very strong ethic of humanitarianism can be a driver for change, but it requires professionals to accept evidence of the nature and extent of damaging discrimination in health and social care (Coker, 2001). Equalities knowledge and transformational leadership are important catalysts to enable the acceptance of the problems because denial remains a big problem, particularly within the NHS (CEMS, 2006; Ruth, 2006; Johns, 2005; Fernando, 2005; Coker, 2001; Gaine, 1995). Transformational leadership has been identified as critical in progressing equal opportunities in the public sector, in particular in care organisations (Goodwin, 2006; Kumar and Kumar, 2002).

Justice and fairness

Justice is a constant theme within discussions about equality and equal opportunities. Justice is acknowledged as the bedrock associated with the right dealings between the many groups and interests that compose society (Clark, 2002), even though the practical importance and consequences of acting justly is open to many interpretations. Liberalism, neo-liberalism and the Third Way perspectives have different 'takes', impacting on processes that are deemed to be fair. What constitutes 'fair' can often be disputed. Disputes resulting from different interpretations could have partly influenced the slow pace of change towards eliminating inequalities.

The 1948 Universal Declaration of Human Rights has become the inspiration for national and international efforts to promote and protect human rights and fundamental freedoms. It has provided the platform for the legally binding international instruments that followed, including instruments addressing the rights of ethnic minorities, women's rights and more recently children's rights. Emerging from this is the idea of equality as a right not to be discriminated against purposely by others. In order to secure these rights to equality of opportunity, liberalism has also been strongly associated with changes in the legislation, as listed earlier in this chapter. Thus rights are enshrined in law (Hughes, 2002).

Whether policy-makers pursue ideas of justice as entailing equality of outcome, fair distribution of resources, or equality of opportunity, depends on the underlying values, ideological position and beliefs about cause and effect. The current political pursuit of equality by the Labour government mainly involves the removal of disadvantage, and the enabling of equality of opportunity through policies relating to education, training and employment that discourage discrimination by sex, disability, age, religion and ethnicity. There is an emphasis on the contract between the citizen and the state in terms of rights and responsibilities. Informing that contract are the traditional values of justice and freedom. Gordon Brown has been quoted as saying 'the road to equality of opportunity starts not with tax rates, but with jobs, education and the reform of the welfare state and redistributing existing resources efficiently and equitably' (Powell and Hewitt, 2002: 17).

Summary

- Equal opportunities policies have been strongly influenced by liberal thought.
- However, liberalism and meritocratic ideas give inadequate attention to social structures of inequality.
- Anti-discrimination legislation provides the framework for liberal policies on equality.
- Effective political and organisational leadership is essential for bringing about positive equality outcomes.

5
Equality and Diversity

Aim

- To provide a historical account of the changes in equality discourse over a period of four decades.
- To show the impact of legislation on the language used within equal opportunities policies.
- To outline the development of the concept of the value of diversity.
- To discuss issues in the management of diversity.

A historical account of the changes in the discourse on equal opportunities from the 1960s to the present day will show how the terminology used in each decade changed to reflect societal attitudes and the legislation of the day. The language used in each decade illustrates the selection of particular equalities terminology to reflect policy. This in turn illustrates the influence of language use on people's reactions and behaviours when issues of discrimination come into the spotlight: 'Language is a very powerful tool. The way we talk about the world can affect the way we regard and interact with other people' (Collier, 1994: 1).

Use of language

As in previous chapters, on-going reflection remains important. Here we encourage reflection on the impact of language in demonstrating anti-oppressive ways of thinking about, and working with, service users and colleagues within the health and social care sectors. Individuals can judge if the impact is negative and, if so, decide on alternatives so as to move away from negativity. Those who have campaigned for change to eliminate discrimination have drawn on linguistic narratives of the day in attempting to win people over. One of the results has been the formulation and enactment of anti-discrimination legislation from the 1960s onward. As a living tool, language grows and changes constantly. Because of this constant change, language is one obstacle in the path to equality that can be easily removed. Therefore, each practitioner can easily make a contribution by removing oppressively negative or exclusionary language from their vocabulary.

Collier (1994) makes an interesting point, commenting on how the use of language to describe specific jobs in nursing was done so as to enhance the status of the those jobs in order to accommodate men working in a traditionally female domain. 'Matron' as a job title became 'senior nursing officer' and 'ward sister' became 'charge nurse'. However, Collier argues that the same accommodation of language has not taken place in situations where women enter traditionally male domains, and she asks us to consider why.

An examination of the historical development of anti-discrimination language used over time from the 1960s to the present day shows the influence of the political ideologies of liberalism, neo-liberalism and socialism on the use of particular frameworks of thought and meaning in relation to issues of equality and justice. By examining the use of language at specific historical points, connections can be made to show how language in current use has emerged, thereby giving a yardstick from which to assess the extent to which genuine progress towards inclusiveness has been made. For example, disablist, sexist, homophobic and racist language offends most people, so health and social care professionals would be expected not to use such language. Such an assessment of progress can be done through the eyes of those who have contested and struggled for equal rights, balanced against those who hold opposing views and wish to retain the status quo in health and social care.

As with any other service organisation, health and social care can be expected to have among its employees and service users a diversity of views about equality and how to achieve it, and language plays an important part in developing shared understanding. For example, among recipients of unfavourable treatment, there have been criticisms about the failures of the tried and tested liberal approaches towards achieving equality. These criticisms have stimulated current debates about diversity and difference (Equalities Review, 2006). Measuring how far and how many citizens have secured their rights to equality of opportunity can identify approaches that could usefully be extended in the future. There is thus a need to look back and take from the past ideas that can inform future debates and action for change.

Exploration of the key stages over recent decades in the establishment of the right of individuals to be afforded equal opportunities, with particular attention to health and social care enterprises, is important because of the care ethos. It is particularly important that those who elect to take on the caring of vulnerable people as a job should not discriminate unlawfully and unfairly. In addition to this, health and social care enterprises play an important role because they employ significant numbers of women and Black and minority ethnic (BME) people whose experience of discrimination is well documented (Collier, 1998; Bagilhole, 1997; Commission for Racial Equality, 1983). Did the use of particular language help or hinder progress?

The 1960s

According to Bagilhole (1997), serious equalities discourse started in the 1960s as women and BME people began to challenge the institutions of the day and demanded protection from discrimination. The language in use at the time is reflective of that era. Employers often saw themselves as dealing fairly when hiring workers on merit from a pool of people who belonged to a restricted group of specific racial identity. At the time newcomers from the Commonwealth were not socially welcome by the white majority population (Francis, 1998; Sewell, 1998). Employers, it would appear, were unable to operate open employment policies due to opposition of white employees to 'coloured' workers, there was absence of references to women and disabled people, and there was concern about possible negative reactions from customers if the status quo was interfered with.

The use of the term 'coloured' was used to refer to people who are not white. So it can be seen that through the use of such language, colour coding and ethnic monitoring of applicants goes back to the 1960s. This use of language can provide some insights into who is being constructed as different. The construction of difference can then lead to discrimination and exclusion. The lack of reference to women and disabled people served to perpetuate inequalities post-Second World War, and yet this was a period in history when the model of social policy in Britain had non-discrimination as one of its objectives, with the goal of abolishing discrimination in society and bringing about equality between people. The contradiction in terms of a socialist political ideal of ending discrimination, and the reality of excluding certain colour-based groups, women and disabled people, was indicative of the complexity of accommodating diversity of opinions among those in leadership positions and the electorate. What is interesting and worthy of note is that, while the discourse was one of exclusion, the employment pattern in the 1960s was different in health and social care and primary school teaching. These areas of social policy were serviced by women as the main workforce in line with traditional values about the role of women as carers, and therefore employable in jobs where the main feature is caring for others. Some of the female health care workers had been recruited from former British colonies to service an expanding welfare state. The Nationality Act 1948 gave Common-wealth citizens special immigration status, enabling them to enter and settle in the UK (Bennett, 2006).

Through state encouragement, many came from the Commonwealth to work in the NHS and other public sector industries such as transport. Their reception and the language used to describe the 1950s and 1960s immigrants were oppressive and exclusionary. The blatant nature of discrimination caused social tensions resulting in riots (Fryer, 1984). The marginalisation of BME people and women through their segregated position in the labour market, despite their participation in important areas of public life, influenced the demands for protection from discrimination (Bagilhole, 1997). This period started the wave of anti-discrimination laws that has continued to mushroom to the present day. Equalities discourse reflects the ever-changing needs and demands made by those on the receiving end of injustice.

The 1970s

The 1970s anti-discrimination legislation on gender and race established the Equal Opportunities Commission and the Commission for Racial Equality. The language of 'equal' was embedded in the duties of the two commissions as they took on the role of:

- promoting good practice by publishing and circulating codes of practice challenging discrimination through formal investigations
- providing legal support to strategic winnable cases that would receive maximum publicity
- undertaking research, so that the evidence would support the argument for change and justify public expenditure towards fighting discrimination.

State funding of the two equality commissions from the mid-1970s reflected government's interest in beginning to tackle discrimination through formally recognised structures. At this stage, the main focuses were sex and race discrimination. The legal framework reflected the demands that were being made by pressure groups and social movements for government to take a lead in fighting the discrimination experienced by women and racial minorities predominantly. The discourse focused particular attention on institutional practices, in line with liberal thought, highlighting to employers the importance of having positive policies to support the realisation of equal opportunities. Legislation defined the categories it applied to sex and marital status in the case of Equal Opportunities legislation, and colour, race, or ethnic origins in the case of Race Discrimination legislation. The legislation applied to all conditions of work, and of crucial importance were procedures to deal with complaints and grievances.

The language used in articulating policy requirements seemed to be about meeting legal requirements in respect of gender and race. Emphasis was on women and men, and minorities and the majority population, working together without fear of discrimination. Discourse tended to focus on employment practices in manufacturing industries, even though the legislation also applied to service delivery. The Equal Opportunities Commission (EOC) and the Commission for Racial Equality (CRE) encouraged and supported employers to formulate equal opportunities policies in order to demonstrate commitment to fair employment practices and to the elimination of gender and race discrimination. Having in place two commissions to support a government social policy objective of non-discrimination arose from liberal ideas and would not have been well received by those who subscribed to neo-liberalism, because of objections to government intervention: 'The demand for social justice for certain groups of people results in legislation which aims to manipulate outcomes, and this corrupts the legal framework which preserves individual freedom' (O'Brien and Penna, 1998: 89).

This view was expressed by Hayek (1982), who argued against egalitarianism and imposed equality because of the likely outcome of a very invasive state. However, this way of thinking is considered by Blakemore (2003) as alarmist and fails to take into account the benefits of equality to society as a whole. This diversity of views again illustrates the complexities associated with finding an appropriate path to achieving equality. In the event, it was decided politically that more legislation should follow.

The 1980s

The 1980s saw a flurry of activity in the development of equality policy statements across the public sector and large corporations in particular. Social services under the umbrella of local authorities produced detailed paper policies and started to implement some aspects of these policies. There was less action within the NHS, even though formal investigations and court cases provided evidence to suggest that sexism and racism were damaging the NHS (Johns, 2005; Baxter, 1988). The work of the equality commissions continued throughout the 1980s and terminology reflected the level of awareness about equality issues. The push was for employers to demonstrate that employees and potential employees were not put at a disadvantage and did not receive less favourable treatment. Legislation had been extended to cover disability, and the discourse (and later the legislation) was further extended to the categories of sexual orientation, age and religious belief. The needs of disadvantaged groups were considered under positive action measures, and managers were encouraged to accept and undertake appropriate training on equal opportunities.

Language helps form the limits of people's perception of the reality of discrimination in the work place. The discourse of 'disadvantage' and 'less favourable treatment' was extended to groups that had not received specific attention during the earlier decades. The limited successes of the 1980s changed people's expectations and disadvantaged groups wanted more.

The language of encouragement, training and positive action reflected a desire to see an increase in the speed of change towards elimination of unlawful and unfair discrimination. The expansion of the categories considered reflected the extent to which diversity thinking was taking hold. It began to be realised that different groups were bound together because of common experiences of discrimination, as well as having specific needs related to each group's specific identity. The equality discourse started to include ideas about diversity and difference.

During this period, reference to service delivery practices is a noticeable omission in the discourse. In health and social care, the omission might be explained by the prevalence of ideas of professionalism and merit, implying that those appointed to jobs within the care sector would act professionally and have the values, knowledge and skills not to discriminate. However, research evidence suggested otherwise (Equalities Review, 2007; Coker, 2001; Collier, 1998; Cohen, 1995; Butt, 1994).

The 1990s

During the 1990s, policies on equality began to address criticism from managers of the quality of training in relation to discrimination, particularly on sexism and racism. The individual-centred approach to training made some individuals feel attacked, so progress in terms of attitudinal and behavioural change was limited. The language of sexism awareness training (SAT) and racism awareness training (RAT) shifted to anti-sexism and anti-racism training in response to criticisms from senior management in industry.

However, explanations and information provided during training sessions about positive action measures were often seen as implying positive discrimination, and some employees felt threatened because it was perceived that disadvantaged groups were receiving too much attention at the expense of the majority. There were serious concerns that powerful decision-makers would become uncooperative and slow down the pace of change (Bennett, 2006). So the language used in writing policies and procedures during this period was aimed at ensuring that the gains made towards equality would be maintained, through shifting the emphasis more on to:

* highlighting the benefits of diversity, particularly to business effectiveness
* nominating staff to champion equality
* including the avoidance of harassment and considering the impact on staff in terms of stress and morale
* the value of training in equal opportunities for the whole workforce
* measuring progress through audits.

These developments were producing improvements in some areas, but persistent inequalities were still evident. At the start of the current New

Labour administration, the Prime Minister expressed his concern about the lack of representation of Black and minority ethnic people (BME) at strategic level within the British establishment:

'We cannot be a beacon to the world unless the talents of all the people shine through. Not one Black high court judge; not one Black Chief Constable or permanent secretary; not one Black army officer above the rank of colonel. Not one Asian one either. Not a record of pride for the British establishment. And not a record of pride for Parliament that there are so few Black and Asian MPs.' (Travis and Rowan, 1997)

The Prime Minister signalled a commitment to tackle inequalities on two fronts, economic and social, placing emphasis on education and employment as means to reduce inequalities. The drive to tackling the root causes of poverty and inequality has shaped social policy since 1997.

The 2000s

Tackling the root causes of inequality as signalled by the Prime Minister is reflected in the policies from 2000 to the present, where many employers show through their literature that they:

- aspire to be a beacon on equality matters
- consider equality and diversity to be complementary
- set realistic and achievable equality goals that are measurable
- mention the importance of employees and customers for business success
- include the notions of social values and communitarianism.

The acceptance of equality and diversity as complementary is reflected in the way top British companies have adopted diversity management policies (Mirza, 2005). Within these policies the main aim is to promote diversity in the workforce to improve productivity. However, the American experience of assessing the impact of diversity on business results has shown that there has been a tendency to over-emphasise the business case and that the groups that are meant to benefit from such initiatives continue to experience discrimination (Hanson, 2003).

Summary of changes

Emerging from this journey between the 1960s and the present day are terms such as equality of opportunity, equality of access, anti-discrimination policies, diversity and more recently a capabilities approach. The changes are noticeable from the 1960s, when the first significant inroads were made in terms of non-discrimination legislation on race, but nevertheless suggested passivity and reactivity rather than taking a positive and proactive stance.

This was followed by recognition of a need to do more than just react to negative discrimination, and to actively fight injustice and support people's rights to equality of opportunity. This active stance was accompanied by monitoring outcomes. Within organisations, this stage in the development process created some resistance, although this resistance appears to be receding somewhat as society generally has become more tolerant. With the move towards equality screening of policies, and equality impact assessments, driven by the Race Relations Amendment Act 2000, it would appear that people are becoming more comfortable and less defensive in their involvement in producing equality data and use of research evidence to inform anti-oppressive practice.

Diversity considerations

Discussions about equality of opportunity, diversity and the management of diversity within organisations are likely to continue to take into account the demands from service users that they remain central to all issues about equality in health and social care. These concepts are distinct and yet interlinked given the historical developments previously outlined.

> Pursuing diversity strategies is essentially going beyond the basic legal requirements. Equality of Opportunity legislation provides a necessary and useful framework for challenging discrimination; however, successful diversity management derives from the commitment to make the best of all human resources. (Auluck, 2001: 9)

Valuing diversity starts from the position that people's differences are an asset rather than a burden to be tolerated. However, for many who have not experienced discrimination and exclusion, being made to consider diversity issues can be received as burdensome. So, for those people who may want to sell the idea to the powerful elite in health care, they need political and financial backing as levers for championing diversity. The government's policy framework through the Positively Diverse Programme (NHS Confederation, 2005) and the Vital Connection Action Plan (NHS Executive, 2000) indicates commitment to see positive changes towards inclusion and a reduction in persistent inequalities as a result of discrimination. Diversity emphasis in relation to equality in the NHS is encapsulated in the following statement:

> There is no such thing as a typical citizen. People's needs and concerns differ: between women and men for example, between the young and the old, between those of different social, cultural and educational backgrounds, and between people with and without disabilities. Some of these concerns have not been given sufficient recognition in the past. We must understand the needs of all people and respond to them. This, too, is a crucial part of modernising government. (NHS Executive, 2000: 6)

It would appear from the above statement that there is an acknowledgement of problems that must be tackled, and diversity thinking cuts across all areas requiring attention. Health and social care employees are therefore expected to understand the needs of service users and colleagues and respond appropriately to those needs. Responding appropriately to need implies anti-oppressive practice.

However, when asking organisational members in health and social care to consider diversity issues, it is important to recognise that diversity gets to the core of people's values, deeply held beliefs and ideologies, and it questions decades of conditioning. This is likely to be found particularly difficult among members of professional groups, because they have their own professional codes of conduct and are used to self-regulation. For example, Sir Donald Irvine, in his capacity as the president of the UK General Medical Council, argued that:

> As a profession we have sometimes concentrated our efforts on quality standards for professional care and services to patients at the expense of considering the ethical context in which we deliver and practise care. (Coker, 2001: 239)

Quality standards of care and services to patients, according to Collier (1998), ought not to be separated from equality, and monitoring of equality should be an integral part of how the quality of performance is measured. Individuals would be expected to incorporate and embed diversity issues within their practice. To do so requires knowledge, skill and a willingness to do things differently.

Exercise

Whatever your role, as student or practitioner, consider what 'incorporating and embedding diversity issues within your practice' might mean for you. What knowledge, skills and motivation might you need to develop?

For newly qualified professionals, valuing diversity and practising in an anti-oppressive way may be less daunting than for seasoned professional practitioners, who may not recognize the need to change their practice in line with anti-discrimination moral and legislative requirements. Enlightened newly qualified professionals are likely to encounter difficulties in attempting to impart inclusive practice techniques to their seniors, due to power differentials, and so it is important to seek out supportive senior staff as mentors. As a result of recognising that structural inequalities are still embedded in health and social care systems, enlightened practitioners need to continue to research, expose institutional discrimination and use the evidence in supporting the direction of change. Public opinion is likely to be favourable towards this (Equalities Review, 2007). Professional bodies such as the General Social Care Council (GSCC), the General Medical Council (GMC) and the Nursing and Midwifery Council (NMC) all accept the need for change and have put out policy statements to demonstrate their commitment to equality and to valuing diversity. An example of such a policy statement reads:

> The NMC is committed to valuing diversity and providing equality of opportunity across all its operations. We intend to do this by rigorously implementing a valuing diversity policy. Valuing diversity can be defined as valuing people and treating them fairly irrespective of their race, colour, religion, ethnic origin, nationality, gender, disability, working patterns, sexual orientation and family circumstances. This is not only right, it will improve the service we provide to the public and the profession. It is good for the employee, the customer, the NMC and the community at large. More than just complying with legislation, the NMC will take the necessary steps to promote fairness and equal treatment, regularly reviewing procedures and practices and monitoring progress. (NMC, 2006)

The diversity interpretation articulated in this statement of policy covers both employment and service delivery, signalling to all its members the nature of conduct expected. This statement ought to be a useful tool and the basis from which all NMC members could make demands for change in areas where diversity is not valued, resulting in discrimination. Along similar lines the other professional bodies, the GSCC and GMC, have their own policy statements on equality and diversity. For the reasons mentioned earlier, of power differentials and discriminatory institutional practices, there are likely to be some complexities associated with policy implementation. However, the recognition of the complexities is a positive step towards effecting desired positive change.

Change drivers

The complexities can be addressed through leadership, research and education. Progressing the valuing of diversity to achieve equality needs effective management and leadership. Kotter's (1990) view is that management is about coping with complexity and bringing order into organisations, in particular to areas like service quality. Leadership is about vision and coping with change towards a desired future. The overlap between management and leadership would suggest that a successful organisation needs both. To effect organisational change to ensure the realisation of equality in health and social care, leadership ought to play a significant role showing how to manage a diverse workforce that has a responsibility to deliver service to diverse user groups. A transformational style of leadership appears to be a favourable one in moving equality issues forward because leaders who adopt this style are concerned with sharing values and developing a sense of doing something purposeful: 'The essence of transformational leadership is that leaders transform the way their staff see themselves and the organisation' (Martin and Henderson, 2001: 40).

In addition to this, Goodwin (2006) suggests that transformational leaders are able to create an environment in which people can grow and contribute all their talents to the performance of the organisation. Such leaders are needed in health and social care, because they are more likely to be able to win the hearts and minds of those who resist change.

Curriculum content of professional courses of study can be inclusive by incorporating the essential elements of diversity to support anti-oppressive practice. Since health and social care are part of the welfare state and are included as specific areas for thorough examination within the academic discipline of social policy, diversity issues ought to be fully explored by students and academics, with service users playing a significant educative role. According to Beresford (2006), a meaningful service-user involvement is yet to happen. He states:

> If social policy as a discipline is to reflect commitments to equality and inclusion, this must change. This isn't just about the inclusion of a specific group of current service users, although this is clearly important. It also raises broader issues about everyone's inclusion in terms of being able to be open about who we actually are, our vulnerabilities, our whole identity, our full selves in social policy. (2006: 149)

While the context of this quotation is the exclusion of disabled service users because of the way social policy has operated, other disciplines involving human subjects can take on board the criticism and stop the exclusion by tapping into the diversity of expertise from marginalised groups.

Exercise

To what extent are service users involved in training or monitoring services in your experience?

Does the involvement reflect the diverse range of service-user identity?

What do you think might be done to increase service-user involvement?

Changes would need to be made to professional undergraduate and postgraduate programmes, as well as post-qualifying courses. Stand-alone diversity training programmes appear not to have made much of a difference over the years. Perhaps it is because training sessions of this nature are seen as something to be endured, get over and done with as quickly as possible, and then get back to real work.

According to Schneider (2001), business pressures are often cited as the reasons why it is hard for managers to think about diversity issues.

This is because diversity remains separated from everyday business practice, and therefore attention to it remains cursory. Despite the potential for resistance to change, it ought to be possible to make some impact through giving attention to a combination of research, publishing evidence of successes and failures, professional inclusive education, and mandatory on-going post-qualifying professional development.

When professional education and training produces health and social care practitioners who understand and value diversity, and have the knowledge and skills to practise in an anti-discriminatory way, such practitioners can expect their managers to create an environment in which they can give of their best. Effective managers working within an inclusive environment would need to acknowledge that people experience the world of work in different ways. They should consider different communication styles in order to relate to and bring the best out of everyone they are responsible for. Diversity champions argue that such a process of management helps to impart positive messages in relation to the benefits that can be accrued by capitalising on the different backgrounds of employees (Baxter, 2001). Difference in this case is accepted as a basis for equality rather than inequality.

Defining diversity

Within health and social care organisations the reality of managing diversity means balancing the differing needs of service users and the contributions of a diverse workforce. Two popular definitions in common use are included here to highlight how diversity can be conceptualised. The extent to which these definitions are useful in stimulating ways of interpreting diversity can be explored.

> The basic concept of managing diversity accepts that the workforce consists of a diverse population of people. The diversity consists of visible and non-visible differences which will include factors such as sex, age, background, race, disability, personality and workstyle. It is founded on the premise that harnessing these differences will create a productive environment in which everyone feels valued, where their talents are being fully utilised and in which organisational goals are met. (Kandola and Fullerton, 1998: 7)

> Diversity management refers to a strategic organisational approach, organisational culture change, and empowerment of the workforce. It represents a shift away from the activities and assumptions defined by affirmative action to management practices that are inclusive, reflecting the workforce diversity and its potential. Ideally it is a pragmatic approach, in which participants anticipate and plan for change, do not fear human difference or perceive them as a threat, and view the workplace as a forum for individuals' growth and change in skills and performance with direct cost benefits to the organisation. (Arredondo, 1996: 17)

Exercise

What is your view of these definitions?

Can you see any drawbacks in them?

Can you come up with an alternative definition of your own of diversity and diversity management?

In both definitions the emphasis is on how people from diverse backgrounds are managed as a means to achieving desired outcomes. Such an approach to management will lead to the creation of a conducive working environment. Even though definitions by their very nature are limited, these two definitions have provided a starting point and stimulated discussion within the field of diversity in the work place and in service delivery.

Lorbiecki and Jack (2000), in their critique of diversity management based on discourse analysis, highlight the issues of the objectification of diversity, control and stigmatisation. The three issues identified are generally associated with oppression. From that standpoint the language used in the two definitions can be seen as unhelpful. Debate has continued and more recently managing diversity has also come to incorporate a growing range of more flexible working practices. For example, the traditional concept of flexi-time has been expanded to include annual hours, home-based working and part-time working. Balancing different needs presents a real challenge to those who are opposed to changing the culture. Such individuals would have specific development needs if they are to continue to function effectively within the new diversity management culture. Anti-oppressive practitioners, while recognising that diversity and difference can be the roots of discrimination, in the sense that it is through identification of differences that discrimination can take place, need to be mindful not to exclude those who have yet to change their ways. In order to win the resisters towards inclusion and diversity thinking, it is possible to create new rules, mirroring what people are familiar with: 'Unwritten organisational rules may need to be changed to nurture and appreciate diversity and to develop sensitivity to individual differences' (Blakemore and Drake, 1996: 189).

Health care professionals fall into this category of practitioners who have consistently resisted changes required to embrace valuing diversity practices and reduce inequalities. Research evidence over the past ten years has confirmed the extent of resistance to change and the continuation of discrimination (Collier, 1999; Agnew, 1998; Esmail and Carnall, 1997). Winning over the resisters remains a tough call because professional groups have dominated the NHS from the time the service was set up. However, as it is a publicly funded service, it is particularly unacceptable that discrimination could lead to less favourable treatment for some at the hands of health care practitioners, or to exclusion from employment or promotion opportunities.

Health and social care organisations provide services for a wide range of people of different ages, both sexes, and from a wide range of backgrounds. So the employment of people to serve these clients should ideally reflect service-user profiles. A mixed work force reflecting the customer base leads to a more culturally sensitive and effective service. In this regard effectively managing a diverse workforce in health and social care is about maximising the benefits that accrue to society. The emphasis ought to be about understanding the many benefits to the service brought about through employing a diverse workforce with different life experiences. Included in the package of benefits is working with difference without fear of the 'other', because valuing diversity strengthens the process of combating prejudice and discrimination.

Benefits of valuing diversity

Some of the benefits of accepting and valuing diversity have been examined from a business point of view. It could be argued that health and social care service users, as tax-payers, will get value for money when diversity policies are implemented, thereby creating inclusive environments in which people are likely to be more contented, to perform well and to take less time off sick. Additionally, making everyone welcome will improve the level of customer satisfaction. Like all modern twenty-first-century organisations, the NHS needs a more innovative and adaptable work culture. Diversity principles and practices offer innovativeness and adaptability. Having had a long-standing history of employing people from diverse backgrounds, albeit in less prestigious positions, a window of opportunity exists for the NHS to tap into an under-utilised human resource. Tapping into the diversity of talent at the disposal of the leaders of health and social care services is the morally right thing to do, but there is also evidence that it would be supported by the general public, who are reported to have become more tolerant and accepting of diversity (Equalities Review, 2007). Leaders have a mandate to act and to support their managers to make things happen and make equality an achievable goal. Dadabhoy says: 'Talent and ability have no racial, ethnic or cultural exclusivity. Racism robs the NHS of both' (2001: 77).

If appointments of some of the people in powerful positions were to be made outside merit and equality principles, for example because of who they knew, their performance might not warrant their position. Discriminatory recruitment practices can result in the appointment of mediocre performing staff, who in turn can produce mediocre service that is unlikely to benefit the diversity of service users from diverse groups. An 'old boy network' approach to staff appointments is unlikely to be good for health and social care business. One of the strong arguments in favour of diversity is that organisations adopting this approach retain staff, utilise the talents of many and get a healthy return on human resource investment. This diversity approach also helps organisations to demonstrate compliance with legislation.

Organisational culture issues

If the business case for adopting the diversity approach is accepted, then the management of change needs to be carefully planned to increase the probability of a successful outcome. The starting position would be an analysis of the dominant organisational culture. It is likely that there will be sub-cultures which contribute towards the dominant culture. This stage is critical because understanding these cultures will provide insights into how the organisation deals with change (Schein, 1992). This analysis can also assist in determining possible reasons for unease when equality issues are raised and for resistance to change among the various professional groups in health and social care. Some unease may be rooted in a lack of understanding of the subject matter and its importance within the context of competing demands in health and social care. Conflict can be anticipated, because conflict is embedded in the discourse of equality and diversity. It is the hidden threat that gives the whole discussion its edge and urgency. Without the threat of conflict the imperatives for change become less impelling. Both the oppressed and the powerful have always known this; the rest – the majority – have assumed for too long that inequalities can go on unchallenged (Hatch, 1997).

Given the diversity of the sub-systems in health and social care and the tribalistic nature of the professional groups within these services, conflict is likely to be intense, but that intensity of conflict should be accepted as an organisational fact of life for these services. With political and financial backing, tapping into that energy, channelling it towards innovation and working out an appropriate way forward are likely to be productive, resulting in measurable success.

The evidence from the Equalities Review (2007) indicates that there has been some progress towards reducing inequalities and that there is strong support from the general public for increased social justice and help for the more disadvantaged in society. Taking this strong support as the starting point, it seems important that caring institutions be seen to do their bit to help the more disadvantaged in society. Since all health care trusts and social services departments have well-developed paper policies on equality and diversity, it should be possible to make some progress and to monitor the degree of success using the capabilities framework. The capabilities approach is a version of equality of opportunity, which focuses on the assets of individuals and gives due attention to what individuals are able to do (Equalities Review, 2006).

However, lasting change is more likely if the main drivers for the change include those on the receiving end of discrimination and oppressive practice. These individuals and groups can seek support from equality champions, and form alliances with others who find injustice intolerable. Because society at large seems much more intolerant of injustice, exposing discrimination within health and social care could bring about positive results.

Exercise

Suppose you are an equality champion within a health or social care organisation. How would you go about the task of exposing discrimination and ensuring justice and fairness for all?

The ideas explored in this chapter will inform the discussion in Chapter 6, developing the radical approach to providing equality of opportunity, given that the minimalist liberal approaches have been less than successful. The cream has failed to rise to the top. It will be argued that it is time for new positive action with the service user at the centre of the debate. The idea is to make a shift towards an inclusive user-led service in which potential employees will be assessed on their ability to work within a framework of equality and mutual respect between workers and service users.

Summary

- Equality discourse and impact have developed over several decades.
- Language is particularly relevant in imparting appropriate messages of equality.
- Valuing diversity is of great benefit in delivering quality services.
- Use of inclusive language is in line with professional codes of practice.
- Diversity management should be flexible and involve service users.

6

Positive Action

Aim

- To develop further the concept of equal opportunities in the context of diversity.
- To provide an interpretation of positive action.
- To illustrate how positive action in a diversity context can inform practice.
- To describe a continuum of progress towards the mainstreaming of equal opportunities actions.

Following on from the discussion on the importance of valuing diversity in Chapter 5, this chapter will explore what could be done in health and social care provision of services and employment of practitioners to redress imbalances that have resulted from past discrimination. Some of the reasons for the inadequacy of a minimalist approach to challenging discrimination within the care sector will again be highlighted to show the need for positive action measures to achieve equality. As before, the basis for the discussion will be legislation. A contrast will be drawn between original pieces of legislation such as the Sex Discrimination Act 1975 and the Race Relations Act 1976, and more recent enactments such as the Disability Discrimination Act (2005) and the Race Relations Amendment Act (2000). The latter demand active elimination of unacceptable practices. These amendments to previous Acts of Parliament were necessary because of clear indications that a social problem remained that needed to be tackled. The stipulations in these Amendment Acts in relation to the setting up of equality schemes will be discussed, giving attention to their implications for health and social care organisations. These implications will be examined with a view to considering their location within mainstreamed equal opportunities discourse.

Anti-oppressive practice in health and social care requires critical thinking and reflection about each of the four strands: a minimalist approach, positive action, equality schemes, and mainstreaming equal opportunities. This is of particular importance to health and social care students, and is relevant to their placements for their hands-on professional practice experience. It is in this part of their training that they can evaluate policy implementation, assess progress and offer suggestions on action for positive change. It is generally acknowledged that students on practice placements are vulnerable because the partnership between placement providers and higher education institutions is not a seamless one (Kemp, 2000). This is likely to impact on the ability of students to apply equality theory to their practice, because there remains a separation of powers between the parties, placing the student in a somewhat precarious and potentially powerless position, having to satisfy demands from both the academic institution and the practice placement agency. However, having access to service users during practice placements can provide real opportunities for students to engage with equality issues and to reflect on specific pieces of work with a view to effecting positive changes within their immediate sphere of influence, as will be highlighted in Chapter 9.

A model of progressive incrementalism incorporating the four levels of minimalism, positive action measures, equality schemes, and mainstreaming equal opportunities ideas will shape and inform the discussion in this chapter, highlighting what could be achieved for each level adopted, as well as acknowledging practice limitations.

The minimalist approach

This approach focuses on ensuring that the organisation acts in line with minimum legal requirements. Equal opportunities legislation listed in Chapter 4 provides the framework by setting down minimum standards of expected behaviour within UK work organisations. This expected behaviour is linked to the provision of services such as health and social care. Individuals who are afforded less favourable treatment in the areas covered by legislation can seek redress through the courts. Equal opportunities laws can be seen as having an essential part to play in supporting all the actions aimed at eliminating discrimination (Dalrymple and Burke, 2006). These laws provide a fundamental underpinning of society's belief in fairness and justice (Bagilhole, 1997).

To demonstrate legal compliance most health and social care organisations have adopted equal opportunities policies and procedures designed to ensure that all those involved within such organisations act in a way that avoids unlawful discrimination (Equalities Review, 2006; Johns, 2005; Butt, 1994). However, three decades have passed since the first piece of active anti-discrimination legislation was put on the statute books and yet discrimination remains a problem, suggesting that a minimalist approach alone cannot deliver fairness and justice for those on the receiving end of discrimination. Nevertheless the legal framework is an essential platform from which individuals working in the care sector can develop ideas for moving forward. Locating evidence of court cases in the public domain for reference can be a helpful springboard for discussion of implications for the care sector and for persuading others to think and act differently. Additionally, current government encouragement for involvement of service users provides a window of opportunity for practitioners to become knowledgeable about the impact of discrimination and to take and accept advice from service users as experts on issues affecting them. Such acceptance of expert advice from service users is in line with equal opportunities thinking, complementing anti-oppressive practice. During the process of interaction with service users, practitioners need to be mindful not to create discursive inequalities because of the danger of reinforcing wider institutional power inequalities (Hodge, 2005).

Genuine service-user engagement would not only add new knowledge and understanding, but is also likely to reduce fear, thereby reducing the erection of unhealthy boundaries of exclusion and shifting some of the balance of power. This aspect of power sharing needs to be handled competently if those on the receiving end of discrimination are to benefit from the involvement. Those subject to unfair or less favourable treatment should not be expected alone to sort out the organisational problems responsible (CEMS, 2002). For example, if an organisation has in place policies that discriminate against workers with caring responsibility at home, or provides a work environment that is unsatisfactory for disabled people, managers should not expect those employees to sort out the organisational problems themselves. There should be a joint and collaborative effort to formulate workable family-friendly practices and disability-inclusive work environments.

An example of the impact of genuine service-user involvement to enable disabled people to undertake their work effectively can be seen among some easily recognised politicians. These politicians as users of the political infrastructure of Her Majesty's government would have been consulted about their specific needs and resources put in place to meet need:

The Houses of Commons and Lords, the main seats of government in Britain and arguably the most powerful policy-making institutions in the country, contain members in wheelchairs, members who are blind and deaf: these politicians are no less capable or effective than their colleagues as a result of these disabilities, because they have the resources to ensure that, with appropriate support and assistance, they are able to avoid or overcome the barriers they face. (Alcock, 2003: 298)

What this political example shows is that disability is not the cause of disadvantage and discrimination, but rather environmental and societal barriers are the problems that must be tackled and removed. Health and social care professionals are well placed to tackle and remove the barriers as an integral part of their work.

An example that illustrates the limitations of a minimalist approach is the way organisations have tended to ignore some well-known barriers relating to women's participation in the labour market: 'Within the labour market women are horizontally segregated from men (they are doing different jobs) and are vertically segregated from men (they are generally at lower grades in the career structure)' (Alcock, 2003: 288).

Vertical segregation has been confirmed over the years, highlighting the under-representation of women in senior positions within UK public institutions and the city (EOC, 2004; Singh and Vinnicombe, 2003). The welfare sector has created employment opportunities for women, but even within this sector women have remained confined to low-status positions when compared to men, reinforcing gender inequalities. Persistent gender-based inequalities are as a result of some of these barriers:

- lack of respect for part-time workers
- inflexible working hours
- sexual harassment and bullying
- intangible cultural factors
- few visible role models
- impact of past discrimination affecting confidence.

Exercise

Have you ever been affected by any of these barriers?

If so, what did you do about it and what was the outcome?

Can lessons be learnt from your experience that can be shared with others?

These barriers can be examined to identify applicability to other groups covered by anti-discrimination laws such as those defined by race or age. While the law sets minimum standards by providing a framework for tackling discrimination, what is needed is for individuals within health and social care to think beyond passive and basic minimum legal requirements, and take into account social divisions that produce structural inequalities. They can draw on guidance from professional codes of conduct as a basis for challenging discrimination in order to do the right thing for service users, students and colleagues. Moving beyond minimum legal requirements could involve taking proactive positive steps permissible within equality laws. This is generally known as 'positive action'. The positive action approach to work and service provision challenges the positive discrimination that has produced a dominance of one group over another. An example of the latter is the dominance of white, non-disabled men in significant positions of power within health and social care institutions to the exclusion of women, minority groups and disabled people.

Positive action

Positive action means:

- special encouragement
- special training
- taking an active stance

Positive action does not mean:

- reverse discrimination
- quotas
- preferential treatment

Under the Sex Discrimination Act and the Race Relations Act of the 1970s, positive action refers to a variety of measures designed to counteract the effects of past discrimination and help eliminate sex and race stereotyping. The interpretation of the meaning of positive action within the confines of the law indicates what is permissible. If rigorously and effectively applied it would go some way to begin to redress the effects of past discrimination. Unfortunately, positive action is frequently confused with positive discrimination, the very thing that positive action is meant to be challenging. This confusion causes concern and discomfort among those who wish to stay strictly within the confines of the law, even if it means persistent inequalities continue, as indeed they have done in a period spanning four decades in respect of gender and race, even though these two areas of discrimination have been outlawed (Equalities Review, 2007). It seems that concern and discomfort caused by positive action measures are greater than concern and discomfort engendered by the evidence of persistent inequalities as a result of discrimination!

Exercise

Why do you think it is that discomfort over positive action is often greater than discomfort over inequality and negative discrimination?

What do you think can be done to address this where it occurs?

You may wish to discuss this with colleagues to broaden discussion.

The concern with regard to employment is that positive discrimination would mean employing someone because they come from a particular background, regardless of whether they have the relevant knowledge, skills and professional qualifications. To offer appointment opportunities in that way would be unlawful and would probably have serious service delivery consequences in health and social care because employees without relevant knowledge and skills would be unable to deliver appropriate care. It can be argued that often in health and social care it is not the case that applicants do not have the basic qualifications such as a nursing degree, a social work degree or a medical degree, but that other unstated criteria such as sex, age, sexuality and race tend to be used to exclude some applicants. This is illustrated by the BMA study on racism in the medical profession (Cooke et al., 2003), focusing on the experience of UK graduates:

> The interview process, even with the structure of the current system, is not transparent. My view is, at a lot of interviews the decision is made before the person's even walked into the room and a lot of the candidates, they're golden boys, they've done the right jobs in the right rotations, they've got the right references and the decision's made before any of the candidates walk into the room. (British male, Indian, cited in Cooke et al., 2003: 11)

> The NHS is a very racist place and mirrors society. Also the referral system favours the status quo. People keep quiet because they want a good reference. (British male, Black African, cited in Cooke et al., 2003: 11)

Within these example it would appear that the unstated criterion as perceived by the respondents is that of 'fitting in' being used to assess suitability, to the detriment of candidates from marginalised and less well-known minority groups. Given the availability of information to confirm the existence of institutional racism in the medical profession (Coker, 2001; Esmail and Everington, 1993), should the medical profession consider positive action measures? Who is likely to be affected the most by such a decision?

The possibility of positive action is included and supported within a clearly defined legal framework under the Race Relations Act 1976. Positive action recognises that certain people in society have been disadvantaged and denied equal opportunities due to the effects of past and continuing discrimination. The evidence from the Cooke et al. (2003) study on racism in the NHS suggests that BME doctors are disadvantaged and are denied equal opportunities on racial grounds. Positive action measures could go some way towards removing the colour-based obstacles, through targeted training, mentoring, encouragement and taking an active stance in challenging discriminatory practices. The following is a gender-based example of positive action.

Positive action: gender

A senior management team in health and social care is all male, despite the fact that the majority of the staff is female. In the next recruitment round, the advertisement states that, 'due to under-representation at this level, women are particularly welcome to apply'. Under the Sex Discrimination Act 1975, this is not unlawful discrimination because the statement is providing encouragement to potential women applicants and openly demonstrating that the organisation is taking a practical step to send out a positive message that women will be given equal consideration. In this example, it does not mean that a female candidate will be given preferential treatment at the point of selection. If the best candidate is male, then that is who will be offered the post. Merit assessment criteria, decided in advance of the job advertisement, remain the overriding factor. To do anything else would be unlawful. This process assumes that recruitment panel members are competent and committed to follow fair employment procedures included within the organisation's equal opportunities policy.

Positive action measures continue to receive mixed reviews from those who see them as unfair and those who see the measures as not going far enough and fast enough to tackle the effects of past discrimination. The Equal Opportunities Commission and the Commission for Racial Equality endorse the use of positive action programmes within the framework of an equal opportunities policy so as to minimise confusion. The following illustrates this with a race-based example.

Positive action: race

Under the Race Relations Act 1976, a positive action management development training programme for Black and minority ethnic (BME) managers in social care was set up and implemented between 2000 and 2004. Under-representation of BMEs at senior management level was the reason for implementing the positive training programme. The project was supported by the social services inspectorate and has since been evaluated. Overall, the programme was considered to have produced positive results on the basis that participants reported:

- increase in confidence
- acquisition of new knowledge
- new skills development
- challenged internalised oppression
- feelings of empowerment.

The reported substantial increase in confidence enabled these managers to compete and gain promotion as well as generally improve their performance and effectiveness (Pascoe, 2004).

For positive action programmes to be set up and implemented as a way forward to tackle discrimination, organisational commitment at senior management level and adequate allocation of financial resources are required. The benefits are linked to maintenance of service quality.

Exercise

In your experience of a health or social care organisation (or an educational establishment if you are a student), what positive action programme for Black and minority ethnic staff might be of benefit?

What positive action programme for women in management might be needed?

Use your creativity to design a programme in each case.

In addition to lawful positive action measures that should be considered and implemented, it is also permissible in very limited cases to consider sex or race as a genuine occupational qualification (GOQ) for health and social care delivery. The laws allow recruitment of only men, or only women, or someone of a particular ethnic origin, for specific jobs. This is because there is sometimes a genuine need identified, such as the provision of welfare and personal care, which can best be met by the involvement of an employee from a particular group. It is a requirement that an assessment be done to confirm that this is the case. A language requirement, for example the need to speak a minority language where that is the mother tongue of a large number of the client group, is not in itself a reason to advertise the post as suitable only for applicants from that minority community, because other potential applicants could have the relevant language skill. Under GOQ an important thing to remember is that the focus is on the recipient of care and how personal care can best be delivered. Therefore employers must be able to justify the requirement objectively. One criticism of positive action is that it is usually group oriented rather than treating people as individuals, and this may run a danger of perpetuating stereotypes and reducing flexibility.

Under the Disability Discrimination Act 2005, positive discrimination is not unlawful. It is permissible to provide more favourable treatment to a disabled person than is provided to a non-disabled person. It is fair that disabled people are appropriately supported through positive discrimination measures, given the history of discrimination experienced by this group due to societal oppressive structures. For example, disabled students may be given extra time in exams, in recognition of the fact that examinations are usually devised with an assumption that those taking them will be able-bodied and without specific learning difficulties.

Exercise

For an organisation with which you are familiar, locate and read its disability policy.

In what ways does it offer positive discrimination in favour of disabled people?

Are there ways in which you think this could be extended to increase fairness and equality?

Anti-discrimination legislation provides a framework to support health and social care organisations to take specific measures aimed at reducing discrimination and its negative impact in the form of oppression. It is incumbent upon individual practitioners and students that they become knowledgeable about the extent of discrimination within their immediate environment in order to put into effect workable strategies within the spirit of a duty of care. It seems inconceivable that the caring professions can continue to ignore issues of fairness and justice. The current realities suggest that the caring professions are complicit in the perpetuation of discrimination in health and social care. The reasons for this state of affairs might be associated with some of the historical developments post-Second World War leading to the evolution of present-day British society.

Taking the example of gender, men have traditionally held most of the dominant positions of power and influence and have therefore dominated the development of the welfare state and the arrangements for the delivery of care (Alcock 2003). Similarly with race, BME people arriving in the UK post-Second World War would not have been entitled to welfare services or to be offered the opportunity to compete for important jobs within the welfare state:

> The development of services within the 'welfare state' of the post-war era was very much a product of the national (and nationalist) politics of the time. The political struggles which underpinned the reforms were dominated by the political parties and campaigning organisations of the white British population. The welfare state was a (white) British achievement, and most of the Black people resident in Britain in the 1960s and 1970s arrived in the country after the establishment of these national welfare services. (Alcock, 2003: 291)

In examining these historical developments in respect of gender and race, it can be argued that the internalisation of the dominance and power bestowed on men, and the subservient and caring role bestowed on women, continue to inform the way services are organised and the appointment of senior staff in health and social care. Internalisation of white dominance and power ensures continued exclusion from senior positions of BME people. It is easier for those in powerful positions just to carry on as before, selecting from a traditional pool for senior employment opportunities within health and social care. The NHS is renowned for an over-representation of BME people working at the lowest grades within the service. Internalisation of oppression among some women and BME people has probably contributed to the lack of confidence in challenging discrimination. Empowered future practitioners could do more to challenge institutional discriminatory practices, tapping into the national policy initiatives of the current administration.

Equality schemes

As a result of intensive lobbying from organised pressure groups, the government has in turn exerted pressure on all public sector organisations to make a measurable impact in reducing inequalities. This pressure is evident from the current discussions about equality schemes. The impetus for these discussions was the Race Relations Amendment Act 2000 (RRAA), following the evidence from the Macpherson Inquiry (1999), and the Disability Discrimination Act 2005 (DDA). The main focus is to engage all public sector organisations to do more than just having equal opportunities policies, by assessing and communicating regularly to government the impact of policy initiatives that are aimed at reducing inequalities.

Equality schemes in respect of race and disability

The main aspects of the RRAA include a general statutory duty to:

- eliminate unlawful racial discrimination
- promote equality of opportunity
- promote good relations between persons of different racial groups.

The statutory duty is for all public bodies in all their functions. The function relates to anything that a public body does in the course of its duties. There is also a specific duty to devise a coherent strategy and an action plan, known as a race equality scheme: 'A scheme must make it clear how a public authority plans to meet both its general and specific duties' (Commission for Racial Equality, 2006).

Similarly, the main aspects of the DDA (2005) include a general duty to:

- promote equality of opportunity between disabled persons and other persons
- eliminate discrimination that is unlawful under the Act
- eliminate harassment of disabled persons that is related to their disability
- promote positive attitudes towards disabled persons
- encourage participation by disabled persons in public life.

The Specific Duty Regulations state that a public authority should:

- publish a Disability Equality Scheme demonstrating how it intends to fulfil general and specific duties
- involve disabled people in the development of the scheme.

For both race and disability the scheme should cover all relevant functions and policies, bringing them within a single framework. Health and social care organisations, and universities and colleges, as public authorities, are all required to have in place equality schemes or a generic integrated equality scheme. As with any planned action, it must be monitored to assess impact. The results should then inform subsequent plans of action. While the equality schemes approach is a welcome development, the tendency to focus on process not outcomes could lead to paper exercises in procedures rather than to lasting institutional change. Critical and creative thinking among practitioners is required on how to address the potential weakness of focusing on process and not outcomes. Measuring outcomes can assist in locating collective institutional failures that can then be highlighted for action. Otherwise, the onus is back on the individual victim of discrimination to complain.

Over the years, the complaints-led model which places the onus on the victim of discrimination to complain has had limited success. Unlawful discrimination is not addressed when victims are not prepared to take the difficult, arduous journey through the courts. The new positive duties on public bodies to promote equality ought to bring about renewed efforts to act. It is to be expected that impact assessments will be acted upon to redress identified imbalances. As a way forward, creating a streamlined single policy document can simplify the procedures that are essential for ensuring that unlawful and unfair discrimination is avoided. Therefore, a single equality scheme covering gender, race and disability as a package can be incorporated into a generic approach to mainstreaming equal opportunities as explained in the next section.

Mainstreaming equal opportunities

The minimalist approach, positive action and equality schemes can all be incorporated into the organisation's business plan as an integrated whole, so as to minimise fragmentation resulting in no action being taken. An integrated approach to equal opportunities is associated with mainstreaming because equal opportunities principles, strategies and practices would be integrated into the everyday work of practitioners.

Taking gender as an example, Mackay and Bilton (2000) suggest that mainstreaming encompasses the normal ideas, attitudes or activities of society. Mainstreaming would be a situation when those ideas, attitudes or activities routinely incorporate a gender perspective and become a normal feature of everyday discourse and action. At national government social policy level, mainstreaming equal opportunities as a strategy can lead to the realisation of the ultimate goal of a fairer society (Mackay and Bilton, 2000). To get to a position where most people working in health and social care think and work in an inclusive and anti-oppressive way, there needs to be a healthy environment and organisational culture that support creativity. Some of the recognised prerequisites for such an environment are:

- specific equality legislation
- clear structures and policy
- disaggregated equality statistics
- knowledge of patterns of social divisions in society at large
- an adequate budget.
  (Mackay and Bilton, 2000)

Identification of these enabling conditions that are based on legislative, social group and diversity analyses is not new. Commentators on successful equal opportunities policies have indicated similar prerequisites (for example, Collier, 1998). The slow pace of change towards the elimination or significant reduction of unacceptable and unlawful forms of discrimination has been attributed to not having in place the enabling conditions. The creation of conducive working environments is the responsibility of senior management. The subject of equal opportunities cannot be expected to grab the attention of the most powerful people in work organisations when there is gender bias as described by Alcock (2003). That failure to grab attention ought to be the focus of attention for the new Equality and Human Rights Commission, to complement initiatives at individual practice level feeding into organisational strategy.

Mainstreaming can be adopted in such a way as to address all areas covered by legislation and to remove irrelevant and artificial barriers between the existing equality specialities. Mainstreaming equal opportunities within health and social care organisations should benefit all, because anti-oppressive practice would become the norm. An integrated mainstreaming equalities approach is likely to produce best results because the process of working out the essential elements to be addressed would involve more people in synthesising workable solutions.

According to Mackay and Bilton (2000), the prerequisites to mainstreaming equal opportunities suggest progressive developmental stages to allow concerns and fears to be acknowledged, especially among those who think that mainstreaming can become 'everyone's responsibility and no one's job', resulting in excuses for doing nothing. Equal opportunities specialists have suffered from such excuses, when equality issues were left to the specialists to sort out, only to be faced with denials and resistance when change to established institutionally discriminatory structures and patterns of behaviour is suggested (Lawrence, 2000). Generally some of the resistance has been associated with the marginalisation of equality and management of diversity. For example, students on placements within the statutory sector report having difficulties in locating equal opportunities information to support their learning, even though these placement agencies have a duty to promote equality of opportunity and are required to have operationally active equality schemes. Students on placements in the statutory sector should not have to struggle to find out about approaches used by the agencies to combat discrimination.

Health and social care organisations, as welfare service providers, ought to provide social care within a clear framework of equality. Equality and the management of diversity within these organisations ought to be treated as part of their mainstream work. But there is evidence to suggest that failure to incorporate equality and diversity into mainstream practices has resulted in discrimination. This is illustrated by some well-publicised cases.

Discrimination

David Bennett, an African-Caribbean man who had been diagnosed with schizophrenia, died after a struggle with another patient was followed by him being restrained in a prone position, face down, by a number of nurses.
The Independent Inquiry into David Bennett's death found evidence of lack of understanding by some in the mental health services of the definition of institutional racism. The Inquiry also remarked that, prior to this case, there had been another investigated and well-publicised death in care, that of Orville Blackwood, a Black patient who was in seclusion. There was thus already major concern about the extent of restraining of Black patients. (NSCSHA, 2003)

A survey by Mind and University College London showed that gay men and lesbians reported more psychological stress than heterosexual people.
The British gay rights organisation, Stonewall, has emphasised that although society is becoming less prejudiced, most lesbians and gay men and bisexuals have experienced a range of difficulties in their lives, which can contribute to mental health problems. The range of difficulties can include:

* bullying at school
* hostility and/or rejection from family
* harassment from neighbours
* casual homophobic comments on a daily basis
* rejection from mainstream religions.

The survey also highlighted that members of this community face discrimination within the mental health system, be they users, carers or professionals. Of particular note was the tendency of some doctors and therapists to perceive sexual orientation as the problem or cause of mental distress, despite the declassification of homosexuality as a mental illness. Such tendencies would suggest that mental health services are not always lesbian- and gay-friendly (King and McKeown, 2003; Hind, 2004).

Examples like these could act as drivers towards synthesising essential inputs into mainstreaming equality in health and social care. However, underestimating the size of the job can result in only partial success (Equalities Review, 2007). The task of embedding equality thinking and discourse within social care environments is likely to be evolutionary, as has been progress so far, as previously described.

Political and executive leadership would be expected to play a significant part in providing the vision and direction for the desired change. However, while the importance of effective leadership is recognised when planning for major change, individual practitioners can do a great deal within their spheres of responsibility. Individuals can take action that is appropriate to the situation and in line with existing agreed procedures, such as challenging unreasonable behaviour, supported by effective political and executive leadership.

The incremental stages to mainstreaming equality – legislation, clear policy, equality statistics, knowledge of social divisions and adequate financial resources – should support health and social care organisations to tackle inequalities comprehensively. The next session introduces four incremental levels as a model that can be used for assessing how far on the equality achievement continuum an organisation locates itself. This can enable senior management to work out what needs to be done, and the financial and other implications of implementing the desired change.

Equality incremental levels

An organisation can be assessed using MPEM (see Figure 6.1) to determine the starting point on the continuum. It can then be decided how best to get to the next level. Progressive incrementalism would ensure that individuals are not overwhelmed, and therefore choose to do nothing and just carry on as before. For example, most health care organisations have equal opportunity policies (Johns, 2005) and are therefore likely to be operating at least at a minimum legal requirement stage. However, often knowledge of legal requirements will not be universal across the organisation and amongst all employees, due to lack of commitment, training, information or adequate resources. Before the next level of positive action can be

1. Minimalism → meeting legal requirements **[M]**
2. Positive action → taking positive and proactive steps **[P]**
3. Equality schemes → coherent strategy of monitored actions **[E]**
4. Mainstreaming equality → integrated approach to equal opportunities **[M]**

M_____ → _____**P**_____ → _____**E**_____ → _____**M**

Figure 6.1 *MPEM continuum*

considered, all employees would need to be fully engaged with the first M stage, commitment in respect of the law. A few health care organisations have flirted with positive action programmes, stage P, with limited success because of inadequate engagement at first stage M. This is like running before walking. To attempt stage E in relation to equality schemes when first stages M and P are not established would be counter-productive. Progressive incrementalism is more likely to produce desired measurable outcomes because it allows enough time for people to gain understanding about the need to change.

Exercise

For an organisation that you are familiar with, try to place its equal opportunities practice on the **MPEM** continuum.

What would you consider to be the next action that should be taken within the organisation to progress it further along the continuum?

Health and social care organisations, as with all social institutions, have developed over time practices that have become institutionalised because they have been followed repeatedly. Adherence to the practices becomes routine and their existence is taken for granted. The shared meanings and understandings among members constitute organisational culture. If institutional practices are found to be discriminatory, then changing those practices means changing the organisational culture. Such a transformation will take time because members of the powerful dominant group might view the change as a threat to the established order and their privileged position, and therefore would be more likely to resist proposed changes. There are well-established strategies for dealing with resistance to change. Institutional discrimination culture change would require the use of robust change strategies.

The stage at which the organisation is operating in relation to equality of opportunity has implications for health and social care students on placement. Progressive incrementalism is likely to take a few years before a health and social care organisation can be confident of its ability to offer genuine equality of opportunity in employment and to deliver relevant and appropriate services to all who call on it. Therefore anti-oppressive practice for students on practice placements is likely to be affected. These students are required to produce assessable evidence within their portfolios, demonstrating their anti-oppressive practice competences. Implicit within the agreement to accept a student on placement is that the student would be afforded equality of opportunity and that there would be appropriate structures in place to support an inclusive learning environment. If the environment is found wanting in terms of anti-oppressive practice, more often than not students will endure and survive their placements. Students should be able to articulate the gaps between the theories and policies of equal opportunities and the reality of what they find in the field. It is not surprising that some health and social care students find some placement agencies wanting. Where health and social care systems have been designed around the powerful elite who lead them, patients and service users who are transient, as they come and go, must fit into the existing system. Likewise for students on placement.

The work of the Equality and Human Rights Commission could offer a fresh approach. Inadequate knowledge has been a stumbling block for some organisations whose leadership was ready to make things happen, but did not quite know how. With so many competing demands, and equal opportunities being seen as an additional other, policies have tended to remain unimplemented. A way forward could be that Equality and Human Rights Commission personnel crystallise their own knowledge base on the subject, then work with individual health and social care organisations to support them to change institutionally discriminatory cultures and work towards the mainstreaming of equal opportunities. Since universities and colleges train the health and social care professionals of the future, educators would need support too, through funding research in this area. Research evidence can be used to create appropriate educational material in collaboration with service users, so that all academic staff within this field would be able to successfully teach and assess anti-oppressive practice.

This chapter has discussed and highlighted the relevance of implementing positive action measures as an integral part of an equal opportunities approach for use in health and social care settings, including those where students are likely to be placed for their fieldwork experience. Incremental stages along an equality continuum were considered, as a method of signposting organisations in their progress towards the development of mainstreamed equal opportunities. It has been argued that some health and social care organisations have inadequate equal opportunities policies, and because of this state of affairs it is likely that students on placement will be affected by the policy and practice gaps in pursuing anti-oppression. The Equality and Human Rights Commission would be expected to play a significant role in helping health and social care organisations to change their institutionally discriminatory cultures and adopt the progressive incremental approach towards mainstreaming equal opportunities that has been suggested.

Summary

- The legal meaning of positive action and its implications for practice need to be understood.
- There is a need to implement positive action in health and social care.
- There are incremental stages on an equality continuum that can support change.
- Mainstreaming of equal opportunities discourse, policy and practice needs to be the goal.

Part III
Individuals

7
A Holistic Approach

Aim

- To explore issues of identity as defined by oneself or others.
- To discuss aspects of identity that can be learned about to assist anti-oppressive practice.
- To present a practical framework for anti-oppressive practice that:
  - is proactive and preventive rather than merely reactive
  - is simple and easily memorised
  - can be applied to groups or individuals
  - can be applied to any person or group at risk of oppression.
- To identify some issues for consideration in applying the framework.

By 'a holistic approach' we mean one which can be applied to any group or individual at risk of oppression, and one that involves the developing of skills and knowledge that can be generalised to apply in any situation of risk of oppression. We believe that these skills and generalisable knowledge can be built up by a process of learning about a wide range of identity groups. This in turn is a process that can and should never end – it involves embarking on a lifelong journey of discovery and learning.

The study of particular identity groups may at first sight seem incompatible with a holistic approach that can apply to any group or individual at risk of oppression. Surely we can develop skills of anti-oppression towards people without needing to know any detail about their identity? This must indeed be true to some extent; we should be able to apply anti-oppressive practice even if we do not know very much about a particular individual or group we encounter. Nevertheless, our contention is that knowing something about people can help to engender respect for them, can put us at ease in interactions with them, and them at ease with us, and can help us in the successful application of a holistic anti-oppressive framework.

A holistic approach involves equipping ourselves with skills and strategies to prevent or ameliorate oppression in relation to any identity. It thus goes beyond the 'isms' approach, that is, the study and development of ways of tackling the oppression of particular specific groups, given names such as 'racism', 'disablism', 'anti-semitism', 'ageism', 'sexism', 'homophobia', 'Islamophobia' and so on. Such specific studies, and the associated development of specific anti-oppressive strategies, can be useful, and we have ourselves discussed racism as a specific example in Chapter 3, for instance. However, there are two issues. First, the 'isms' approach makes it appear that there are many separate strategies of anti-oppression that need to be separately developed by students or practitioners: anti-racism, anti-sexism, anti-homophobia, anti-ageism and so on. This seems a daunting task! Second, there are identities that may be associated with a risk of oppression that are not covered by the 'isms'. There is no such thing as 'single parentism' or 'homelessism', for example.

Therefore, in this chapter, we present a framework that can be applied to groups or individuals of any identity. But first we will consider the nature of identity itself.

Identity

A wide variety of aspects make up a person's identity, both as seen by themselves and by others (Woodward, 1997).

There is a charming children's story (Reeves, 1992) of a girl who meets an elephant who tells her she is small, then a mouse who tells her she is big, then a giraffe who tells her she is short, then a hedgehog who tells her she is tall. A snake tells her she is fat and a pig tells her she is thin. A bird tells her she is slow, and then she meets a tortoise. 'I suppose you're going to tell me I'm quick,' she says, but the tortoise, being wise, says to her, 'It depends how you feel, not what people say.'

We need to acknowledge that everyone is different and that people may not view their own identity in the same way that we may initially do. To be welcoming towards a person we need to know which aspects of their identity are important to them. It may be ethnic or cultural origin, it may be religion, it may be family role, it may be job, it may be gender or sexual orientation, it may be physical characteristics, it may be political allegiance. Some aspects of identity are associated with a risk of oppression, while others are not. We may take pride in an aspect of our identity, or we may wish it were different. Our perception of a particular aspect of our identity may differ from that of others. The characteristics of our identity that we hold as most important, or as unimportant, may be held by others as less or more significant respectively.

This chapter is based on the premise that the more we can learn about the identity characteristics of people, their feelings about those characteristics, and the potential or actual responses of other people to those characteristics, the better we will be able to be anti-oppressive towards them. For example, if we have at least some basic knowledge of the history of gay people and their personal and political struggles for recognition, respect and rights, the contribution of gay people in society (Cowan, 1992), gay literature, accurate terminology used by gay people and so on, we will develop a personal respect for gay people, we will feel at ease with them, and we will come across as welcoming to individual people we meet if we know they are gay.

Each aspect of our identity we share with some people and we differ in that respect from others. In our efforts to be anti-oppressive we can show solidarity with those with whom we have characteristics in common, and we can respect the differences that others have from us and try to lessen any negative perceptions others may have of our differences from them.

As part of a holistic approach we need to acknowledge that there is a very wide range of identities that can be associated with a risk of oppression. If there is an aspect of the identity of a person we meet that is associated with a particular risk of oppression from others, we can express an anti-oppressive stance especially in relation to that aspect. Here is a list of categories within each of which there may be such identities:

- Country of birth
- Country of parents' birth
- Nationality
- Skin colour
- Ethnic membership
- Place of current residence
- Membership of community group
- Religion
- First language
- Age
- Size
- Personal appearance
- Social or economic class
- Gender
- Sexual orientation
- Impairment or health status
- Care status
- Lifestyle
- Housing status
- Employment status
- Financial status
- Current job
- Educational status
- Marital status
- Parental status
- Family role
- Community role
- Political stance
- Particular skills or interests
- Life experiences and personal history

Exercise

Choose five or six of these categories and consider what identities within each category might be associated with a risk of oppression.

What information about these identities might it be useful for you to know in order to develop an anti-oppressive stance towards people with those identities?

The WISE principles

Having seen the wide variety of areas in which an identity characteristic may be associated with a risk of oppression, we now present a simple, easily memorised framework for proactive and preventive (rather than merely reactive) anti-oppressive practice, which we have developed to guide our students. It can be applied to groups or individuals, and to anyone at risk of oppression. We call the framework 'The WISE Principles' (Williams, 2004). Its elements are:

- **W**elcome
- **I**mage
- **S**upport
- **E**mpowerment

Anti-oppressive practice that is preventive needs to include all four elements of welcome, positive imagery, support for equality, and empowerment to be effective. It needs to prevent the imposition and experience of all four of the negative elements of oppression which are the opposite of the WISE principles, as described in Chapters 1 and 2: dislike or hatred, negative stereotyped imagery, lack of support for equal functioning, and disempowerment. The WISE framework is a set of interactive principles that operate together to form attitudes and practices in everyday life that increase the likelihood of avoiding other people experiencing oppression from one's actions.

Some aspects of identity, whether fixed or changing, are out of our control. Others we choose for ourselves. However a person has arrived at their identity, if that identity is associated with a risk of oppression from others this chapter addresses the questions: What information about the person, or about the identity group to which the person belongs, will help us

- to be anti-oppressive towards them?
- to help the person – if they need it and would welcome it – to develop self-esteem and confidence in their identity, as a protection and survival strategy to avoid or overcome oppression?

The purpose is to give us knowledge that will help us to avoid stereotypes and prejudice about people, to respect them as people and their strengths and contribution, to provide appropriate support if required, and to empower them.

Welcome

In this first principle, the primary attitude is one of welcoming diversity in society. In practice it involves actively welcoming individuals or groups who may be at risk of oppression.

By developing ways of welcoming groups that have a particular identity we can learn ways of welcoming individuals, while remaining sensitive to the fact that individual people may not identify with the groups we assume they belong to, nor subscribe to the ideas, beliefs or practices of other members of those groups. For example, it is helpful if we wish to be welcoming towards Jewish people for us to learn about Judaism and Jewish culture and history (Jewish Social Work Interest Group, 2000). An individual person whom we may discover is Jewish may or may not see being Jewish as their primary identity, they may or may not believe in or practise particular elements of Judaic religion or tradition, and they may or may not have strong knowledge of or interest in Jewish history. However, if we have some knowledge and appreciation of these things, they will help us to practise the welcoming element of anti-oppressive practice if, when we get to know the person, we discover the specific importance of Jewish identity to them.

Exercise

Find out some traditional practices of many Jewish families on the Sabbath (Friday evening and Saturday).

Consider how this knowledge may help you to be welcoming to a Jewish person, acknowledging their identity and putting them at ease.

If students or practitioners in health and social care learn something about Jews it will help them not to be anti-semitic towards Jewish people they encounter. Our contention is also that learning about Jews, or any other identity group, helps to develop general skills and knowledge to be anti-oppressive towards any identity group at risk of oppression. By learning, and practising, how to welcome Jews, or gay people, or single parents, or homeless people, we learn and strengthen general skills of being welcoming.

The first step is to be sensitive to and respectful of the identity, and especially the self-defined identity, of people. Within that context, we can explore areas of knowledge relating to that identity that will help us to be welcoming and to pursue the other elements of the WISE principles. We will discuss six areas here:

- History
- Survival
- Culture
- Language
- Belief system
- Contribution

Appreciating history

It is useful for anti-oppressive practice to know the history both of individuals and of identity groups.

Knowing the history of individuals can help us to be welcoming towards them. We can appreciate the struggles they may have been through, the contribution they have made to family or community, the skills and abilities they have shown, the experience, knowledge and wisdom they have gained. This helps us to see people as survivors rather than victims, and to work in partnership with them through mutual learning, rather than being in a one-sided giving but not receiving role.

The history of individual people can be very important in gaining the full respect and appreciation of them that will help us to be anti-oppressive towards them. The history of older people, for example, is likely to be particularly rich in terms of their experiences and their contribution. If the person is unable to communicate or to remember easily, or if contact with family and friends has been lost, this history may be lost too. Researching the history of older people, and of members of other groups at risk of loss of their history, can be extremely valuable.

Knowing the history of refugees and asylum seekers can engender great admiration for their struggles. Likewise for people who have experienced domestic abuse, or people who have had mental health problems. We can again respect the people as survivors rather than victims, and learn from their resilience, coping skills and enterprise.

The general history of groups of people who share an identity can also help us to appreciate these things in order to welcome the presence of those groups in society and to welcome individual group members. The history of a group is not just the history of their oppression. Nor is it just the history of services, interventions or legislation that might have been provided for the group. It should include the positive history of the group itself: how it has survived oppression, its positive contribution in society, and the historical roots of its pride in its identity. This knowledge should engender respect for members of the group, rather than attitudes of pity or suspicion.

The history of particular identity groups can give us an appreciation of the experiences people have had and their responses to them. For instance, to use the example of Jews again, the major contribution of Jewish people to all the communities where they have resided is remarkable in view of their experience of oppression throughout their long history, as recounted in Chapter 1. By learning about Jewish history we can gain an understanding of Jewish people's pride and determination to survive (Ausubel, 1984).

Knowing that homosexual behaviour between gay men was illegal in Britain until 1967 can help us understand why few gay people were able to 'come out' and live openly as gay people before that time. This will have constituted major oppression for many gay men who are now in their older years. Knowing also that gay men and lesbian women played as strong a role as heterosexual people in the World Wars gives us an impression of how prejudice was overcome so that an equal contribution could be made – again a story of survival that deserves great respect (Miller, 1995; Cook et al., 2007).

History from non-European perspectives can help us not to be Eurocentric in our beliefs and stereotypes of members of other cultures and nations. Writers on Black history, for example, have described how explorers from West Africa almost certainly made the journey to 'discover' America long before Columbus. The ancient civilizations of the Middle East, China, Egypt and North Africa were in place long before the development of equivalent European knowledge and culture (Karenga, 1993; de Bary and Bloom, 1999; Ebrey, 1996; Braudel, 1994).

Many identity groups have developed their own responses to oppression, and from them we can learn valid anti-oppressive strategies deriving from the authentic voice of the people themselves, rather than from others speaking for them. The study of the history and nature of the feminist movement, the disability rights movement, the Black freedom movement, the gay liberation movement and so on will equip us with this knowledge.

The history of services for particular groups can also help us to appreciate what *not* to do. For example, there is a salutary lesson in services for disabled people. Samuel Howe, speaking in 1866, said:

> All great establishments ... where the sexes must be separated, where there must be boarding in common, and sleeping in congregate dormitories, where there must be routine and formality and restraint and repression of individuality, where the charms and refining influences of the true family relation cannot be had – all such institutions are unnatural, undesirable and very liable to abuse. We should have as few of them as possible, and those few should be kept as small as possible ... Beware how you needlessly sever any of those ties of family, of friendship, of neighbourhood ... lest you make a homeless man, a wanderer and a stranger. Especially beware how you cause him to neglect forming ... relations of affection with those whose sympathy and friendship will be most important to him during life ... If the field were all clear, and no buildings provided, there should be built only ... school rooms, recitation rooms, music rooms and workshops, and these should be in or near the centre of a dense population. For other purposes ordinary houses would suffice. (Howe, 1866, quoted in Wolfensberger, 1969: 138–41)

We took no notice of this advice for around 120 years until the advent of modern conceptions of community care. Disabled people suffered great oppression throughout most of the twentieth century through the isolation and segregation of the large institutions that formed much of health and social care provision (see for example Morris, 1969).

Survival

One particular piece of knowledge about a person or group that has experienced oppression, or is at risk of oppression, that can engender respect and appreciation is how they have survived, and the skills, resilience and character that that entails. We have already mentioned the usefulness of individual stories of survival by asylum seekers, those who have experienced domestic violence, and those with experience of mental health problems.

For groups of people there are sometimes stories of triumph over oppression, as in the case of the ending of apartheid in South Africa. Other stories are of the resilience and contribution of groups that have been greatly weakened by historical violence and oppression, such as the Aboriginal people of Australia, Maoris in New Zealand, the Inuit people in Canada, and the native Indian population in North America.

Exercise

Find out from the Internet or books or other sources what is being done in Australia to ensure the survival of Aboriginal people and their culture, particularly actions by the people themselves.

There are many organisations, such as Amnesty International, Greenpeace, Oxfam, the United Nations, with which we can ally ourselves to support the survival strategies of groups that are currently being oppressed. We can also learn from the survival stories of individual people whom we encounter in practice or about whom we can read in biographies and other literature (some examples are given in Chapter 1, pages 17–18).

Valuing culture

The culture of a group of people is the beliefs, practices, stories and creations of those who share the group identity. Knowledge of this can again help us to form welcoming relationships with people at risk of oppression. The best source of information is from the people themselves, to avoid misrepresentation and stereotyping. For example, some of our students who have chosen to research the culture of Irish people in Britain have benefited greatly from visiting an Irish social club and speaking directly to members.

An interesting question is whether all groups have something that can be called their 'culture'. Do disabled people have a culture? Do tall people have a culture? Do people who are surviving mental health problems have a culture? It can be argued that they do, if we use the definition of culture given above. There are certainly particular perceptions amongst disabled people that are expressed in academic writings by those people (for example Abberley, 1987), and in a wealth of stories and accounts and creations by the people themselves (for example Finkelstein, 1992), that have a distinctive nature and a consistency that can be called 'disability culture'.

Thus, we can envisage that there is a 'culture', not only of different nationalities, religions and ethnic groups, but of any identity group. Where people who share an identity are able to meet together or communicate with each other, it is likely that something that can legitimately be called the 'culture' of that identity group will emerge. Sharing of group culture will depend on mechanisms for people having contact with other group members. For many groups there are clubs, support groups, Internet sites, magazines, social events or actual communities that live together on a daily basis, which ensure contact and a sharing of culture. These sources of knowledge can be tapped into by those of us who wish to learn about a group's culture.

A good way to find out about the culture of a group is by identifying organisations for members of the group. The Internet is an extensive source of information about such groups, though there is no substitute for actually visiting an organisation to see and hear first-hand how it functions and what it does.

Exercise

Choose four or five identity groups from different categories listed at the beginning of this chapter. See if you can find a self-help or self-interest site on the Internet that relates to each group.

It is important to remember that individual members of an identity group may or may not subscribe to the group culture expressed by the group as a whole. For example, individual disabled people may not agree with the culture developed by disabled activists (see Shakespeare, 2006). Individuals who have experienced mental health problems may not agree with the 'mental health system survivor' movement. The current controversy over dress, particularly women's dress, within the Moslem community in Britain is an illustration of the wide range of views and practice that may exist.

Nevertheless, many groups have their own literature, websites, artistic performances, modes of dress, political stances and so on that constitute their 'culture'. By finding out about these things we can learn respect, understanding and welcoming of diversity.

Valuing language

Closely tied into culture are communication and language. There are many easily available sources to learn some basic communication in different languages, which can be a very helpful, simple and immediate way of expressing welcome for a person. There is a wide variety of methods and systems that have been developed to aid communication with disabled people. Taking the trouble to communicate with a person through their primary language or communication method is well worthwhile as a basic act of welcome to counter the risk of oppression.

Learning one or two foreign languages in depth is good educational discipline and is obviously very useful for communication in those languages. However, from an anti-oppressive practice viewpoint, it may be more useful to know a small number of useful words and phrases in many languages. To greet people in their own language is a mark of respect, it can put people at ease and convey that they are welcome, and it shows an interest in their background and culture.

There are some very useful Internet resources giving how to say 'Hello', 'Thank you', 'Goodbye' and other useful words or phrases in many different languages. For example, http://www.elite.net/~runner/jennifers/hello.htm has greetings in over 800 different languages. Another similar resource is http://www.plattbridger.pwp.blueyonder.co.uk/hello.htm. Some examples of greetings ('Hello') are:

Albanian	Tungjatjeta
Arabic (Moslem)	Asalaam-aleikum
Bengali	Gamon Ashen
Chinese (Mandarin)	Ni Hao
Chishona (Zimbabwe)	Mhoroi
Czech	Ahoy
Dutch	Goeden Dag
French	Bonjour
German	Guten Tag
Greek	Yassou
Hindi	Nomoshkar
Indonesian	Selamat
Japanese	Konnichi Wa
Kiswahili (East Africa)	Habari Bwana (to a man)
	Habari Bibi (to a woman)
Latvian	Sveiks (to a man)
	Sveika (to a woman)
Mende (Sierra Leone)	Bua
Polish	Dzien dobry
Russian	Priviet
Spanish	Hola

Temne (Sierra Leone)	Seke
Thai	Sawasdee Krup (by a man)
	Sawasdee Kaa (by a woman)
Welsh	Dydd Da

Exercise

Find out how to say 'Hello' in at least three languages not on the above list. Also find out how to say 'Thank you' in at least four or five different languages of your choice.

Valuing beliefs

Knowing about different religions also helps to engender respect and understanding. Especially if we are caring for a person, we need to know about their religious beliefs in order to respect them in our day-to-day practice.

It is easy to find references to the basic beliefs of the major religions of Judaism, Buddhism, Islam, Christianity, Sikhism and Hinduism (for example Knott, 1998; Solomon, 1996; Ruthven, 1997). It is also useful to know some of the particular beliefs of sects within the religions, for example Orthodox Judaism and Reform Judaism, or, within Christianity, Mormons, Jehovah's Witnesses, Catholics, Methodists and so on. The history of particular groups can be useful. For example, Jehovah's Witnesses are often stereotyped as excessively evangelical, constituting a nuisance on the doorstep. They are pacifists and refuse to bear arms, so in times of war they are conscientious objectors and may find themselves imprisoned. Because of this belief, and the assumption that 'Jehovah' in their name gave them an affinity with Jews, they suffered great oppression in Nazi Germany and many were killed (Chu, 2004).

The perception of members of a group as menacing or dangerous can be defused by appreciating their religious beliefs. An example of this is the Rastafarian movement. Knowing it is a religion, based on a belief that King Haile Selasse of Ethiopia was descended from the same Jewish line as Jesus, and symbolically represents the saviour of people of Black African origin, helps us to understand the symbolism of dreadlocks and other Rasta religious practices (Pollard, 1999; Barrett, 1998; Hausmann, 1997; White, 1998).

Awareness of contribution

Many individuals, and certainly most groups as a general feature, will have made and be making a positive contribution to family and society. This can be brought out in the study of the person's or group's history, and in finding out their current strengths. For example, through sources such as Peter Fryer, *Staying Power: The History of Black People in Britain* (1984), we can become aware not only of the presence of Black people in Britain since the Roman occupation (some Roman soldiers were from North Africa), but of the consistent contribution of Black people to British life throughout history.

It is useful to have a sense of the immense contribution to our society and economy by many groups that are looked down on and are at risk of oppression. Older people are often regarded as economically dependent and a drain on the economy. We need to appreciate not only their lifetime contribution to the economy, but also their current roles in teaching and caring for the young, for example in their roles as grandparents, godparents, aunts or uncles within families. They also continue to be consumers, and hence active participants in the economy.

Immigrants to Britain, including asylum seekers, are educated to the same level as British nationals (Bell, 1997; Dustmann and Theodoropoulos, 2006). They are likely to make a major contribution to the country's need for skilled workers. Dustmann and Theodoropoulos (2006) found that 30 per cent of immigrants were university educated or had a professional or trade qualification equivalent to A-levels, compared with 35 per cent of comparable British nationals. Indeed, one of the most valid arguments against immigration is not the bad effect on the country to which people go, but the draining effect on the country they leave (see for example Eke, 2006). We benefit from other countries' loss of some of their most gifted people.

In this context, it should be recognised that many immigrants continue to support families and communities in their original home country. Countries like Somalia in Africa and Bangladesh in Asia are heavily supported by people working in Western developed countries sending money back to those countries. Sometimes whole villages are sustained by resources provided from income from members working overseas. This generosity and assumption of responsibility often arises from strong commitment to a religion, especially Islam.

For example, most 'Indian' restaurants in Britain are run and staffed by men from Bangladesh. Many of them have qualifications, but can earn more money here as waiters and chefs than they could as teachers, doctors or accountants in Bangladesh. However, many of them live simply, have deeply embedded moral principles, and work very long hours in order to send substantial sums of money back to extended families and to support poor people in their home villages. Many endure years, and even a lifetime, of separation from loved ones because they cannot bring them to live with them in the West. Such contributions deserve great admiration and respect.

We can also become aware of the historical contribution made by particular groups. An example is the Irish. In the times generally known as the 'dark ages', roughly 500 to 1000 AD/CE, Irish monks travelled through Europe rescuing and preserving the literature of the Greek, Roman and other civilizations, without which much would have been lost (Cahill, 1995).

And in the seventeenth and eighteenth centuries, Britain's canals and railways were largely built through the hard and dangerous work of large groups of Irish 'navvies' (Coleman, 2000). The current contribution of identity groups to British cultural and social life can also be studied: for example, the positive and vibrant Black British culture described in Owusu (2000).

Image

Compared with the care taken (and massive amounts of money expended) on imagery in industry, human services are very careless. People are often surrounded by negative images that portray danger, sickness, childlikeness and even sometimes ridicule. For example, it is not unusual to observe on a notice board in a waiting room at a hospital or social services office a poster about domestic violence, a poster about AIDS, and a notice of a fund-raising event picturing clowns.

The framework of ideas known as 'social role valorisation' (Wolfensberger, 1998; Wolfensberger and Glenn, 1975; Wolfensberger and Thomas, 1983, 2007) contains an analysis of sources of imagery in human services. Table 7.1 gives some examples, both negative and positive:

Table 7.1 Imagery and social role valorisation

	Negative example	Positive example
Language about people	Speaking of adults as 'boys and girls'	Guests, tenants
Language about services	Calling a residential home 'Rivendell' (home of elves and mythical creatures in Tolkein's stories)	Describing a service as 'achievement through partnership'
Buildings	Use of an old primary school for a day service for adults	Use of ordinary housing for residential care
Service structures	Hospitals being used for residential care	Supported apprenticeships in industry for disabled young people
Juxtaposition of services or people	Advice service for single parents next to a probation office	Course for people with learning difficulties situated in a Further Education College
Relationships	Unnecessary wearing of uniforms by staff	Friendship, informality, mutuality
Location	Home for older people situated next to a cemetery	Residential service close to local shops and leisure resources
Pictures	Posters of monkeys, donkeys, clowns	Art or photographs of beauty or constructive activity
Notices	Prominently displayed health and safety notices	Accounts of achievement
Personal appearance	Scruffy, unclean	People supported to present themselves well
Funding	Dependent on charity or supported from proceeds of gambling	Statutory funding as of right

Exercise

Consider what image of a person is likely to be conveyed by each of the negative and positive examples in Table 7.1.

Here is our list of some of the images that may be evoked:

Negative
- childlike
- strange
- inhuman
- sick
- contagious
- dangerous
- anti-social
- different
- to be avoided
- associated with death
- stupid
- trivial
- irresponsible
- unpleasant
- object of pity
- associated with vice or exploitation

Positive
- responsible
- contributor
- participant
- citizen
- community member
- skilled
- capable
- achiever
- friend
- consumer
- adult
- cultured
- appreciative
- attractive
- good to meet
- worthy of rights

Imagery is of course not the sole preserve of services. The media often portray people or groups in simplified stereotypical ways, and sometimes in highly negative ways for dramatic effect.

Anti-oppressive practice requires us to avoid negative imagery. This requires an active stance of awareness, since much negative imagery is produced unintentionally without consciousness of the issue. Anti-oppressive practice also requires us to provide positive imagery that reflects value, equality, respect, dignity and citizenship. We can evaluate our own environments with this in mind, and we can strive to reflect positive imagery in everything we provide for or do with people who may be at risk of oppression.

Avoiding stereotyping

A related issue is that of avoiding stereotyped assumptions about people of particular identities. Not all Jews are rich; not all large people are unhappy with their size and wish to diet; not all blind people read Braille; not all disabled people use wheelchairs. Again, we need to get to know individuals really well before we make assumptions about them. On the other hand, it is often possible to make valid generalisations about groups; there is such a thing as group identity and culture. We just need to make sure we know the facts and that our information is accurate. Learning about the characteristics of individuals or identity groups, as described in the previous section on 'Welcome', can provide us with knowledge and information that will help to prevent stereotyping. In particular it will help to replace negative stereotyping with positive perceptions.

Support

People at risk of oppression may need support to function equally in society. Obvious examples would include interpreters for users of other languages, or aids and equipment for disabled people. More subtle needs may include better access to buildings and services, clear and positive presentation of information, and respect for cultural practices and provision of resources for their expression (for example, halal or kosher food).

Attention to the comfort of people and to their health needs may be an important support. Older people, disabled people or people of unusual size may be unable to function well if they are uncomfortable. People need to be receiving effective health care if they have conditions that affect their functioning.

People may need information and practical support to achieve contact with other people who share their identity or interests. This can help to develop friendships and supportive networks for people.

As with imagery, the ways human services operate can provide support for the development of competence by people that will help them function well and equally in society, or services can severely damage the prospects of that. Again, social role valorisation provides an analysis (Wolfensberger, 1998; Wolfensberger and Glenn, 1975; Wolfensberger and Thomas, 1983, 2007). Some negative and positive examples are given in Table 7.2.

Support may need to be provided directly to individual people to avoid oppressive experiences. For example, hospital staff may have little experience of meeting the needs of people with learning difficulties (Williams, 2006). Such a person may well need the continuing support of those carers who look after their needs when they are not in hospital. This may include family members or residential care staff or supported living facilitators. Hospitals need to welcome the input of these people, and financial arrangements need to be in place to pay for the extra care they provide for the person while they are in hospital. If such arrangements are not in place, a person with severe disabilities may be at risk of oppression. They may feel abandoned and they may be at risk of neglect, harm and even death through lack of appropriate informed support. Mencap (2004, 2007) and the Disability Rights

Table 7.2 Support and social role valorisation

	Negative example	Positive example
Opportunity	Service in isolated location with poor transport	Service situated close to learning resources
Environment	All risks avoided	Appropriate challenges presented
Activities	Lots of time sitting around doing nothing	Appropriate activities supported with good frequency and intensity
Grouping of people together	People with severe disabilities served together in a segregated setting	Integrated education in schools
Numbers of people served together	Home for older people with 60 residents	Highly individualised provision through Direct Payment
Choice and responsibility	No choice, little responsibility expected	Encouragement of choice and responsibility
Relationships	Control	Learning and partnership
Aids and equipment	Few aids to learning or functioning	Individualised provision of good technological, physical or communication aids

Commission (2006) are currently carrying out campaigns against the oppression of disabled people through lack of appropriate support in health care settings.

Support can also be provided to groups. The following is taken from some advice by Catherine Jones on white people giving support to Black and minority ethnic groups:

Do your homework. There *is* stuff going on in your community. Find out what it is and how you can support the work. Give Practical Support! What are your resources that you can share with organisations of color? Maybe you can provide food or childcare or translation at meetings, maybe you can help phonebank for specific events, maybe you can volunteer to work at the front desk, give people rides, find out where a group can get donated computer equipment, or throw a fundraising party at your house. There are tons of ways for white folks to give necessary behind-the-scenes support to organisations of color. Figure out – don't assume you know – what people need, and find a way to help out.

Don't wait for people to come to you out of the blue 'cause they won't. Be proactive about letting organisations and allies know who you are and what you do. Figure out when it's appropriate to get involved, and do it. Be willing to do what's needed. Maybe you really want to be working with some amazing and popular organisation of color that doesn't actually have a whole lot of opportunities for you to plug in, while another organisation down the street is doing less high-profile work but really needs some folks to help them with fundraising. Take the opportunity to be of use.

This is my motto – say less, think less, do more. Remember that you're not a whole lot of use to the movement if you're sitting in a workshop. Put your knowledge to use. The struggle needs you! (2004)

Empowerment

Self-help

As we have already indicated, practically every identity group has its own organisation providing a voice for its members, and information, support and help from a position of informed knowledge and empathy. There are organisations in Britain for support to a very wide variety of nationalities. There are organisations catering for women, men, gay people, people of all classes, homeless people, people recovering from addiction or illness, lone parents. There are organisations for people with different kinds of disability, and umbrella organisations pursuing rights for all disabled people. There are organisations representing older people, carers, children, children in care, young people, ex-offenders, exceptionally large, tall or short people, and people of all religious or political creeds. Many of these organisations combine three functions: advice and help for individual members, pursuing a political agenda for greater rights and treatment, and a social function for people to meet together. The emphasis on each of these will vary between the organisations.

It will help us to be anti-oppressive if we are aware of these organisations. We can put people in touch with a relevant organisation if that is appropriate to their needs. We can learn how the organisations function, and the benefit they give to members, to inform us about helpful strategies to prevent and counter discrimination and oppression.

Very many groups have structures for self-help and self-advocacy. Anti-oppressive practice can involve providing information about these groups to relevant people, supporting the groups with practical help, and ensuring that the views expressed by the group are heard and listened to in relevant places. In nearly all places in Britain there are literally hundreds of small special interest groups catering for an extremely wide variety of identities and interests (see Chapter 11, pages 191–3). The Internet is a good source of information about national, and some local, groups. Local libraries or Citizens Advice Bureaux can provide information about local groups.

If individuals are not already in contact with a group relevant to their needs or identity, it can be very helpful to them to be put in touch. This not only helps people to develop and retain a positive sense of identity, but it encourages them to participate in community life and to develop friendships and networks of common interest.

Individual people, and groups representing particular identities or interests, should be involved in discussions and decisions that involve them. For example, since the publication of a government White Paper on services for people with learning difficulties, called *Valuing People* (Department of Health, 2001), there has developed a discussion and communication network through which people with learning difficulties themselves can express views and influence policy and service development. There are Partnership Boards at local level, in which people participate along with carers, policy-makers and service providers. There is a regional and national structure of forums in which people meet to discuss issues, and there is representation from these on a taskforce which monitors implementation of the White Paper (see Williams, 2006).

Advocacy and rights

One powerful way of supporting empowerment of people is advocacy (see Chapter 2, pages 29–30). Advocacy may be by paid specialist advocates (for example a solicitor), or by other professionals as part of their job (for example a social worker), or it can be voluntary and unpaid. It can be by an individual or an organisation. Each type of advocacy involves standing up for people and helping to represent their views and needs.

As analysed in Chapters 3 to 6, a further mechanism for empowerment is legislation. Anti-discrimination legislation, and the equality commissions that derived from the legislation, have given people legal rights and provide support for protection of those rights. At the level of organisations, equal opportunity and anti-discrimination policies protect the rights of people and provide empowerment.

All these mechanisms for enhancing empowerment can be supported and used to ensure anti-oppressive practice towards people, and the avoidance of oppressive experiences by them.

Authentic reading

One general act of empowerment is to ensure that one's own information comes from a first-hand source. In Chapter 1 we gave a short list of reading that some of our current students are studying in order to learn from the authentic first-hand voice of people themselves who have experienced, or are at risk of, oppression: Bauby (1998), Crisp (1996), Mandela (1994), Turney (1997) and Williams (1998) (we have also used Picardie, 1998, and Robert, 2005). They illustrate the wide range of such materials that is available.

Interaction

There is a great deal of overlap between the descriptions above of the four elements of the WISE principles. Indeed the elements interact with each other. You welcome people by surrounding them with positive imagery, offering them practical support and ensuring they are empowered.

You provide a positive image of people by welcoming them, supporting them and empowering them. You support people by welcoming them, presenting positive images of them and empowering them. You empower people through welcome, positive imagery and practical support.

Putting it all together

It may seem a daunting task to gain the knowledge background to help us to avoid discrimination and oppression towards those we meet. In practice, we are likely often to have an opportunity to prepare to meet a person we know to have a certain identity. Hopefully, a general approach of respect and empathy will enable us to form a good enough relationship that we can ask and learn from the person themselves how to be anti-oppressive towards them. For example, if a person is very large we may have natural concerns about their health and fitness. Do we also know the views of large people about facilitating pride in size, countering exploitation by the diet industry, securing rights to equal treatment in health, travel, fashion and so on, countering bullying, facilitating relationships and a good social life, maintaining fitness even though of large size and so forth? (See the next chapter, pages 154–5.) Knowing these things will help us to avoid prejudice and stereotyping, and will engender respect for the person's own view of their identity. Where people's self-esteem is very low, we can encourage pride in their identity, and put people – if they wish – in touch with others who proclaim that pride.

Learning about the history and survival strategies of oppressed groups, learning some basic phrases in different languages, reading authentic accounts by people at risk of oppression themselves, identifying self-help and self-advocacy organisations: all of these will help us pursue a personal anti-oppression strategy.

Critiques and issues in practice

A first criticism of the approach we have described in this chapter is that a little knowledge is a dangerous thing. By acquiring superficial and simplistic knowledge of a particular identity group, we may simply increase our stereotypes and erroneous assumptions about the group, and particularly about variety and diversity within the group. It is also true that we cannot know everything about all groups; there will always be large gaps in our knowledge and understanding, and there will be some identities about which we will know nothing.

While we agree with these caveats, we do not agree that the answer is to remain completely ignorant of different identity groups! The more authentic, complete and accurate knowledge we can gain, the better we will be able to be anti-oppressive towards people. As we have said, this is a lifelong journey that is never complete. We believe that while one should always remain aware of the danger of mistakes and of stereotyping while embarking on this journey, nevertheless the journey is essential for anti-oppressive practice.

A second argument is that our approach colludes in the negative consequences of 'identity politics'. This is a term given to the political struggles of particular identity groups which focus on the aggrandisement of that identity and the seeking of power and self-determination by that group, at the possible expense of two things: the interests of other groups and the acceptance and inclusion of the group in mainstream society. Indeed, some groups may come to argue that they have no wish to be accepted by mainstream society or to join it. Some gay people hold this view, as do some disabled people, and some Islamic adherents, for example. Those who believe that all identity groups should be accepted within the institutions and culture of mainstream society – otherwise there will be conflict, misunderstanding, hatred and possibly bloodshed – fear this consequence of 'identity politics'.

One of the most forceful writers about this is the American author Arthur Schlesinger (1999). He claims that the original American 'dream' was that new arrivals would sever their allegiance to self-centred ethnic roots and would engage in a new cooperative beginning as equal citizens of a new world. He considers that this dream has been destroyed by identity politics. He also gives the example of the former Yugoslavia where, he says, celebrating ethnic differences had a disastrous effect. Some of these arguments are similar to those against multi-culturalism, discussed in Chapter 2 (page 23).

Another critique of identity politics is that it draws attention away from underlying forces of oppression that are not related to specific identities, such as poverty, capitalist economics, exploitation, and abuse of power (which we have discussed in Chapters 3 to 6; see also Lipsitz, 2006). And a further argument is that it imposes supposed identities on people which they otherwise would not arrive at by self-definition: the familiar case against labelling.

Despite these objections, we still believe that sensible acknowledgement of different identity characteristics, and study of the accompaniments of those identities for people who share them, is worthwhile, and is necessary for the pursuit of the WISE principles which we propose as a practical framework for anti-oppression.

However, in applying the framework of the WISE principles there are a number of practical considerations. There are likely to be some individuals or groups to whom it is very difficult to apply the principles: serious criminal offenders, for example. Even in such cases, some elements of the WISE framework may be relevant. Everyone has aspects of their identity that are positive and can be supported. In relation to negative identities, for example as an offender, people can still be welcomed in personal relations if not in open society, a positive image can be held of their potential, they can be supported towards reform and rehabilitation, and they can be accorded at least some rights and some voice in decisions that affect them (see for example Williams, 1999; Williams and Dale, 2001).

In pursuing this framework for anti-oppressive practice, it is often necessary to be bold. We should not fear making mistakes, or being embarrassed. People are generally very forgiving of attempts to be helpful if they are clearly well-meaning, even if the results are not ideal. For example, a student from Kashmir was having difficulties on a social work course which might have been related to racism. To support the student it was agreed to find a mentor, and an experienced social worker was identified who also came from Kashmir and who was willing to act as mentor. Unfortunately, it turned out that the student was a Moslem from the Pakistan-controlled area of Kashmir, while the mentor was a Hindu from India-controlled Kashmir. Although in fact they formed a good relationship, it was not an ideal choice.

We have occasionally come across situations where attempts to speak at least a few words to a person in their first language is not appreciated, especially where they have made recent attempts to become fluent in their English; the attempt can be interpreted as denigrating their wish to communicate in good English. Sometimes too, especially in languages like Chinese where tones of voice can convey completely different meanings to the same basic sound, one can actually be saying something very different from what one intends. In Chinese the word for 'teacher' is very like the word for 'mouse'; no doubt on many occasions distinguished Chinese professors on visits to Britain have been greeted with 'You are welcome, dear mouse!'

We can also be seen as very patronising in these attempts to be anti-oppressive. After all, the notion of welcoming someone rather assumes that you are the host (permanent and having control) and the person is the stranger or visitor (temporary and subservient). The notion of supporting someone assumes you are in possession of greater resources, and the other person is dependent on you. The notion of empowerment can come across as a process of powerful people according just a little more influence to other people, but with the amount and the results always still in their control.

Conclusion

Despite these caveats, we believe that a framework such as the WISE principles can help us to develop routine practice towards anyone we meet that increases the likelihood of an anti-oppressive experience for them, and the avoidance of the accidental, unconscious oppressive acts that a less careful and thoughtful approach might allow.

Summary

- A holistic approach can be adopted to becoming anti-oppressive towards anyone at risk.
- This gets away from the 'isms' approach that focuses on a narrow set of identities.
- However, studying specific identities can help to develop generalisable skills and knowledge for anti-oppression.
- A useful framework for applying these skills and knowledge is the 'WISE Principles': Welcome, Image, Support and Empowerment.
- There are dangers in this approach, but they can be overcome.

8

Examples of Researching Identities

Aim

- To outline a curriculum for teaching anti-oppressive practice.
- To give a range of examples of researching specific identities.
- To illustrate the process of gaining general skills through study of specific groups.

It is a general principle on all courses in the School of Health and Social Care at Reading University that anti-discriminatory and anti-oppressive values will permeate all activities and all learning. Thus, all lecturers and practice assessors are expected to be familiar with anti-oppressive principles and to refer to them and reinforce them whenever possible. In addition, on some courses, there are specific teaching modules on anti-oppressive practice. For example, on social work courses in recent years at Reading these modules have been entitled 'Social Justice and Inclusion', taught in Years 1 and 2 of the 3-year degree. This chapter will describe the basic curriculum of these modules and give some examples of the study of identity groups that we have used in our teaching.

Curriculum and assignments

In Year 1, basic concepts in anti-oppressive practice are covered, such as those in Chapter 2, and students are introduced to issues of equality and diversity, as discussed in Chapters 3 to 6. The overall structure of the module is based on the themes of relevant professional Codes of Practice, and there is teaching of helpful frameworks for understanding the scope of anti-oppression and developing good practice, such as the PCS framework of Thompson (see Chapter 1, pages 18–19) and the WISE principles (Chapter 7).

An assignment is set for completion towards the end of the students' practice placement. It requires each student to draw up a personal plan for their own anti-oppressive practice. This can focus on the placement, providing evidence for the values requirements of the placement, but it can also cover past experience and practice. Students are expected to make some statements about their intentions for anti-oppressive practice in their future careers as health or social care professionals. Placements are discussed in Chapter 9, and Chapter 10 gives some examples of students' personal plans for anti-oppressive practice.

In Year 2, students are introduced to specific areas of study to illustrate greater depth in acquiring knowledge. There is coverage of Gender Studies, Disability Studies, Class Studies, Sexuality Studies, Black and Minority Ethnic Studies, Religion Studies and Age Studies. Each is taught within the overall context of the holistic model, with the aim of developing general skills of study and understanding that can be applied to good practice in relation to any identity that may be associated with a risk of oppression from others.

This more holistic process is then illustrated through two assignments for students. One is to choose an identity group of each student's own choice, and to write about the application of principles of social justice, inclusion and anti-oppression to that group. For the second assignment, students work in pairs or threes to prepare a presentation to the whole student cohort on a specific identity group, covering positive knowledge about that group that will help anti-oppressive practice. In both the essay and the presentation, students are encouraged to be creative in choosing the group they will cover. As a result, a very wide range of groups has been studied by students over the years. Here, for example, are the groups about whom presentations were given by Year 2 Social Work students in 2007:

- Rastafarians
- Homeless people
- Women prisoners
- Kaballists
- People with Down syndrome
- People living with HIV/AIDS
- Ex-offenders
- Children with Attention Deficit Hyperactivity Disorder (ADHD)
- Jehovah's Witnesses
- Gay men
- Teenagers who identify through music
- Men survivors of domestic violence
- Australian Aboriginals
- Kosovans
- People who have experienced schizophrenia

- Children in gay families
- Christians
- Sex workers

Examples of researching specific identities

We begin with some examples that we have prepared as illustrations for students of the sort of information that can be collected on:

- Albanians
- Muslim brides
- People of short stature
- Lesbian and gay people
- Transgendered people

This is followed by examples of students' research into:

- People living with HIV/AIDS
- Children with Attention Deficit Hyperactivity Disorder (ADHD)
- Homeless people
- Young homeless people
- Working-class youth from disadvantaged areas
- Fat people

Albanians

Albanians in Britain may have come from Albania itself or they may be ethnic Albanians from Kosovo, possibly refugees from the war in Kosovo in the 1990s. Kosovo was until recently a self-governing region of Serbia, part of the old Yugoslavia, but the majority of its population are ethnic Albanians. Kosovo unilaterally declared independence from Serbia in February 2008.

Albania is situated on the eastern side of the Adriatic Sea, opposite the heel of the foot of Italy. It is bordered to the south by Greece and to the east and north by the former Yugoslavian republics of Macedonia and Montenegro and by Kosovo.

If you have been to the Greek island of Corfu, the mountains of Albania can be seen clearly just a few miles away. They look rocky and barren, but behind them lies a beautiful country of lakes and forests. Originally named Illyria, the country came to be known as Albania after one of the main tribes inhabiting the area, the Albani. The Albanian name for the country is *Shqiperi*, meaning Land of the Eagles. The flag of Albania is a black two-headed eagle on a red background. The population is around 3½ million. Albania is one of the poorest countries in Europe. Most of the population are Muslim.

In the fourteenth century, Albania became part of the Turkish Ottoman Empire, and remained part of that Empire until 1912, apart from a 25-year period that is famous in Albanian history. An Albanian prince and military commander named Skanderbeg liberated Albania from the Ottoman Empire in 1443, until it was recaptured in 1468. In Tiranë, the capital of Albania, there is a statue of Skanderbeg and a square named after him in the centre of the city. The two-headed eagle on the flag of Albania was originally the emblem of Skanderbeg.

For a time in the 1930s, Albania became a monarchy, after its leader, Ahmet Zogu, declared himself King Zog. Occupied by Italy and then Germany in the Second World War, Albania was liberated in 1944 by Communist forces led by Enver Hoxha (pronounced 'Hodge'). As a Communist state, Albania was allied with Russia until 1960 when it broke away and formed an alliance with China. In the 1970s and 1980s, Albania represented the extraordinary phenomenon of a Chinese Communist state in the heart of Europe. However, despite investment by the Chinese, Albania remained extremely poor. Hoxha died in 1985 and moves took place to establish democracy. Elections were held in 1991. In 1997 there was a brief civil war in Albania precipitated by the collapse of exploitative 'pyramid investment' schemes, through which large numbers of people lost their meagre life savings. Albania is now trying to develop its education and health services, its infrastructure and its economy, and is developing new industries including tourism.

Albanian life centres around the family and the local community. Women generally stay in the home and take great pride in their houses, which are kept spotlessly clean. In the evenings, men will gather in the centre of villages or towns and walk around in a circle, known as a *xhiro*, holding conversations and exchanging news. Families often visit each other for coffee, the serving of which is treated ceremoniously on silver trays.

The downside of community life is the extensive possession of guns, which are sometimes used to imprison people in their homes if there are feuds between families.

Albania has a strong culture, especially of literature and poetry. Much of this expresses the pride of Albanian people in their survival of so much upheaval and conflict in their history. Here is an example:

A Couple of Words to Poets to Come

We had no time to write of love
Though we were impetuous lovers,
The country needed songs of freedom,
The country needed songs of grain ripening in the fields.
The country demanded of us poor poets,
That we teach courses to fight illiteracy,
That we build dams on the rivers,
That we light the flame of socialism in the mountains.

Do not wonder, oh poets yet to be born,
And do not judge us for what we have not accomplished.
Compared to you, we will look like simple monks
Laden with grain and heavy iron chains.
We, who spent many a sleepless night,
We, who accomplished many a great deed,
Could we not at least have written a couple of love poems,
Could we not have stammered, 'Oh, my beloved?'
Do not believe we were heartless! If only you could have seen
The passions we felt for the girls we loved and heard
What sweet nothings we whispered in their ears on those radiant evenings!
But we lacked the time to publish those sweet nothings.
Our printers were busy with more important things.

© Copyright. Written by the Albanian poet Dritero Agolli and translated by Robert Elsie in his anthology of Albanian poetry (Elsie, 1993), reproduced by kind permission of the translator.

Reading: Olsen (2000), Elsie (1993, 1996), Vickers (1999) and Roberts (2000).

Muslim brides

Through a friendship with a Bangladeshi family in Britain, one of us was invited to a wedding in Bangladesh. A video was made of the Muslim wedding which we show to students. Throughout the ceremony the bride looks extremely sad. At the end she bursts into tears as she kneels to kiss her father's feet before departing with her new husband.

The first question asked by at least some students is 'Was it an arranged marriage?', with the implication that the bride may not have wished to marry that man, or to get married at all, and that the video shows the unhappiness of a woman being coerced against her wishes. However, we know that the couple were very happy before the wedding and have been very happy since.

In fact the wedding was semi-arranged. Muslims traditionally see marriage as not just between two individuals but between two families. The bride is moving from her family to be a member of the groom's family. It is important that both families are happy with each other. In the case of this wedding, the groom's mother had chosen three or four young women from families known to her. Her son then met the women and chose one to get to know better. The two of them met frequently during a period of several months before the wedding, and both of them proclaimed that it was a marriage of love.

Although individual practice varies at Muslim weddings, it is traditional in many cultures for the bride to look sad throughout the ceremony, as a mark of respect and love for her family that she is leaving. Indeed it can be regarded as an insult to her family if she looks cheerful. At many Muslim weddings, therefore, whether arranged or not, the bride will deliberately look thoroughly miserable. Tears and even wails of anguish are part of the ceremony at the end of the wedding when the bride says goodbye to her father and he formally presents her to her new husband.

Necessarily interpreting the behaviour of the bride as indicating coercion and unhappiness is an example of misunderstanding a cultural practice through lack of knowledge.

People of short stature

From 1966 to 1986 there was a General Practitioner in Aylesbury who was only just over four feet tall. He was also distinguished by a grand and historic name: Sir William Shakespeare. His father, Geoffrey Shakespeare, was an MP who played a key role in international negotiations during the Second World War. As a result he was made a Baronet, a hereditary title enabling him and, after his death, his first-born son to call themselves 'Sir'. William was born in 1927 with achondroplasia, a condition that results in shortened arms and legs, and hence overall short stature. Despite this he trained as a doctor. He married a woman of average height and in 1966 his first son, Thomas, was born. Tom is now a well-known researcher, writer and broadcaster on disability issues (see Shakespeare, 2006).

William Shakespeare was a founder member in the late 1960s of the organisation in Britain which represents the interests of people of short stature, now called the Restricted Growth Association. One of the functions of the Association is to publicise the achievements of people of short stature, to inform professionals who may become involved with them and to present role models to people of short stature themselves. In his autobiography, William says:

> Small people are perceived in the public eye as dwarfs who appear on the stage and as clowns in circuses. I think this is a pity because ... it suggests that small people are less intelligent and are only able to earn a living by offering themselves in a rather demeaning way to the entertainment industry ... I think there is a general misconception that if you are small in body you are small in mind and therefore not blessed with great intelligence. This is quite wrong and everyone who is small should do their best to disprove it. (Shakespeare, 1996: 89)

William's son Tom wrote in 1997:

> Recent letters [in the magazine *Disability Now*] have asked how disabled people could call themselves 'proud' to be disabled. Being disabled means belonging to a social group which faces discrimination and prejudice in society. We are proud because we are part of a group who are strong, support each other and achieve great things. It is this collective of resistance that helps us survive as individuals, and makes us glad to be disabled people. We realise that the problem does not reside in us, it resides in

society; and so we are able to be positive about ourselves and our bodies. We are proud of our achievements in work or family life. It would be foolish to feel ashamed of who we are. None of this is to minimise the pains and problems that having an impairment brings. Instead it is about celebrating our achievements, working to make being disabled less restrictive, and ultimately empowering ourselves. And it is about remembering that many major figures in history, from Roosevelt to Cole Porter, Proust to Plath, Hawking to Handel to Harriet Tubman, were themselves disabled people. I think that is something to be proud of too. (Shakespeare, 1997: 14)

The Restricted Growth Association has recently supported a survey of people of short stature by Thompson et al. (2007) at Newcastle University. The results showed that the sample of 81 people had higher educational qualifications than average, and were equally likely to be employed, but were more likely to be restricted to lower occupational roles. They were likely to have suffered from public ignorance and hostility, through stares, mockery and harassment, leading to insecurity, isolation and sometimes depression. They faced physical and attitudinal barriers in everyday life. There were difficulties in accessing benefits and public services. They experienced a range of medical complications throughout life, but often had difficulty obtaining appropriate medical services or informed professional advice.

The survey ends with the statement that, despite the negative aspects, many respondents were positive and resilient people, quoting one person as saying, 'I'm totally happy the way I am.' In a recent edition of its magazine *Small Talk*, the Restricted Growth Association launched a campaign to be known as 'p2bs', standing for 'Proud to be Small'. The campaign is described as 'a celebration of the restricted growth community being proud of who they are, and that being small should not stop you attaining whatever you want in your life'. The magazine states: 'Many people within the restricted growth community lead successful lives during their careers, home lives and other interests and it is about time that this is celebrated. To this end, over the coming months the campaign will post profiles of people with restricted growth who have been successful in their lives, whether it be career, sport, hobbies, home lives, etc.' (Restricted Growth Association, 2007: 8).

Website of the Restricted Growth Association: www.restrictedgrowth.co.uk.

Lesbian and gay people

To give an example of the sort of information that can be researched about a group, here are some of the questions we give to students about gay and lesbian identity, history and culture, to review their existing knowledge and to indicate the sort of useful information they might acquire. The answers we give are accurate as far as our present knowledge goes, though research by students and contact with the gay community are always likely to refine, expand or correct them.

1. *What does LGBT stand for?*

   Lesbian, Gay, Bisexual and Transgendered. Transgendered people are those who need or wish to adopt a gender identity opposite to their original gender, either temporarily or permanently. Although solidarity with gay men and lesbians against oppression is often shown by transgendered people, their identity is a gender issue, not one of sexuality (see the next section in this chapter).

2. *What is the origin of the word 'lesbian'?*

   The Greek poetess Sappho founded a college for women on the island of Lesbos around 600 BC.

3. *Is it ever appropriate to use the word 'queer' in talking about gay men or lesbians?*

   Gay, lesbian or transgendered people may use the word 'queer' about themselves, illustrating a process of claiming control over language used negatively by others. Some academic courses and writings are called 'Queer Studies' (for example, Corber and Valocchi, 2003; Lovaas et al., 2007). The word is thus being rehabilitated, but should probably still be used with caution by non-gay people.

4. *What objections do many gay and lesbian people have to the word 'homosexual'?*

   'Homo' is often taken to have male connotations, so may not be understood to incorporate lesbians. 'Homosexual' emphasises 'sex', whereas there is of course much more to the identity. It also has medical connotations: at one time it was classified as a disease in the World Health Organisation's Classification of Diseases!

5. *What is the significance of the Pink Triangle?*

   Many gay men were interned in concentration camps, or were killed, in Nazi Germany between 1933 and 1945. They were made to wear a pink triangular badge to identify their homosexuality. More recently, the pink triangle has been worn by some gay people as a mark of pride in their identity.

6. *What happened at the Admiral Duncan pub in Soho, London, on 30 April 1999?*

   A nail bomb was thrown into this pub, frequented by gay people, killing several people including some non-gay customers.

7. *How many cases of homophobic hate crime are reported each year to the police in London, and what proportion is this of the total occurring?*

   In 2005, 1,359 cases were reported to the Metropolitan Police. The police believe that 90 per cent of cases go unreported.

8. *What is the significance of 'Stonewall' in the history of the gay rights movement?*

   A bar in New York where gay, lesbian and transgendered people gathered, was raided by the police in 1969. Instead of meekly accepting this, the customers rioted, and this 'Stonewall Riot' is usually taken as the beginning of a really powerful international Gay Pride and Gay Rights movement. 'Stonewall' has been adopted as the name of a prominent British Gay Rights group.

9. *What is 'Mardi Gras', and why is it significant to the lesbian and gay rights movement?*

   Mardi Gras, 'Fat Tuesday' in French, originally referred to Shrove Tuesday, the day before Ash Wednesday, the beginning of the 40 days fasting of Lent. It was thus a day of feasting ready for the fast. It has become the name for celebratory festivals, particularly used by the Gay Rights movement to name their marches and Pride events.

10. *What colour is the flag adopted by the Gay Pride movement, especially in America?*
    The rainbow flag, symbolising diversity.

11. *What was the significance of the Sexual Offences Act 1967 in England and Wales?*
    It made consenting sex between two men over 21 in private legal. Sex between more than two men, sex involving a man under 21, and sex in public places were still illegal. 'Public' places were defined as anywhere to which the public had access – that is, anywhere outdoors, cubicles in public toilets, and even hotel rooms.

12. *Whose autobiography was called 'The Naked Civil Servant', and why?*
    Quentin Crisp. At one time his occupation was as a male model for art students, employed by a government-financed college. He therefore described himself as a civil servant, and he was of course, for his job, naked. The autobiography describes what it was like to be gay when homosexuality was illegal.

13. *What is 'cottaging' and why is it called that?*
    Many public toilets in the past, especially in parks, were designed to look like little cottages. Cottaging is seeking meetings with other gay people in or around public toilets. This is illegal and in the past led to the arrest of many gay men by the police.

14. *What were the changes in the age of consent for gay male sex, passed in Parliament in 1994 and in 2000?*
    The age at which a man could have legal gay sex was reduced to 18 in 1994 and to 16 in 2000.

15. *Are gay men and lesbians banned from serving in the British armed forces?*
    Many gay people served with distinction in the two World Wars, and gay men were accepted for National Service until it was ended in 1960. Since then the armed forces adopted a policy of not accepting gay people, and discharging people who were discovered to be gay. The Gay Rights group 'Stonewall' took the Ministry of Defence to the European Court of Human Rights over this issue in 2000, and won the case, resulting in the ban being lifted.

16. *In which jail did Oscar Wilde serve two years' imprisonment for homosexuality?*
    Reading. He wrote a famous poem there: 'The Ballad of Reading Gaol'.

17. *Is there a society for gay and lesbian students at Reading University?*
    Yes. Most universities have one.

Main sources:

Alyson (1993), Cook et al. (2007), Miller (1995) and Richardson (2002).

Reading University Lesbian, Gay, Bisexual and Transgendered Group: www.readinglgbt.org.

The Knitting Circle (Lesbian and Gay Staff Association, South Bank University, London): www.sbu.ac.uk/~stafflag.

The Home Office: www.homeoffice.gov.uk/crime-victims/reducing-crime/hate-crime.

Transgendered people

Interesting correspondence took place between us and a transgendered person (a woman who had been born a man) after she had seen some literature by us which placed transgendered people under the category of 'sexual orientation'. The dialogue illustrates the importance of learning from the people themselves and avoiding assumptions.

First letter:

I wish to take issue with your claim that transsexual people belong in the 'sexual orientation' bracket. It would be more appropriate, and more factual, to place transsexual people into the 'gender' bracket, as what you are talking about is oppression based on gender identity and not sexual preference, which plays no role in the individual's gender formation.

Be sure this is a very common mistake made by a lot of people and organisations (thankfully no longer by the government) and has caused untold problems for the trans population. The BBC also altered its positioning of trans issues within a sexual orientation area for precisely the reasons I have outlined.

The term itself, transsexual, popularised by Harry Benjamin in the mid-20th century, is of dubious benefit in identifying individuals who fit this description, as Harry Benjamin himself lamented. As a trans woman myself, I can state that my sexual preference, or lack thereof, plays no part in my gender identity.

The correct bracket to place transsexual people in is under 'gender', as that is the basis for their minority status, not who they choose to sleep with.

Our reply:

Thank you very much indeed for this very helpful clarification. One of the reasons for including transsexual people under sexual orientation is that there has been a certain amount of solidarity shown between transsexual people and gay, lesbian or bisexual people. For example, many groups in Britain call themselves LGBT groups – lesbian, gay, bisexual and transsexual (or transgendered). And we believe the original Stonewall riots in New York that gave a boost to the lesbian and gay rights movement strongly involved some transsexual or transgendered people. However, we do very much take your point and we will endeavour to be more accurate in future.

Second letter:

Collusion in self-advancement or not, gender and sexuality are in fact exclusive, and the distinction should be remembered and understood. It isn't down to want, but necessity. We all share oppressions and some wounds, trans and gay people more than most. Feinberg (1997, 1999) writes with a burning passion about cooperation between gay and trans activists, as well as other oppressed minorities.

Part of the reason why there is in fact a crossover with gay oppression is that some (not all) trans people are gay. However, the truth is that we are a very diverse part of the population. Sexually, socially, educationally, politically, religiously . . . being trans is just a part of our identity, not the be all and end all.

The oppression isn't simply due to ignorance of difference, because we are dealing with the most basic forms of identification in our cultures. It is almost impossible to explain adequately to people in terms they would understand from their own experience. The very first thing you do when meeting a new person, without even thinking about it, is assign a gender to them. When you later learn that this gender may have been different from their birth sex, it throws up all sorts of societal complexities that most people just can't cope with.

So please ensure that trans issues are discussed under 'gender'. Thank you.

People living with HIV/AIDS

(Adapted from a student presentation by Maddie Willems, Nalene Edwards and Louisa Stock, University of Reading, 2007.)

This presentation is a celebration of people living with HIV/AIDS.

HIV stands for Human Immuno-Deficiency Virus. AIDS stands for Acquired Immune Deficiency Syndrome. Information in this presentation is taken from the Internet sites listed at the end.

HIV was first identified in the UK in the 1980s. Specific groups of people most affected with HIV are intravenous drug users, gay men, sex workers, and individuals receiving blood transfusions. Recently, increasing numbers of heterosexuals have become affected by HIV. The United Nations and the World Health Organisation estimate that in 2005, 38.6 million people were living with HIV. In the UK, 60,000 people are living with HIV and 7,000 people are newly diagnosed every year.

Over and above the stigma associated with illness and disease, this is increased in the case of HIV because of its association with taboo social topics: sexuality, death, sexual practices, gender roles, morality, race and mental health. This stigma leads to a risk of oppression and discrimination in public attitudes, access to services, employment, housing, relationships and other areas of social life.

Oppression and discrimination can be tackled through:

- Accurate information
- Support groups
- Shared narrative
- Positive language
- The global community

Support groups provide a positive forum for sharing experiences, information, advice, identification, peer support and self-empowerment. People can gain confidence and solidarity through 'being in the same boat'. An easily accessible network of supportive friends and family can be fostered and developed.

Examples of support groups include:

- Thames Valley Positive Support: www.tvps.org.uk
- Positively Women: www.positivelywomen.org.uk
- National Long Term Survivors Group: www.nltsg.org.uk

Support groups can provide a forum for sharing narratives of experience. Other channels for this may be the Internet or publications. Narrative is a powerful vehicle for expression, awareness, self-empowerment, education, achievement and survival. The power operates not only for those who write the narrative but also for those who read it, fostering cross-communication and understanding.

It is important to use anti-discriminatory language in the pursuit of social inclusion and equality. The use of terms such as 'aids sufferer' and 'aids victim' imply powerlessness and a lack of control over circumstances. The terms 'living with HIV' and 'HIV positive' have replaced older, more negative terms. The move to use anti-oppressive language signifies an important recognition that positive language can communicate positive messages.

Because it is a worldwide phenomenon, there is a global feeling of unity amongst people living with HIV/AIDS, and there are many examples of positive support being provided in different parts of the world:

- The United Nations has a programme operating under the GIPA principle (Greater Involvement of People). This emphasises the centrality of groups of people living with HIV in planning, coordinating and implementing HIV/AIDS awareness and education programmes. Empowering people through the GIPA principle, and establishing an environment in which people living with HIV can flourish and contribute meaningfully, are at the heart of tackling stigma and oppression.
- 'Talk to Me' is a national television and radio campaign in South Africa. It is aimed at encouraging parents and carers to talk to children about HIV – both about protection from HIV and about positive living with HIV. It uses a much loved South African children's character, 'Kami' the Muppet. The campaign is based on the conviction that young children have the capacity to understand HIV and its effects.
- The Targeted Intervention Project in India involves a self-help group of gay men, living with HIV/AIDS, designing and selling jewellery. Young men can become economically independent and enjoy the support of a group in tackling stigma and discrimination. Methods such as dance, music and counselling are also used as a forum for education and awareness.
- World Aids Day represents a positive global effort to unite everyone in raising awareness about HIV/AIDS and breaking down barriers of stigma, fear and prejudice. It provides the opportunity to talk openly about HIV and AIDS. The red ribbon is the international symbol of World Aids Day.

Just as other groups at risk of oppression have developed a feeling of pride in their identity, so there are many people who have lived and are living positively and proudly with HIV around the world today.

The following Internet resources provide information and are a vehicle for the expression of positive attitudes towards people living with HIV/AIDS. Several of them contain narratives by the people themselves.

- www.comminit.com
- www.dipex.org
- www.nat.org.uk
- www.nltsg.org.uk
- www.positivelywomen.org.uk
- www.thebody.com
- www.tht.org.uk
- www.tvps.org.uk
- www.unaids.org
- www.worldaidsday.org

Children with Attention Deficit Hyperactivity Disorder (ADHD)

(Adapted from a student presentation by Nikki Osborne, Matt Neads and Natasha Hutchings, University of Reading, 2007.)

ADHD is a cluster of learning and behaviour problems in children that includes poor self-control, physical restlessness, poor concentration and short-term memory, and failure to follow instructions (www.adhdtraining. co.uk). It was first described by Dr Heinrich Hoffman in 1845.

In the UK, 2 per cent of young people aged from 11–16 years are diagnosed hyperactive, with over 30,000 diagnosed with severe ADHD. The effects on a young person's family life, education, social friendships and overall well-being can be profound. Treatment tends to focus on drugs, such as Ritalin, which are believed to have a beneficial effect on behaviour. However, often the young person is confused about the condition, afraid of its consequences and even unsure about the nature of the medication they are being prescribed.

There is no national support service available for families in the UK. Families are often referred to child and adolescent mental health services (CAMHS), where they may be offered a psychiatric assessment and treatment. Some authorities may offer specialist parenting courses aimed at dealing with difficult behaviours. However, this appears to be a postcode lottery.

In school, negative behaviours, which may often be a cry for help, can be misinterpreted as wilfully bad behaviour. Often, additional classroom support is not available. The child may be excluded from activities and relationships by peers. Teaching staff can find it frustrating and difficult when a child is disruptive.

A person's behaviour is likely to be profoundly affected by the role expectations that are placed upon him or her (Wolfensberger, 1972; Wolfensberger and Thomas, 1983, 2007). This can lead to self-fulfilling prophecies, with children living up (or down) to expectations of them. Some negative perceptions of children with ADHD are:

- Naughty
- Unwilling to learn
- Coming from a family with poor parenting skills
- Watching too much television
- Having a poor diet
- Being lazy
- Lacking intelligence
- Not wanting to socialise

Responses such as exclusion or over-medication reinforce these negative views.

Anti-oppressive practice towards the children might involve:

- Having positive perceptions of the children
- Having high expectations of the children
- Supporting positive social roles
- Supporting inclusion
- Providing high-quality education
- Better training for teachers
- More classroom support
- More informed media coverage
- Improved community awareness
- Early assessment and intervention
- Support for families
- Local support and self-help groups
- More knowledge and understanding by GPs

To illustrate how ADHD need not be a career limiting or choice restricting condition, here is a list of some of the well-known people who have had ADHD but who have gone on to achieve their career goals:

- Albert Einstein
- Anthony Hopkins
- Bill Cosby
- Bill Gates
- Cher
- Dustin Hoffman
- Elvis Presley
- George Bush Senior
- George W. Bush
- Guy Ritchie
- Henry Winkler
- Jack Nicholson
- Jim Carey
- John Lennon
- Kirk Douglas
- Robin Williams
- Stephen Hawking
- Steve McQueen
- Steven Spielberg
- Stevie Wonder
- Sylvester Stallone
- Tom Cruise
- Whoopi Goldberg
- Will Smith

Reading: Mental Health Foundation (2000), Green and Chee (1997) and Honos-Webb (2005).

Homeless People

(Adapted from a student presentation by Laura Pitman, Alison Miller and Jane Lynch, University of Reading, 2007.)

Around 20,000 people live in accommodation for homeless people in London, but this presentation is focused on those people who regularly sleep on the streets, of whom there are about 300 in London and about 2,000 nationally. Statistics here are drawn from the website of St Mungo's (see Resources below).

Over 90 per cent of people sleeping rough are men. About 15 per cent are under 25, 60 per cent are 25 to 50, and 25 per cent are over 50. Around 25 per cent are of non-white or non-British ethnic origin. Almost 20 per cent have been sleeping rough for more than 10 years, a further 10 per cent for more than 5 years, and 30 per cent for between 1 and 5 years.

There are many myths about people who sleep rough. It is not true that the majority are young. It is not true that they receive extra benefit money to feed their dogs. And it is not true that homelessness is never a choice.

For as long as historical records have been kept, Britain has seen homelessness. In the seventh century there were laws to punish and round up 'vagrants'. In the sixteenth century the state first tried to house vagrants rather than punish them. It began introducing bridewells, which were intended to take vagrants in and train them for a profession, though this was rarely achieved. By the eighteenth century, workhouses replaced the bridewells, but these were intended to discourage over-reliance on state help. The successor to the workhouse was the spike (dormitory housing provided by local boroughs).

From a post-war low of six people found sleeping rough in London in 1949, by the 1980s the numbers had risen to more than 1,000. The reasons for this include:

- a change in benefits, stopping 16- and 17-year-olds from claiming housing benefits
- the closure of many of the dormitories for homeless people and their replacement with hostels with single rooms, which meant that while the housing standard rose the number of beds fell
- a general increase in the number of people with drink, drug and mental health problems.

Government action has included programmes like the Rough Sleepers Initiatives and the Homeless Mentally Ill Initiative to fund extra hostels and other services (ODPM, 2003). In 1998, the Rough Sleepers Unit was established to coordinate the government's approach and the efforts of the homelessness charities. As a result the numbers of people living on the street have fallen again.

There is legislation designed to improve services for homeless people. As well as the Housing (Homeless Persons) Act 1977, the Housing Act 2004 brought in several reforms to bring empty homes back into use through

Empty Dwelling Management Orders. In 2000, the National Health Service introduced new flexibility to primary care services; a Personal Medical Service with new contracts for GPs made it easier for them to work with marginalised groups such as homeless people.

There are barriers to access to educational facilities and employment for homeless people, due to them not having a fixed address. A survey commissioned by St Mungo's of almost 200 people sleeping rough in London, Manchester and Edinburgh found that only 8 per cent were in full-time, part-time or casual work while on the street, though 53 per cent said they were looking for work, 28 per cent had educational attainments to O-level standard (8 per cent to A-level standard or above), and 87 per cent had worked at some time in their lives.

There are also major health concerns for homeless people. Tuberculosis amongst homeless people is 25 times the national average and at least 1 in 5 homeless people suffers from a severe mental health problem. Homeless people are 40 times more likely not to be registered with a GP than the general population.

On the positive side, public perceptions of homeless people have become less negative. They are no longer treated as criminals and no longer exploited in workhouses. Housing provided is no longer unsanitary. Legislation and policy dictates minimum standards for temporary accommodation, should people wish to access these provisions.

Homeless people now have a voice through self-help groups, reality television programmes and voluntary organisations.

Some people choose to be homeless:

> Ben Taylor has no house, heat, bed, television or computer. He sleeps in a tent and sleeping bag in weather most people wouldn't want to step out in, much less sleep in, and he loves it. Taylor attends Utah University. He enjoys it so much he would want to continue with this way of life through all of college. At first, Taylor said he was embarrassed to be seen around campus with his gear, but now he would rather people ask him what he is doing carrying around a tent than not say anything to him.
>
> Taylor says it is an inexpensive and creative way of living. He says sleeping outside is a good way to learn the difference between 30 degrees and 40 degrees at night. He also can't sleep in beds anymore; the floor is more comfortable. Sleeping inside is really hard now as well, because he is used to silence. He claims that living outdoors has prepared him for any challenges life will throw him in the future. (Betts, 2003)

The Big Issue was established in 1995. The aim of the Big Issue Foundation is to assist homeless people by enabling them to gain control of their lives and achieve greater self-reliance and independence. Each issue of the magazine is sold by over 2,000 vendors. In the London area alone, the Foundation has helped over 400 people to go into further education or attend courses; almost 300 people have been rehoused; and 75 have been helped into permanent employment.

There are some well-known people who were once homeless. The DJ and singer Sonique spent some time as a homeless person when she was 16. The singer Ella Fitzgerald slept on the streets of Harlem in New York for a year as a teenager before winning a singing contest that launched her career. Film director Gordon Parks used to sleep in empty trolleys at night while a teenager, after his mother died. And Jesus of Nazareth had no permanent home and often slept in the open.

There have been films about homelessness. For example, *Pursuit of Happyness* portrays a father and son who are evicted from their home and forced on to the streets where they spend their nights in homeless shelters and public restrooms. Television films about homelessness include *Cathy Come Home*, a 1966 drama which helped to raise awareness and led to the founding of the national charity Shelter. There have been many books about homelessness and homeless people, as for example, George Orwell's account (2003), originally written in 1933, and Alexander Masters' more recent (2006) biography of a homeless person. Poetry by homeless people often appears in *The Big Issue*. There are stories and biographies of homeless people on several Internet sites (see Resources below).

Resources:

- www.shelter.org.uk: Shelter is the major voluntary organisation campaigning on behalf of homeless people.
- www.mungos.org: St Mungo's provides advice and services for homeless people and has carried out surveys and research.
- www.crisis.org.uk: Crisis also provides advice and help for homeless people.
- www.streetwiseopera.org: Streetwise Opera provides cultural activities to raise the self-esteem and employment prospects of homeless people.
- www.bigissue.co.uk: The Big Issue Foundation supports homeless people and provides income for them through selling *The Big Issue* magazine.
- www.housemate.co.uk: Housemate is an advice service for young homeless people in Wales, run by Shelter.
- www.salvationarmy.org.uk: The Salvation Army provides services and advice for homeless people.
- www.citizensadvice.org.uk: Citizens Advice Bureaux provide advice and support for homeless people.
- www.resettlement-agency.co.uk: REAP is a resettlement agency for single homeless people, based in Reading.
- www.homeless.org.uk: Homeless Link is a partnership of agencies working with homeless people.

Young homeless people

(A summary of a student essay by Daniel Jones, University of Reading, 2006.)

Definitions of 'homeless' and of 'youth' (under 25) are given. Relevant current legislation is then reviewed, mainly the Housing Act 1996 and the Homeless Act 2002. The emphasis in the latter is much more on prevention. Explanations for youth homelessness are explored under two categories: 'structural' and 'agency'.

Structural explanations include insufficient public housing stock and high rents for private rented property (Hutson and Liddiard, 1994). A second structural factor is youth unemployment, running at 12 per cent in 2003 according to the Office of Public Sector Information (www.opsi.gov.uk). Legislation has made it difficult for young people to obtain benefits, and almost impossible for 16- to 18-year-olds. Some employment available to young people is poorly paid and does not provide sufficient income for accommodation. Poverty, unemployment and legislation thus interact to cause homelessness.

Agency explanations for young people leaving the parental home include escaping violence and physical and sexual abuse, response to family poverty, and breakdown of family relationships (Rees, 1993). Wishing to, or having to, leave the care system is a factor for those in care. For many homeless young people, multiple factors have operated (Ploeg and Scholte, 1997).

An anti-oppressive approach to preventing youth homelessness needs to operate at both structural and agency levels. There needs to be less dis-crimination against young people by employers, and efforts to reduce youth unemployment. There is also a need for more affordable housing options. However, there is also a need for direct work with young people at local level. Rees (1993) found that young people wanted better advice on the realities of leaving home, and services where they could discuss their problems and hence prevent them leaving. Levitas (2005) suggests that empowering people to address their own circumstances can create changes at structural level. (In Thompson's PCS model this would be an instance of the personal influencing the cultural which in turn influences the structural.)

Centrepoint, an agency supporting young homeless people, has worked with teachers, youth leaders and young people themselves to develop inter-active activity packs on housing issues, covering such issues as budgeting, communal living, cookery and access to employment (www.centrepoint. org.uk). The Supporting People programme has been developed to provide housing-related support to vulnerable people at local level (ODPM, 2004). Mediation services can be provided for families to rebuild relationships, for example through Family Group Conferences.

At the cultural level, media portrayal of homeless young people can change perceptions and attitudes. Organisations such as Shelter and Crisis have done much to show this group in a sympathetic light.

In summary, tackling youth homelessness requires a holistic approach involving many simultaneous strategies addressing different levels and types of cause.

Working-class youth from disadvantaged areas

(This is a verbatim summary from a student essay by Myrleene Beckford, University of Reading, 2006.)

This essay suggests that the collective identity 'youth' has within its culture trusted and protective networks that give young people a sense of belonging and unity. The strength of peer group support and sharing of local knowledge allow working-class youths from disadvantaged areas to become resilient and self-protective (Joseph Rowntree Foundation, 2006).

The strengths and positives within youth culture can be highlighted to combat societal perceptions of 'yob' culture. Youth Action* strategies could mobilise working-class youths within their neighbourhoods to use their culture and local knowledge to create initiatives that benefit the community. One way of tackling discrimination could be through giving youths support to promote and publicise their positive initiatives, to help create better understanding of the meaning of popular youth cultures. Events like 'Rebel Youth'** have been used to highlight young people's achievements and to promote inclusion, via supporting media coverage of young people's projects. In this way, young people have been able to raise their profile within society, proving their worth and claiming their rights to be regarded as true citizens.

Working-class youth have resilience but need help, guidance and support – empowerment – to effectively address the impact of inequalities, oppression and discrimination. Social work practitioners can empower youths to achieve inclusion using advocacy skills and through the promotion of participation and youth involvement via partnership (Trevithick, 2005). Community action groups and local councils could involve local youths more in the development of their policies, working in partnership to create community initiatives that can be informed, managed and run by youths.

Power differentials, inequalities and imbalances are intrinsic in issues of social conflict and can determine and control social relationships (Lukes, 2005). In the relationship between working-class youth and the government, it could be perceived that youths are powerless as the government exercises its authority through legislation such as the Anti-social Behaviour Act 2003. However, the power relations existing amongst young people and the flexibility of their informal rules can be utilised positively through the choices they make about how they react, or not, to the oppression they experience. Social work practitioners can assist working-class youths to make those choices wisely and, using the resources available to them as statutory agents, social workers can utilise their power to address issues of social justice for working-class youths.

* Youth Action: see www.youth-action.net.

** 'Rebel Youth': an event organised in European Youth Week, November 2005, by the British Youth Council, involving 'hard to reach' young people, mainly from Black and minority ethnic backgrounds, making their views and needs known at a European level (see www.byc.org.uk).

Fat people

(A summary based on a student essay by Kathryn Holman, University of Reading, 2006.)

This essay first discusses terminology. The author decides to use the word 'fat' rather than 'big' or 'large' or 'overweight' or 'obese', stating a rationale based on research into the preferences of the people themselves. Others may prefer alternative terms, but this is a good example of application of the principles in Reading University's guidance to students on language (see Chapter 2, pages 28–9).

Issues for fat people are discussed in relation to social inclusion (Pierson, 2002), social justice, a person-centred approach to assessing and meeting needs (Coulshed and Orme, 2006), social role valorisation (Kendrick, 1994), the WISE principles, and inclusion discourse (Levitas, 2005).

The following Internet resources are identified and discussed:

- www.cat-and-dragon.com
  An extract from 'Stef's Home Page' on this site:
  'Size acceptance is the notion that people are OK (and should be treated with respect and feel good about themselves and enjoy life) at whatever size they are: thin, fat, or in-between. Size acceptance usually includes the notion that consciously manipulating one's weight (either gaining or losing) is not desirable and may even be harmful, and the idea that dieting for weight loss usually leads in the long term to higher rather than lower weights.

  'The political side of size acceptance includes calling for public accommodations and public products to be accessible to all people, regardless of size. (This means, among other things, that movie theatres should have seats that are wide enough for large folks, and clothing stores should carry attractive clothing in large sizes.) Size acceptance addresses the discrimination that fat people often face because they are fat; promotes a wider range of beauty standards than is usually shown in the media; publicises the studies that indicate harmful effects of dieting; and educates people (for example doctors) about interacting respectfully with large folks.

  'On the personal side, size acceptance involves feeling good about one's body, treating oneself well (for example enjoying good food, fun activities, nice clothing), and expecting to be treated well by others (that is, not accepting, or at least not internalising, size-hating remarks). Not everyone who believes in size acceptance completely accepts their size. This is a problem of a fat-hating culture, and one we are working to minimize.'

- www.naafa.org
  Site of the National Association to Advance Fat Acceptance. This American organisation documents discrimination against fat people, gives advice on health, provides useful information and links to resources, and campaigns against oppression of fat people.
- www.casagordita.com
  The personal website of Mary McGhee, giving information about her life and about fat acceptance. Here is an extract:
  'Here I am, fat, forty-eight, and more at peace with my body that I've ever been. It's been a tough fight, and it's not altogether over – I still have twinges of doubt and self-reproach every now and then – but mostly I like how I look and what I'm able to do with my body. I'm certainly a lot less willing to passively accept all the crap – the fat jokes, the lack of public accommodations and products and services that meet my needs, the misinformation, the discrimination that fat people face every day – than I used to be. I guess I just must be an educator and an agitator by nature, because it only feels right for me to stand up against injustice and ignorance, and to work to empower other people to stand up for themselves, too.'
- www.sixteen47.com
  A website on clothes for big women, run by the actress Dawn French.
- www.sizewise.com
  A site covering health and fitness, the politics of being large, relationships, resources and personal stories.

Summary

- A wide variety of examples of research into identity groups has been given.
- A range of methods and sources for gaining information is illustrated.
- A wide variety of aspects of a particular identity can be studied.

9

Practice Placements

Aim

- To explain practice placement processes.
- To describe some of the difficulties that can arise during placements.
- To show how an effective placement process can support anti-oppressive practice.

This chapter will discuss issues concerning practice placements for students training for health and social care professions. Drawing particularly on the processes for social work and community nursing students, the focus will include:

- placement suitability
- student preparation
- the learning contract
- supervision
- assessment
- evaluation of the placement.

First-hand experience of working directly with health and social care users plays an important part in students' education. Fieldwork placements are compulsory and the length of these placements is stipulated by the professional bodies who award the professional qualification. For example, as required by the Nursing and Midwifery Council (NMC), to ensure consistency and quality, community nursing students' placements are normally organised by the sponsoring health care trust as part of their responsibility to create appropriate learning environments for students. The placement experience constitutes the equivalent of 50 per cent of the course. The placement experience will enable students to relate and apply theory to their practice and to produce evidence to demonstrate professional competence. Similarly, social work students are required by the General Social Care Council (GSCC) to successfully undertake 200 days of supervised fieldwork practice during their programme of study and to produce evidence that they have met the key roles set out in the National Occupational Standards for Social Work. Here too, the 200 days constitute 50 per cent of the degree programme of study.

It is expected that students, while on placements, through interaction would seek to understand the everyday life of individuals, groups and organisations by entering their social worlds. They should try as much as is possible to see things from the point of view of service users (Clark, 2000). For each student, the process of interaction with all the constituent parts within the placement agency is likely to be influenced by social characteristics such as age, gender or class. Some of these social differences can play a significant role in the placement process and in the quality of experience and learning. Entering someone else's social world and seeing things from their point of view is challenging but congruent with the ideas about anti-oppressive practice. In support of this line of thought, professional bodies governing health and social care curriculum content expect students to be adequately prepared in terms of what is expected of them, to receive appropriate guidance on conduct and to be fully informed on how they will be assessed on their anti-oppressive practice competences.

Specific aspects of practice placements have been identified for their importance in ensuring that students have relevant and appropriate educative experience inclusive of anti-oppressive practice. The type of placement, and the nature of supervision within the placement environment and the university, are critical to enable students to make the links between theories of equality and discrimination and their own anti-oppressive practice. Fieldwork experience for social work and community nursing students will be the illustrative examples. However, the issues discussed are also applicable to other professional vocational programmes within the care sector.

Placement suitability

To comply with anti-discrimination legislation, all health and social care organisations within the UK should have written policies on equal opportunities and the management of diversity, and most of these organisations do have such policies (Johns, 2005; Butt, 1994). In addition to such policies, public sector service providers are required to have equality schemes that are monitored for impact on diverse constituencies, under the Disability

Discrimination Act 2005 and the Race Relations Amendment Act 2000. These social care organisations are the agencies that would normally provide practice placements to students. Establishing the suitability of a placement opportunity is the responsibility of the university or college.

For example, nurse educators assess the suitability of clinical areas for the placement of student nurses, based on the partnership that exists between universities and health care trusts in relation to nurse education. The nurse educators need to be satisfied that any student placed with such a provider would be afforded meaningful learning opportunities, so that the theoretical taught content has relevance. In social work, locating suitable practice placements for social work students is primarily the responsibility of the university or college. The partnership that exists between universities and health care trusts appears not to be so clearly defined between local authority social services departments and universities. The tenuous arrangement between education providers can make the assessment of suitability of placements difficult. This is particularly so when trying to establish an agency's commitment to anti-discriminatory and anti-oppressive practice. In addition to the statutory local authority social care sector, placements can also be provided by the voluntary and the private sectors. These providers would need to be assessed for suitability along similar lines to the statutory sector.

Within that tenuous relationship between academic and practice education for social workers, the approved universities and colleges who deliver social work education programmes seek to find the best placement match for each student with due regard to their prior experience and current needs. Employers of social care workers are expected to provide written policies and procedures to deal with unsafe, discriminatory or exploitative behaviour and practice. Checking that such frameworks are in place for all placement providers would give reassurance that when students are accepted for hands-on practice within these agencies, they would be enabled to develop anti-discriminatory and anti-oppressive social care practice. This is particularly important if anti-oppressive practice is to become a normal way of working. Having appropriate procedures in place would imply that placement providers would be prepared to accommodate critical comments from students on aspects of practice that are found wanting.

In seeking to find the best match for each social work student, programme providers need to make use of evidence about fieldwork experiences of students from diverse backgrounds. For example, some Black and minority ethnic (BME) students do encounter racist attitudes when interacting with service users, at the same rate as they would in society at large. Having in place a clear and unambiguous mechanism for acknowledging the existence of such negative and disempowering attitudes and challenging them is particularly beneficial towards promoting anti-oppressive practice. Another example relates to the practicalities of getting to a placement and undertaking assigned work. A student needs to be able to get to the placement agency and carry out agreed work without having to constantly worry about their safety. If students feel vulnerable for any reason, they are not likely to have a satisfactory learning experience. Such a situation can constitute a breach of health and safety rules, as well as breaching equal opportunities and anti-discrimination policy.

Suitable placements should demonstrate that they support critical practice. This means providing opportunities for students to question personal assumptions and underpinning values, work with service users towards empowerment, and evaluate knowledge gained in the process of interacting with those around them. According to Barnett, 'critical practitioners must be skilled and knowledgeable and yet remain open to alternative ideas, frameworks and belief systems, recognising and valuing alternative perspectives' (1997: 44). Placements ought to provide students with opportunities to become critical practitioners who can challenge discriminatory hurdles within the framework of respectful and equal relationships.

Unfortunately, the reality is that, for some local authority social services departments and health care trusts, equal opportunities paper policies have tended to be just that because of the institutionalised nature of discrimination. Equal opportunities policies have yet to have positive impact on the cultures of health and social care organisations so that practitioners adopt new ways of working, in order that anti-oppressive practice becomes routine in such a way as to be taken for granted. The preparation for practice process can include an evaluation of documented policies on equality from different placement providers to assess progress made towards a culture of inclusiveness. If such an impact assessment is made prior to starting placement, the results can be beneficial to students, practice assessors and tutors in determining a baseline against which progress can be measured during the placement.

The pace of change towards positive equal opportunities impact has been slow because some of those in leadership positions continue to deny the existence of institutional discrimination. One factor may be that of unwitting prejudice as one of the defining features of institutional racism (MacPherson, 1999). The concept of unwitting prejudice highlights the fact that discrimination by individuals is not solely the result of conscious, intentional actions, but may be behaviour that has been unconsciously influenced by an individual's ideas and feelings. Such behaviour may be an important factor generating discriminatory outcomes at the organisational level, even though at the individual level their origin may be subtle and difficult to identify.

A frequently cited example of how institutional discrimination operates relates to seniority and professional status within work organisations. So, for example, when an ethnic minority person arrives with a white colleague at another department for a meeting, it is often the white colleague who is perceived to be the more senior, the one 'in charge'. There are issues here of non-recognition, belittlement, invisibility and questioning of credibility, that echo the features of some of the major historical oppressions described in Chapter 1. There are similar issues in relation to gender.

Until individuals question their assumptions, they can continue to act out their unwitting prejudice, contributing to institutional discrimination at work. The more recent anti-discrimination legislation (DDA 2005 and RRAA 2000) requiring public authorities to adopt equality schemes, confirms the extent to which institutional discriminatory practices have continued to be present within the statutory sector. Given this state of affairs, the process remains problematic of finding a suitable placement for a community nursing or a social work student that will offer a rounded experience, including opportunities to be supported to develop equal opportunities and anti-oppressive skills.

Does this mean universities and colleges are knowingly sanctioning unsuitable student placements, or are they caught up in the web of collective failure to recognise institutional discrimination? The stated position of each university or college would influence the nature of student preparation necessary prior to fieldwork experience. Community nursing and social work practice placement arrangements are illustrations of similarities as well as differences in emphasis, as informed by the respective professional institutions that award the appropriate licences to practice. The specifications from the nursing and midwifery council (NMC) and the general social care council (GSCC) are taken into account during the period of preparation prior to students going out on practice placements. In addition to the stipulations from the NMC and GSCC, it needs to be acknowledged that nursing and social work as professions are at different stages in their development, hence some differences in emphasis on how to educate students on equality issues.

Community nursing student preparation

Students are supported through written information and discussion about the roles of tutors, practice teachers and mentors in supporting supervised practice, including enabling students to be clear about equality objectives. The infrastructure and support network for students is conducive to tackling unprofessional and oppressive practices, thereby realising the main aim of appropriate education on equality issues. Three broad objectives identified for appropriate education for students include:

• to develop their disposition to act impartially
• to enhance their capacity to be critical
• to extend their understanding of oppression.

Students are encouraged to reflect on ways to achieve these broad objectives.

Impartiality

Community nurses are required to be impartial in their dealings with clients. This is a matter of professional ethics and general morality. It entails, in particular, fairness in the allocation of resources. Fairness involves differences in treatment between clients being solely related to need, and not to such characteristics as class, disability, gender, race or sexual orientation.

Criticality

This is a prerequisite for effective practice. It entails preparedness to examine assumptions and to step back from generalisations, which, if uncriticised, may vitiate a true understanding of particular persons and situations. Critical practitioners are, therefore, suspicious of stereotypes in general and of negative stereotypes in particular; they are also self-aware and able to identify, hold in check and question any prejudice, for example racist attitudes, that may be derived from their socialisation.

Understanding of oppression

Since community nurses practise in a society characterised by differences in power, and may typically work with clients who are relatively powerless, they need to understand the political context of nursing and the structures of oppression, as outlined in Chapters 3 to 6.

In addition to encouraging students to consider ways of working towards achieving these broad objectives, the relationship between students and tutors, and between students and practice teachers, should foster fairness and empowerment in preparation for placements. Practice teachers, who are experienced practitioners, bring into the learning experience teaching on equality issues that should be up-to-date, credible and evidence-based (University of Reading, 2006a: 43).

Having the broad equality objectives stated at the outset of a course provides an important reference point. As students work through the course material, they need to take into account equality implications at every turn, as part of the educative process. Practice placements offer to students the opportunity to reflect continuously on their thoughts, behaviours and actions. This method of learning lends itself well to promoting equality, as students progressively question, evaluate and challenge discriminatory and oppressive practices. The course objectives in relation to equal opportunities give the students the permission to find ways to effect change within their sphere of influence.

Social work student preparation

Students are supported through documented information on the university's equal opportunities policy and the GSCC's policy on service user and carer involvement in social work education. Contents of the policies are discussed with students as an integral part of preparation for practice. Students must successfully complete this assessed element of their preparation prior to attending for their placement in the field.

The taught module assessable outcomes include:

- demonstration of the student's ability to engage with service users
- demonstration of professionally acceptable behaviour within a social care agency
- recognition of the relevance of codes of practice to their work
- a demonstration of ability to reflect on their experience and identify learning needs. (University of Reading, 2006b: 22)

The General Social Care Council Codes of Practice provide guidance on acceptable forms of professional behaviour. Students have the opportunity to engage with codes of practice discourse and the underlying values within the preparation for the practice module. Equal opportunities promotion and anti-oppressive practice are an integral part of this expected professional behaviour. GSCC code 1 states that 'as a social care worker, you must protect the rights and promote the interests of service users and carers.' Subsections 1.5 and 1.6 highlight the importance of promoting equal opportunities for service users and carers and respecting diversity and different cultures and values.

Codes of practice

Nursing and medical practitioners have similar codes of practice. The General Medical Council (GMC) states within its Code of Conduct that doctors are to avoid bias on grounds of sex, race, disability, lifestyle, culture, belief, colour, gender, sexuality or age. Additionally, under the duties of a doctor, members are expected to show respect for human life and make sure that their personal beliefs do not prejudice their patients' care. The Council offers practical tips with regards to anti-discrimination and states:

> Whilst compliance with the legislation is essential, do not be drawn into mere legal compliance. Focus instead on what will add value to your services and what information would be useful to identify and measure in order to continually improve your professional practice. (GMC, 2003: 5)

For nurses and midwives there is a Code of Professional Conduct (NMC, 2002). Under section 2.2, nurses and midwives are accountable for ensuring that they promote and protect the interests and dignity of patients, irrespective of gender, age, race, ability, sexuality, economic status, lifestyle, culture and religious or political beliefs. Additionally, section 2.4 requires nurses and midwives to promote the interests of patients and clients by helping individuals and groups to gain access to health and social care information and support relevant to their needs. Adherence to the laws of the United Kingdom is a requirement and is an integral part of the overall Code of Conduct.

Implicit in the information contained in all the codes of practice/conduct is the need for professional practitioners to acknowledge the power invested in their profession and to use that power wisely for the benefit of service users. Because of this professional power invested in practitioners it is possible to make a real difference in equal opportunities and anti-oppressive practice if there is a will and commitment. Unfortunately, there has been a lack of vigilance because it is just accepted that those who work in health and social care genuinely care, and therefore would not discriminate. The framework through the codes of practice to enable professionals to do the right thing is in place, and yet a snail's pace of change continues (Cowden and Singh, 2007; CEMS, 2001). This might be because institutional discriminatory practices are embedded routines which members regard as normal without realising the contradiction to the professional code of conduct. However, students, as the practitioners of tomorrow, are uniquely placed to take a questioning stance with the support of universities and colleges in the interest of service users on issues of vulnerability and oppression. Information and taught sessions as preparation for practice play a significant part of initial support for this.

Exercise

How does the preparation so described square up to what you know?

What changes would you make to improve the process?

Student and practice teacher/assessor

Student preparation for fieldwork involves also matching a student with a practice teacher and a tutor. They will provide ongoing support for the duration of the placement. To be able to offer appropriate support for professional development on anti-oppressive issues, practice teachers and tutors are expected to work within the codes of professional practice and not to collude with injustice and oppression. This remains a real challenge to many health and social work practitioners and tutors who aspire to the equality ideal and yet operate within structures that are institutionally discriminatory and oppressive with regard to some service user groups and staff (see the MacPherson Report, 1999). There is a cultural tradition of service users being expected to fit in within a prescribed system (Cowden and Singh, 2007).

Practice teachers can acknowledge the shortcomings of the existing structures, so that consideration of this can be included within the student's learning contract to guide their ongoing critical and reflective accounts. For some students, it may be that prior to joining the course their experiences of discrimination and oppression acted as a springboard to seek professional training. In view of the different motives at entry, some students may be euphoric, some may be angry and some may be fragile. A skilled practice teacher would tailor-make their responses according to individual needs. Identified needs will inform decisions and actions to be taken to enable each student to flourish.

Research into the experiences of BME students on social work courses suggests that some of them have not always fared well (Dominelli, 1997). Responding to individual needs is a normal way of working in health and social care, suggesting that those who work with students can readily work in an anti-oppressive way if there is commitment, because the normal way of working enables rather than disables. Vulnerable as they are, students can also make the most of this needs-based approach to working and articulate their needs as clearly as they can. An example of such needs is shared here to illustrate some of the complexities associated with marrying equality theory with practice:

A BME student's placement within a local authority social services department fully exercised all parties. The duration of the placement was 80 days. As with most local authorities, this placement agency has an equal opportunities policy. It also had a track record of offering placements to students, and hence the placement was deemed to be suitable. Within three weeks of starting fieldwork experience, the feedback to the education establishment suggested that the student was distressed because they were made to feel different due to their colour, religion and accent. All the protocols were acted upon to sort out the oppression as expressed by the student, including the offer of an alternative placement. The student decided to remain within this placement agency, so additional support from an experienced practitioner external to the organisation was offered and accepted by the student. The student successfully completed their practice placement. Formal written feedback received from the student and written assessment records revealed the gaps between anti-oppressive theory and practice. Attempts by the education establishment to work with the placement agency to explore the gaps between theory and practice, and improve the knowledge base for both institutions, were swiftly rebuffed. It was decided that no students from that education establishment would be placed with that agency until equal opportunity issues and anti-oppressive practice were jointly addressed.

Such issues are not likely to apply just to BME students. For example, guidelines from the Disability Rights Commission about learning and teaching have suggested that a great deal more attention is required to make sure that appropriate support is available to students with disabilities to enable them to flourish. There is a need to review existing structures, education processes and materials available at educational establishments and on placements, to eliminate discrimination and consequent negative learning experiences. This demands that teaching is delivered in an inclusive and anti-oppressive way.

Exercise

To enable disabled students to be treated equally and to perform well when on placements, what actions do you think are required by a) the educational establishment, b) the placement agency, c) the student's tutor and d) the student's practice teacher/assessor?

Placement contract/learning agreement

The elements in negotiating and drawing up a learning contract (adapted from Boud et al., 1996) are:

- exploring learning needs
- establishing learning goals
- identifying learning resources
- developing a plan
- dividing responsibilities between student and teacher
- agreeing on a timescale
- evaluating achievement of goals together
- re-negotiating or terminating the contract.

Using this process enables the student's learning needs to be formalised, and ensures all parties are involved, agree and are committed. Normally two organisations would be directly involved: the placement agency and the university or college. Representatives from each organisation and the student would agree the details of the learning contract, setting out as clearly as possible available learning opportunities, the nature of support for the student and how the assessment would be carried out. It is important to include within the contract the starting position of the student and what must be achieved for the student to pass the placement. In addition to this, the contract formalises how the two organisations will work together in the interests of the student. Issues of empowerment and the promotion of equal opportunities should be included in the contract in an explicit way. As a working document, the learning contract would guide all parties to continually check the quality of human relationships in an effort to avoid oppression. Such relationships would be between:

- student and service users
- student and practice teacher
- student and tutor.

The student would be expected to have constructive engagement with all three above, if the placement experience is a positive one. Service-user involvement is of particular importance. This involvement is a central part of current discourse in training and in services, although its achievement is still fraught with difficulties because of the power dynamics. However, within the context of anti-oppressive practice, this change towards full user involvement is particularly helpful in enabling those who have previously been marginalised to gain some power.

Students on placement are well placed to assess impact, confirm what works and incorporate the ideas into their own practice. From a learning point of view, students can be encouraged to reflect on the process of negotiating a learning agreement and take from that process aspects that can be adapted for use between themselves and service users. The adaptations can be discussed in supervision.

Student supervision

Supervision has been defined as: 'A quintessentially interpersonal interaction with the general goal that one person, the supervisor, meets with another, the supervisee, in an effort to make the latter more effective in helping people' (Hess, 1980: 25).

Health and social care students need to be enabled through supervision to be effective in helping service users. According to Kadushin (1992), supervision has both a supportive and an educative role. Through reflection and exploration of students' work through supervision, students can better understand service users and can review their interventions and the outcomes. Supervisors can also help students to explore alternative ways of working in similar situations as well as sharing strategies for coping with stress or distress.

As part of their learning, students should be encouraged to be proactive within supervision. At the contract stage, expectations of supervision should be clearly stated as well as indicating how it will be carried out. Location, frequency, recording and duration of supervision sessions need to be negotiated and agreed. Both parties should adequately prepare for each session. Hawkins and Shohet (2000: 118) cite a blueprint of some of the responsibilities for students and supervisors, shown in Table 9.1.

Table 9.1 Supervision responsibilities

Student responsibility	Supervisor responsibility
To develop self-awareness	To ensure safe space for laying out issues
To identify practice issues	To help with exploration and thinking
To be open to receive feedback	To challenge unsafe or incompetent practice
To monitor effectiveness of supervision	To share experiences and skill appropriately

Source: Adapted from Proctor, 1988

These responsibilities, if accepted and acted upon, would ensure that supervision forms an important part of students' continual learning and development. Practice teachers as supervisors have an important role to play in ensuring that supervision is of good quality. Good-quality supervision helps students to become critical and reflective practitioners (Hawkins and Shohet, 2000). If students are proactive within supervision, this suggests that they are in control of their student life for maximum performance, and are thereby well placed to help service users to take control of their lives. This way of working sits comfortably within the framework of empowerment and anti-oppression.

Power dynamics need careful attention, because all students in training are vulnerable, particularly students who belong to marginalised groups in society at large, as illustrated by the example given earlier in this chapter. This vulnerability requires recognition and acknowledgement of power differentials between supervisor and student. These power differentials can be explored within the context of the equal opportunity policy of the agency and the value of anti-oppressive practice. Addressing the power issues as an integral part of professional development means that the impact of discrimination can be tackled openly and honestly. Students can be equipped with skills for future use as and when the need arises when relating to service users or colleagues. The openness with which the subject of discrimination is tackled can enable students to appreciate how liberating anti-oppressive practice can be. Anti-oppressive practitioners are able to make judgements that are based on careful and thorough assessment of the specific realities of a given situation (Dominelli, 2002a, 2002b). The following is an example of that:

A student with limited hearing and an excellent lip-reading ability informed her tutor that she would want to be allowed to take charge of when to disclose her disability to those service users she would be working with on placement. Initial concerns were expressed by the placement agency about potential impact if people were not informed in good time to enable them to relate appropriately in the process of engagement. This student used her university's stated position on equal opportunities and the importance of promoting anti-oppression and empowering service users as a basis for clearly articulating her needs.

The student clearly placed herself within the context of a university service user and asked to be supported in her decision. Fortunately for this student, all her requests, which were not unreasonable, were accommodated.

Her fieldwork experience was a success. The fears that had been expressed initially by the placement agency were not realised. The student's engagement with service users was exemplary. Sensitivity to the student's needs and preparedness to adapt practices to suit her specifications contributed towards a successful outcome. The course team and the placement agency team gained additional knowledge from working with this student.

The student was aware of the discriminatory nature of the existing structures and practices but was able to negotiate her way through them for a successful outcome.

This example illustrates what can be achieved through negotiation, even where a student identifies discriminatory policy or practice within the agency in which they are on placement. The important requirement is that a support structure exists for students to raise and pursue issues.

When things go wrong

Things can go wrong for students on practice placements at any stage of the process. It is therefore important to have in place procedures to deal with placement-related problems as they arise. In most cases the problems can be sorted through discussion involving the student, the practice teacher and the tutor, or through re-negotiation of the learning contract. If the problem cannot be resolved, it may be decided that the placement has broken down and the student should be spared further distress. An alternative placement would be sought and a new learning contract negotiated.

A useful joint exercise for practice teachers and tutors is to review the impact of equality policy and practice, both within the education establishment and the placement agency, on specific identity groups of students, for example those categorised by disability, gender or race. Sharing and discussing the analysis of the data could then inform change if needed, or confirm good practice that can be shared with a wider audience.

Equal opportunities tasks on placement

As part of their learning about equal opportunities and implementing anti-oppressive practice, students can:

- research a specific topic within the subject of equality
- discuss their findings with their peers, practice teachers and tutors

- use language appropriately to avoid causing offence
- be aware of what they do not know
- ask individuals what they require rather than avoid contact out of embarrassment
- be active learners
- adopt a questioning stance and continuous reflection
- make use of up-to-date evidence on the subject to inform practice
- remain open to alternative ideas.

This learning process can support students in gaining knowledge, skills and confidence. With confidence comes improved quality of engagement with service users from diverse backgrounds, leading to the delivery of good-quality service. This learning process is significant because local authority social services departments and health care trusts, as with most public bodies, have yet to mainstream equal opportunities. Individual employees are at different stages in their understanding of the best techniques that can be used to support anti-oppressive practice. Pressures of work have been cited as reasons for limited capacity for ongoing critical reflection on how to challenge discriminatory and oppressive practices. However, in this regard students are in a somewhat privile-ged position as learners and can ask awkward questions to stimulate constructive debate, in spite of the 'fire-fighting' nature of the working environments.

Practice assessment

Community nursing and social work students are assessed through portfolios. A practice portfolio is a collection of documents which provide the evidence that a student has or has not reached the required standard. The terminology used does differ between professional programmes of study. For example, UKCC (2001) refers to 'core learning outcomes', while the National Occupational Standards for social work refer to 'key roles'. However, for both programmes students are required to produce evidence to support the level of competence achieved. The competences include students' knowledge of the nature of discrimination within the UK and knowledge of how equal opportunities policies inform anti-oppressive practice.

Social work students must satisfy the core values requirements as follows:

- identify and question own values and prejudices and their implications for practice
- respect and value uniqueness and diversity and recognise and build on strengths
- promote people's rights to choice, privacy, confidentiality and protection, while recognising and addressing the complexities of competing rights and demands
- assist people to increase control of and improve the quality of their lives, while recog-nising that control will be required at times in order to protect children and adults from harm

- identify, analyse and take action to counter discrimination, racism, disadvantage, inequality and injustice, using strategies appropriate to role and context
- practise in a manner that does not stigmatise or disadvantage individuals, groups or communities.

These core values requirements can be cross-referenced to the broad equality objectives for community nursing students, confirming similarities across professional groups while accepting the differences in emphasis in relation to specific jobs or tasks.

Students prepare reflective accounts of practice linked to each key role and the associated pieces of evidence. Within these reflective accounts, students should demonstrate how the value requirements are integrated into their practice with particular attention to anti-racist and anti-discriminatory practice. If practice supervision is effective, producing the evidence and reflective accounts should produce no surprises, because problems would have been dealt with as an ongoing process, in preparation for the final assessment.

These values are comprehensive and laudable, and students do work very hard to produce the evidence to demonstrate how these values inform their practice. Service-user feedback generally confirms that students practise in an anti-oppressive manner. However, in some instances, students may not have opportunities for first-hand experience of working with individuals from particular communities, and their ability to engage effectively in future, post qualification, may be questioned. Countering racism and racial discrimination is one such area when there is lack of exposure to BME groups. Perhaps the important point for practice teachers and tutors is to support students with workable strategies that are likely to produce the desired effect, while acknowledging that there is no one best way because every situation is unique and contextual. Giving appropriate support to students assumes knowledgeability and competence on the part of practice teachers and tutors. Similar issues are being raised within nursing and midwifery contexts and research is underway to try to establish what is required within curriculum content and practice placements to equip nurses and midwives for working in multi-ethnic Britain (Gerrish et al., 1996).

Exercise

What methods do you think might be employed to teach students about anti-racism if there is little or no opportunity offered by the placement for contact with BME clients?

Might these methods also be introduced in relation to other identities that are under-represented?

Some of the points raised in Chapter 4, about limited progress on the implementation of equal opportunities policies within public authorities such as social services departments, contribute to the concerns expressed by some students. If practice assessors, as practitioners, are operating within structures that are not conducive to the realisation of equal opportunities, what do they tell students? This concern is compounded by the fact that practice-teacher training is being phased out. Student supervision and assessment are to be the responsibility of experienced social workers, but this will be at a time when many practitioners still find themselves operating institutionally discriminatory procedures created by their employers. How realistic is it to expect that front-line social workers will challenge their employers on discriminatory service structures while giving due attention to the needs of students?

Overall, the codes of practice and the set of core values provide a sound base from which students can develop their anti-oppressive practice and feel confident that the evidence presented in their portfolios will meet practice requirements. They can use this framework to critically evaluate the work of placement agencies and offer feedback. Learning organisations ought to welcome feedback from students and act on it in order to improve their effectiveness.

Monitoring and evaluation

Universities and colleges do formally monitor the quality of practice learning and teaching, and students are encouraged to be honest. The feedback from students is used to improve the service to the students across the spectrum of processes and experiences. Confidentiality is guaranteed to all respondents. The main areas on which students are asked to give feedback include:

* how the learning contract was adhered to in relation to anti-oppressive practice as well as gaps in relating theory and practice
* how the student was supported
* frequency and quality of supervision
* achievement of learning objectives
* suggestions for improvements.

For each one of these areas, equal opportunities thinking provides an overarching framework from which students can give constructive feedback and suggestions for improvements.

The analysed information feeds into the cycle of searching for and approving placements. It is expected that for most students, the process of evaluation can help them to reflect further on their overall fieldwork experience and the extent of their learning as they progress to the next level of their training or join the graduate labour market.

Using a themed approach and practice examples, this chapter has described the value of fieldwork practice for students on professional programmes of study, focusing on some of the essential processes involved and some of the difficulties that can arise with regards to equal opportunities and anti-oppressive practice.

Summary

- Practice placements are a valuable vehicle for demonstrating anti-oppressive practice.
- Vetting practice placements for institutional discrimination is important.
- Students' learning contracts are important to ensure appropriate practice and support.
- Student supervision is vital and requires careful planning.
- Ongoing review of the learning contract is necessary, including the possibility of termination if things go wrong.
- Students' placement evaluations are important in reviewing placement effectiveness.

10

Examples of Personal Plans

Aim

- To illustrate personal plans for anti-oppressive practice drawn up by students.

As described in Chapter 8, an assignment for social work students at Reading University is to prepare a personal plan for anti-oppressive practice. This assignment is due during a practice placement, and students may, if they wish, relate the plan to their placement, with the advantage that it can contribute to their portfolio of evidence. On the other hand, students may make the plan more general and consider issues for their future career after graduating. This chapter gives illustrations of plans that recent students have devised.

Work with children and families

(Extracts from a student's personal plan for anti-oppressive practice, developed by Jane Lynch, University of Reading, 2007.)

1. Pursue and Protect Rights and Use of Legislation

Long-term actions:
- Join organisations that canvas and campaign for children's rights.
- Encourage local authorities to sign up to policies that promote children's rights.
- Strive to amend existing and influence new legislation and government policies through above campaigns and lobbying.

Short-term actions:
- Research organisations that offer children support and are independent from Social Services/Government organisations.
- Compile a resource file of the above organisations.
- Make it an agenda item for team away-day to create a team process that promotes children's rights and relevant organisations to children and their carers.
- Volunteer as an advocate for children in care.

Current actions:
- Always seek the child's views, wishes and feelings.
- Provide opportunities and appropriate methods for the child to convey their views, wishes and feelings to those involved with them – professionally or personally.
- Advocate for the child when decisions are made that are not in their best interests; this includes at care plan meetings and court hearings.

Future actions:
- Make time on each contact with a child to raise the issue of their rights and discuss these.
- Ensure the children I have contact with have access to age-appropriate information surrounding their rights.
- Draw colleagues' attention to resources on children's rights.
- Highlight children's rights through the training I deliver.

Actions re personal relationships and interactions:
- Recognise, welcome and appreciate and absorb information about diversity and individuality when meeting people, and interpret and relate these differences to children's rights.

Actions to improve the service I work in:
- Deliver training to service colleagues across the county, in both social services and education departments, that promotes children's rights.
- Keep children's rights on the agenda by attending strategic meetings and making use of communication events and systems.

Actions to improve the organisation I work for:
- Deliver training to organisation colleagues across the county, in both social services and education departments, that promotes children's rights.
- Write articles for internal publications.

Actions to improve social acceptance:
- Be a good role model to all those I come into contact with.
- Empower children to stand up for their rights.
- Display posters in the public areas that I work within, which highlight children's rights.
- Write articles for local and national publications.
- Raise awareness of children's rights through workshops and giving talks at community organisations, e.g. women's institutes, lions clubs, religious meetings, etc.

2. Management of Power Relations, Empowerment and Advocacy

Long-term actions:
- Create review consultation documents that are child friendly and age-appropriate.
- Join independent advocacy service for children and campaign for changes for children in care.

Short-term actions:
- Gather from teams across the county any resources they use to discuss reviews with children, and compile a resource file.
- Draw up a team-specific procedure for setting up reviews for children that involves them and highlights the need to ask and consider if an independent advocate is needed.

Current actions:
- Make available consultation documents to children to complete prior to review.
- Discuss with the child prior to review how they feel things are going.

Future actions:
- Contribute to re-designing review consultation booklets that are more child friendly and age-appropriate.
- When children are accommodated, make them aware of the review process and explain it to them and its purpose, and leave information with them.
- Make contact with local independent advocate organisations and establish links with the workers.
- Always ask (age-appropriately) the child if they wish to have an independent advocate present at the review.

Actions re personal relationships and interactions:
- Promote the advocacy service to fellow practitioners and foster carers.
- Raise public awareness of the life chances of children in care by spreading facts and knowledge in my social circles.
- Continue to build my skills in direct work with children.

Actions to improve the service I work in:
- Publicise through departmental publications and intranet the contact details for independent advocacy services for children.
- Encourage children in care to join children's steering groups.

Actions to improve the organisation I work for:
- Instigate the promotion of department-wide policies and procedures around children's involvements in their reviews.
- Promote empowerment of children and advocacy through the training I deliver.

Actions to improve social acceptance:
- If there is not one available, promote the need for a local independent advocacy service for children.
- Help to set up a local independent advocacy service for children.
- Join national advocacy service for children and campaign for improvements for children in care.

3. Cultural Awareness, Positive Imagery and Support

Long-term actions:
- Carry out an evaluative study of life-story books and their worth and impact on cultural awareness and positive identity.

Short-term actions:
- Create and use a before and after qualitative questionnaire when carrying out life-story work with reference to cultural awareness.

Current actions:
- Research and seek information from relevant organisations to obtain and provide cultural awareness.

- Experience different cultural features with the child, e.g. food, language, music, etc.
- Gather information from and involve birth parents in production of life-story book.

Future actions:
- Establish links with different cultural organisations.
- Expand my repertoire of approaches to life-story work to meet altering needs of children and parents of varying abilities.

Actions re personal relationships and interactions:
- Explore cultures of those I come into contact with.

Actions to improve the service I work in:
- Continue to promote culture and positive images in the training I deliver.

Actions to improve the organisation I work for:
- Help to develop a county-wide policy for life-story work, paying attention to culture, positive imagery and support.

Actions to improve social acceptance:
- Encourage life-story work for children other than those placed away from family, either as a home or school activity.

4. Welcoming Diversity and Equal Opportunities

Long-term actions:
- Become involved in the recruitment and training of potential adopters.
- Become involved with national adoption organisations to lobby government for consistent, open and fair national policies.

Short-term actions:
- Attend adoption information day road-shows for potential adopters.
- Explore how my placement team choose adopters for the child.

Current actions:
- Challenge individual practitioners' thinking and reasoning around adopters.
- Reflect upon my practice in assessing the adopted child's needs.

Future actions:
- Be creative and flexible in assessment of post-adoption support needs.
- Assess each child's family requirements individually and look for individual families.

Actions re personal relationships and interactions:
- Take time to get to know potential adopters and value their diversity.

Actions to improve the service I work in:
- Initiate debate on restrictions on potential adopters.
- Improve communications between teams.

Actions to improve the organisation I work for:
- Promote and encourage diversity at road-shows for recruitment of adopters.
- Encourage working with other local authorities on policies around the recruitment of adopters.

Actions to improve social acceptance:
- Attempt to influence marketing material used in the recruitment of adopters.
- Join adoption organisations and promote diversity.

Working with fathers in child protection procedures

(Extracts from a student's personal plan for anti-oppressive practice, developed by Paul Brewster, University of Reading, 2007.)

Area of practice to be considered:
- Initial contact with the father following a Child Protection referral.

Potential area of discrimination:
- It might be the case that the parents are seen as joint perpetrators of the alleged abuse.

Action to be considered to counter potential discrimination:
- Immediate: In such a situation seek to deal with both parents on an individual basis.
- Long-term: To develop a practice style which reinforces an individual approach to male partners as well as all other parties concerned.

Area of practice:
- Conducting an interview with the father.

Potential discrimination:
- Men might be perceived to be more likely to be perpetrators than women.

Action:
- Immediate: To carefully read all Child Protection referrals, to make sure that the issues/allegations are fully understood prior to making contact.
- Long-term: Undertake further research into the abusive patterns of men in Child Protection cases.

Area of practice:
- Ascertaining what part the father can take within the Child Protection Plan.

Potential discrimination:
- It is possible that the role of the father might be overlooked, especially if he does not live in the family home.

Action:
- Immediate: Take steps to ascertain the role, if any, that the father is taking. If it is active and positive, attempt to engage him and develop this further. Otherwise consider the use of resources such as Family Group Conferencing.
- Long-term: Consider the use of additional training to develop a professional understanding of the needs of fathers.

Area of practice:
- The participation of the father in the Child Protection Conference.

Potential discrimination:
- The father of a child subject to a Child Protection Conference might be reluctant to take part in it.

Action:
- Immediate: Offer advice and support with regard to the process of the conference. Also make available details concerning the father's right to be supported by an advocate (independent of any advocacy provided for other significant adults).

- Long term: Liaise with the Child Protection Co-ordinator to develop strategies to promote fathers' rights during conferences.

Area of practice:
- Enabling the father to deal with the decision of the conference.

Potential discrimination:
- As with the mother of a child whose child becomes subject to a Child Protection Plan the father might well consider himself stigmatised by the label that comes with it.

Action:
- Immediate: Reflect upon one's own feelings and ensure that any element of 'them and us' is removed from the practice arena. Consideration should also be given to practical information that can be offered to him and again it might be appropriate to empower him by reinforcing the notion of him making use of independent advocacy. Whilst it is accepted that society might be prejudiced against him because of his action, he should be supported in taking ownership of this.
- Long-term: Continually search for local resources and support that is available to fathers in such situations. Also challenge any anti-discriminatory language/behaviour towards this group, either from professionals or the larger community.

Area of practice:
- Supporting the father in coming to terms with the issues raised.

Potential discrimination:
- Assumptions might be made as to the father's ability to understand the process that he has experienced. Thus, not offering professional support, based upon a misinterpretation of his ability to cope.

Action:
- Immediate: Offer a one-to-one session with the father after, or near to the end of any Child Protection process so as to gauge his comprehension of the issues and consequences. Use this information to signpost him to appropriate resources. Such support should be tailored to the individual and could be presented through a variety of different media, so as to engage him effectively.
- Long-term: Work with fathers from this group with an aim to help them set up a self-help network within their community. One objective of this support should be to raise the awareness of the need for their participation and inform their expectations.

Professional work generally in health and social care

(Extracts from a student's personal plan for anti-oppressive practice, developed by Francesca Booth, University of Reading, 2007.)

Issue: Inappropriate language used within the team room about service users.

Action:
- Address this within a team meeting.
- Challenge existing behaviours within the team.
- Ensure all individuals are respected.

- Be aware of language myself and other team members use.
- Continuous personal reflection is needed. I would do this in supervision. In the past I have used supervision for personal reflection as well as taking on board advice on this subject. Supervision is confidential and it would be a good place to highlight an area such as language. This could make my manager aware of the language being used in the team room as well, as the manager sits in a separate office to the rest of the team.
- Feel confident in challenging this oppression within a group setting.
- Recognise my own values and challenge without imposing them on others.
- Encourage positive imagery of all service users with team, other agencies and wider community. I could do this by researching into a specific group, such as gay men, and giving a presentation in a team meeting.
- Acknowledge that language changes and recognise that what is 'politically correct' now may not be in the future.
- Promote the need for the use of positive language within the team and wider community.

Issue: The disadvantages that face service users with differing ethnic origins within a predominantly white, middle-class area.

Action:
- Apply the WISE principles in multi-professional working: W–Welcome; I–Image; S–Support; E–Empower.
- Acknowledge the impact of racism on both staff and service users.
- Service users to receive the same service regardless of their ethnicity, race or cultural background.
- Service users not to feel stigmatised in any way.
- All service users to feel valued and be proud of their background and beliefs.
- Challenge existing practices and ensure equality is paramount.
- Keep up-to-date on training about different ethnic cultures/backgrounds.
- Welcome diversity within team and wider community. Talk to colleagues about the positive aspects of diversity and the advantages of having a diverse team. Encouraging the growth of minorities in the team would be a good way of learning about other cultures and races.
- Empower service users to find support networks within the community.
- Think about how social care practice can disadvantage either directly or indirectly those from differing ethnicities/cultures. Ensure my social work practice does not stigmatise individuals in any way. I could do this by obtaining feedback from service users and colleagues about my practice.
- Direct service users to information available in the community, such as internet sites, libraries, etc.
- Assist service users in gaining the confidence in seeking help from official statutory agencies such as police, department for work and pensions, etc.
- Make translators readily available for service users.
- Promote positive imagery of all ethnicities within the social care team and other agencies as well as in the wider community. Again, I could do this in a team meeting.
- In my previous position as a family support worker, I worked with a Muslim family. I researched into the Muslim religion and culture so that I could understand their way of life better. This helped me relate to the family and provide support that best suited them.

Issue: Power dynamics – professionals using their powerful role inappropriately.

Action:

- Recognise that the role I am in is one of power.
- Be aware of the Human Rights Act and other legislation associated with my practice.
- Every service user to be aware of their rights.
- More support to be given within the family home environment – where service users feel most comfortable.
- Every service user to have easy access to an advocate or a legal representative so that their voices can be heard.
- Reflect on my practice continually. I would do this on my own and in supervision.
- Ensure that the service that I provide is needs-led as far as possible.
- Research the services that are available in the local community that would meet service users' needs.
- Work within current policies and legislation.
- Recognise the impact of power within relationships. Discuss this with service users if difficulties occur. Get advice from colleagues.
- Recognise that because of power dynamics within service user/practitioner relationships, service users may be at the receiving end of oppressive practice.
- Be open to change and take on new ideas and ways of working, so that best practice in services and social care is undertaken. I would do this by listening to my service user and taking advice from colleagues in how best to work in a certain situation.
- Help service users access advocacy services within the community. I would do this by firstly making them aware of the services available, for example giving them a leaflet on advocacy, and then supporting them through the process such as finding a suitable advocate for their needs.

Issue: Disabilities – service users being unable to access services.

Action:

- Be aware of current legislation, e.g. Disability Discrimination Act 2005.
- Work in a needs-led manner.
- Ensure that meeting rooms, etc. are accessible to those in wheelchairs.
- Ensure that easy-read versions of documents, etc. are available for those who need them.
- Ensure that service users feel supported.
- Increase self-esteem and independence.
- Encourage and enable full and equal participation in society for all service users.
- Keep up-to-date with legislation relating to disability.
- Never assume that a disabled person is unable to do anything.
- Good communication is essential to assess needs.
- Focus on positives, rather than on difficulties.
- Provide support that the service users feel would be in their best interest.
- Listen to what the service users think would help them.
- Assist service users in accessing advocacy services if needed.
- Support choice, and advocate for the family or individual.
- Ensure equal opportunities.

Issue: Lack of service user evaluation of practice.

Action:

- Ensure service users feel empowered.
- If the evaluation process is made as anonymous as possible it is more likely that service users will feel that they can participate in this process.
- Ensure that an appropriate feedback method is given to every service user, including children of an appropriate age, when work is coming to an end. This should include group work and individual casework, and when a change of worker is being implemented.
- Service users to be part of the social care process in which they are involved, by providing feedback.
- Make sure that the service users' voices are heard and taken into consideration when shaping social care services.
- Learn from service users' feedback – acknowledge that this will highlight areas of knowledge and skills that I lack.
- Always seek feedback after working with a service user.
- Promote the need for evaluation with my team. Do this at a team meeting and seek others' thoughts about the evaluation process and how best to conduct it.
- Ensure equal opportunities by providing evaluation forms in a form that each individual will be able to access, e.g. in braille, easy read or large print, etc.

Issue: Structures of health and social care services – inequalities for both service users and staff within services.

Action:

- Instead of working under a top-down model of intervention, it may be best to work from a bottom-up perspective, i.e. a needs-led service would be in place.
- Equal rights are paramount for all service users and workers involved in the health and social care services.
- Each employee and service user to have the opportunity to challenge existing structures and to be heard when challenging.
- Every service user to be party to changes in the service structure.
- Promote service user involvement in the delivery of social care services.
- Be aware of employment/training and promotion issues within services – challenge any discrimination.
- Think about how hierarchies within service structures disadvantage either directly or indirectly those from differing ethnicities/cultures.
- Challenge the lack of services available or language barriers that create oppressive practice.
- Recognise that structures within the service can often be invisible. Look deeper.
- Involve service users in decision processes where possible.
- Protect service users' rights through knowledge of their entitlements in law.
- Ensure equal opportunities.

Issue: Lack of choice/independence of service users.

Action:

- Implement Person-Centred Planning.
- Service users to take control of their lives and the services that they receive.

- Empower service users to gain support from their families and friends and circles of support.
- Always make sure that the service user is in the centre of their plan.
- I will encourage person-centred planning by making service users aware of the process and providing information on how they might be able to gain support in this way. I believe that this will provide an opportunity for services to adapt to service users' needs, preventing a top-down model of intervention.
- New ideas will be invented to try to fulfil the service users' aspirations.
- Be understanding and appreciate the need for choice for all service users.
- Research by reading policies and looking on the Internet at service users' perspectives of services, and learn from these.
- Assist service users in fulfilling their full potential by supporting them in gaining choice and independence within the community.
- Acknowledge what the service user has achieved and focus on potential and need.
- Give positive feedback to raise service users' self-esteem and empower them to continue to make changes.
- Support self-help and self-advocacy.
- Listen to the service user's wishes and feelings.
- Work in equal partnership with service users to seek solutions to their problems. Do this by communicating effectively with them, for example get an interpreter if there are language barriers, or a signer if the service user communicates in sign language. This will ensure equal opportunities.

Issue: Inaccurate recording of service users' details – marital status, dates of birth, ethnicity, religion, etc.

Action:
- It is important to establish all service users' true identity on files and on computer databases used in the social care system.
- Check details with service users when beginning working with a service user and their family.
- Make sure everything is recorded accurately to maintain and enhance service users' identities.
- Promote the rights of all individuals by recording information accurately.
- Do not pre-judge anyone on the information presented to you on file.

Summary

- Personal plans can be drawn up for anti-oppressive practice in a wide range of areas.
- Actions can relate to specific current tasks, or to longer-term or more general practice.

Part IV
Reflection

11

Assessment and Evaluation

Aim

- To present a series of questions that can be asked by a student or practitioner in an educational, health, social care or other human service setting, at three levels of anti-oppressive practice:
    - *The personal* – our own knowledge and actions
    - *The organisational* – the characteristics and performance of organisations
    - *The community-based and cultural* – fostering anti-oppressive practice within communities and society.
- The organisational and community questions can also be used to evaluate the student or practitioner's own experience within those settings.

The personal level

Becoming informed

We have argued that anti-oppressive practice is helped by becoming informed about people of particular identities – their history, beliefs, communal actions, writings, traditions, creative productions and so on – their 'culture'. Researching the facts about a social group at risk of oppression from others can help us to avoid stereotypes and prejudice, to support and advocate for members of the group, to show solidarity where appropriate, to have a positive image of the group, and to empower members of the group and treat them equally.

List some specific identities in some of the categories listed in Chapter 7 (page 115) that you are likely to encounter, or that you would wish to encounter, in your education, practice placement or human service work. For each identity ask:

- Do you know any sources of information about people of that identity?
- What do you know about the 'culture' of people with that identity?
- Do you know any of the language that may be used by those people?
- Do you know of any self-advocacy or self-help groups for those people, or representing their interests?
- Is there any additional knowledge that would be useful to you?
- What can you learn from people of that identity?
- How have people of that identity survived or protected themselves from oppression?
- Do you know any mechanisms for complaint, use of legislation or other formal action that can be taken to remedy any instances of discrimination against or oppression of a person of that identity?
- Do you feel you have rid yourself of stereotyped views, assumptions or prejudice about people of that identity?

Your own actions

For each identity, ask:

- How can you use your knowledge to make people of that identity welcome and put them at ease when you meet them?
- How can you convey respect for people of that identity, both directly to them and as a model to others?
- Is there any support that you can offer or arrange to enable a person of that identity to function equally in situations they encounter?
- How can you ensure that the voice of people with that identity is heard, respected and, where appropriate, acted on?
- What methods do you have of learning from people of that identity?
- How can you act in partnership with people of that identity?

Evaluation and learning

Ask yourself:

- How often do you review your knowledge and actions in relation to each identity?
- How often do you review your general knowledge of and commitment to anti-oppressive practice?
- Do you need to plan further learning and development for yourself?

The organisational level

As we have discussed in various places in this book, discrimination and oppression can operate within an organisation, through organisational structures and practices, even when individual people within that organisation are personally striving to be anti-discriminatory and anti-oppressive. It is therefore important to pursue anti-oppression at an organisational level as well as at a personal level. Depending on our role in the organisation, our power to do this may be limited, but there are pieces of knowledge about organisations that can inform our efforts and make them more effective.

What are the ways in which anti-oppression is pursued? Is there good access to the building, and good facilities for mobility and comfort inside? Are different cultures, religions and languages catered for? Is there genuine equality of opportunity within the organisation, and how is this monitored? Are people of a wide variety of identities welcomed and supported as required? Are people of different identities empowered to have a voice and be listened to within the organisation?

Within your organisation, you may need to decide whether it is best to try to influence the part of the organisation in which you are most closely involved, and are likely to have the most influence, rather than trying to influence the organisation as a whole. For example, seeking more effective support for disabled students on your course may be more feasible than attempting to change the policy of the whole educational establishment – though of course you may wish to attempt both.

A first step you might consider is to carry out a survey of existing practice in a particular area. You might count up how many people from ethnic minorities there are in different roles, as students, as service clients, or as employees in various positions, and come to conclusions as to whether the representation is appropriate or may reflect (however unconsciously) some discrimination.

You might join existing groups or agencies within your organisation that can provide a base for action that you wish to pursue, for example the Students Union, a Trade Union, a group for lesbian and gay students, a forum on minority ethnic issues and so on.

Within our organisations, we can explore the application of the WISE principles. We can review the use of different languages for communication and other aspects of a welcoming strategy, such as comfort, inclusion in activities, information for and mentoring of new arrivals, good introductions to colleagues and so on. We can review the images in our organisational environments, trying to ensure they are positive and representative. We can review the support given to people to enable them to function equally in social situations. This can include arranging interpreters, providing aids to communication or mobility, giving extra time for activities, physically helping or verbally encouraging people and so on. We can review whether people of particular identities have a voice to express their interests and any concerns they may have, and whether they are adequately included in contexts of decision-taking or influence. Even if people have these opportunities, are they genuinely listened to and their views respected and appropriately acted on?

Having found out what policies your organisation has adopted, especially those that are in writing, you may wish to comment on them and suggest further improvements. Equal opportunities and anti-discrimination policies, and complaints procedures are often being reviewed and updated by working groups, and you may wish to put yourself forward for membership of such a group.

The following information should be useful to seek out about your educational establishment if you are a student or employee, or if you are employed in, or on a practice placement in, a health or social care agency.

The organisation's knowledge

For each organisation that you are carrying out this exercise for, list some specific identities that the organisation encounters, or should expect to encounter. This can include your own identity, so that you are evaluating your own experiences within the organisation. Then ask:

- Is there sufficient knowledge of the 'culture' of these identity groups for the organisation to act with cultural competence?
- Does the organisation have a knowledge base available to its personnel to support cultural competence in relation to each identity?
- Are sources of information known in relation to these identities?
- Are self-help or support groups or other resources known about in relation to each identity?
- Does the organisation receive any input, for example evaluation of its service, from any of these groups or resources?
- Is it known within the organisation how to make contact with people of each identity in the context of recruitment or information about the service offered?

The organisational setting

The physical setting, location, neighbourhood, building design and décor of a human service can indicate respect for people of particular identities and can provide appropriate opportunities and facilities to meet their needs, or it can fail to do these things. For each identity you have listed, ask:

- How close is the location of the service to where people of that identity are likely to live?
- How good is physical access, including transport, to and at the site for people of that identity?

- Is the service situated in a neighbourhood that is appropriate to its function, and safe for users of that identity?
- Does the external design send out a message of respect and welcome for people of that identity?
- Do the internal design and décor signal respect and welcome for people of that identity?
- Is the service setting likely to be comfortable for people of that identity?
- Are the name of the service, and the terminology used to refer to clients, conducive to people of that identity feeling respected and welcome?
- What could be done to improve these things?

The organisation's practices

Are the language, demeanour and relationships between personnel and clients of that identity appropriate, respectful and welcoming?

- Does the organisation treat people as individuals without stereotyped or prejudiced assumptions about them?
- Is there any evidence that people of that identity are treated in a way that constitutes negative discrimination?
- Does the organisation correctly assess the needs of people of that identity?
- Is the organisation efficient and effective in meeting the needs of people of that identity?
- Does the organisation ensure full integration and participation of people of that identity?
- Does the organisation in any way stigmatise people of that identity, through negative imagery or behaviour towards them?
- Does the organisation provide support for people of that identity to enable them to function equally within the organisation, as personnel or clients?
- Does the organisation seek and use feedback from people of that identity about its performance?
- Is there any evidence that people of that identity are under-represented amongst the personnel or clients of the service, is this monitored, and is under-representation addressed?
- Does the service regularly evaluate its performance in relation to people of that identity?

The organisation's commitment to anti-oppression

We can find out what policies there are for anti-oppression. Are there any policies? Are they written down? Who devised them? Do they represent a minimal response to legal duties, or are they genuinely proactive and being reviewed and developed all the time? How are the policies disseminated? Does everyone know about them? What checks are made to ensure that people follow policy? Is training in the policy made available, and is it mandatory or optional?

We can find out what the structures and processes are to pursue anti-oppression within the organisation. Who sets policy, and how? What is the procedure for complaints, and how and by whom are they dealt with? To whom can positive suggestions be made? Who evaluates the effectiveness of anti-discrimination or anti-oppression policy, how is it done and how is it acted on?

Does the organisation provide access to resources for learning about anti-oppression – for example information about different cultures, religions and languages? How extensive is this information? Are there forums or discussions to explore or inform people about issues for people of particular identities, for example ethnic minorities, gay people, women or disabled people? How is information disseminated? Are there checks on the knowledge of personnel, and how effectively that knowledge is used?

The following questions can be asked in general, or in relation to people of specific identities:

- Does the organisation have an active policy of anti-discrimination and anti-oppression?
- Is this policy proactive and preventative, not just reactive to problems when they occur?
- Is this policy available and made known to all personnel and clients?
- Does the organisation have appropriate, user-friendly and effective mechanisms for complaint and remedial action about harassment, discrimination or oppression?
- Does a 'culture' of anti-discrimination and anti-oppression exist, and does it permeate the whole organisation?
- Does the organisation train and supervise its personnel in the knowledge base and the practice of anti-discrimination and anti-oppression?
- Does the organisation regularly update its policy on anti-discrimination and anti-oppression?
- Is the organisation open to outside scrutiny of its performance, for example by groups representing particular identities?
- What more could the organisation do to improve its practice?

A plan for your actions

Where you have identified any areas of need for improvement, prepare an action plan for how you might approach the task of facilitating that improvement.

There is a lot we can do as individuals to foster anti-oppression, but we are likely to be more effective – and less lonely – if we get together with others to pursue this agenda. Some years ago, a paper was written on achieving change in organisations called 'The myth of the hero innovator' (Georgiades and Phillimore, 1975). It described how most organisations will eat you for breakfast if you try to go it alone, and it advocated extensive networking to find and enlist like-minded people before you try to influence organisational policy or practice.

The knowledge gained of who in the organisation is formally charged with addressing issues of anti-discrimination or anti-oppression, and which colleagues are informally committed to achieving these, can help us to build up a network through which we can gain personal support and pursue action to achieve change.

Who are the people in the organisation who appear most concerned to develop anti-oppressive policy and practice? We can learn from these people, we can support them in their efforts, and they can be our allies in what we seek to achieve ourselves. People may have a formal role, as Equal Opportunities Officer for example. They may represent a particular interest within the organisation, for example the Students Union, or a gay and lesbian staff group. Or they may have an informal commitment to anti-oppression, being known through their actions or conversation to be active in challenging or preventing discrimination, inequality or lack of welcome.

- Who might you enlist as allies in taking action?
- Who are the best people to approach within the organisation to raise issues?
- How will you document and present your evidence?
- How will you present your constructive suggestions for improvement?
- How will you seek to minimise upset and conflict?
- Are you sure the people you will be advocating for agree with your judgement and your actions, and if not how will you ensure this?
- Are you the best person to raise the issues, or should you empower people to do it themselves, or enlist other, perhaps more experienced or skilled, people to do it?
- What outcome are you seeking, and how will you follow up outcomes of success or failure?

The community and cultural level

Developing a sense of community

As well as information about the organisations in which we receive education, are on placement or are employed, we can gain knowledge of the communities in which we live or have other activities. Knowledge of the communities in which we work, or from which our health or social care clients come, may be useful to us in being anti-oppressive in our work. Knowledge of the community in which we live will help us to contribute to anti-oppression within that community.

One useful area of knowledge is that of community organisations and groups. It is often thought that nowadays communities are crumbling and have few resources for self-support. However, a systematic listing of community resources can give a very different picture. For example, in the London Borough of Tower Hamlets, renowned for extensive poverty and social problems, a group called the Community Organisations Forum carried out a survey of self-help or special interest groups in the borough.

They found around 700 separate organisations, including 90 for ethnic minority groups, 33 for women, 51 giving advice or information, and 72 concerned with recreation (King's Fund Centre, 1988).

Kretzmann and McKnight (1993) suggest headings for assembling what they call an 'association map', that is, a comprehensive list of community organisations that may be helpful in building up contacts for and participation by people at risk of social exclusion (for example people with learning difficulties):

- Artistic organisations (e.g. painting, theatre, writing)
- Business organisations (e.g. Chamber of Commerce, trades unions)
- Charitable groups and voluntary organisations
- Churches and church groups
- Organisations for civic events (e.g. exhibitions, fairs, carnivals)
- Collectors' groups
- Community support groups (e.g. hospital friends)
- Groups for older people
- Organisations for ethnic minority groups
- Organisations for other minorities (e.g. gay men, lesbians)
- Health and fitness groups
- Special interest groups (e.g. pets, cars, gardening)
- Local government agencies
- Local media
- Men's groups
- Women's groups
- Mutual support or self-help groups (e.g. disability organisations, Alcoholics Anonymous)
- Neighbourhood groups (e.g. Neighbourhood Watch)
- Outdoor groups (e.g. ramblers, bird watching, local tours)
- Political parties and groups
- School groups (e.g. parent–teacher organisations)
- Community service groups (e.g. Rotary Clubs, Round Table, Lions)
- Social cause groups (e.g. Greenpeace, rights groups)
- Advocacy groups (e.g. Citizen Advocacy schemes, welfare rights, People First)
- Volunteer groups (e.g. Community Service Volunteers)
- Sports groups
- Veterans (ex-services) groups
- Youth groups

Even this is likely to be only a partial list of possible community organisations and resources that could be identified. Such community groups cater for common interests, providing self-esteem, welcome and support for members. Knowledge of them can help us to impart information about resources to those we encounter who may need or benefit from them, and direct contact with them will keep us informed about issues for people of particular identities.

Related to the collection of information about community groups is the gaining of a picture of the different identities, cultures, religions, languages and so on that are represented in our communities. The town where one of us lives, for example, is in an area that one might assume to be predominantly white, middle-class, with little presence of people from minority ethnic groups. In fact it has the largest population of Moroccan people outside London, a large long-standing Polish community, and smaller but significant communities of people from Bangladesh and people of Chinese origin, mostly from Hong Kong and Malaysia. These groups have well-developed systems and networks for the expression of interests and for support of members. They are generally very welcoming of non-members who wish to find out more, especially if they take the trouble to know a few words of greeting in Arabic, Polish, Bengali, Cantonese or Mandarin.

Within your communities, you may wish to make contact with particular community groups that represent particular interests or that support people with particular identities. Almost invariably, our experience and that of our students has been one of being very much welcomed when contact has been made with mosques, synagogues, temples, churches, chapels or meeting houses, with Irish clubs, community centres for ethnic minorities, deaf clubs, gypsy camps, self-advocacy groups of people with learning difficulties and so on.

- Which community groups or organisations might be of particular interest or relevance to you?
- Do those groups or organisations exist at national or local level?
- How can you find out information about each one?
- Should you consider joining any of them?

A broad view of cultural acceptability

One area of controversy in public debates around identity, culture, discrimination and oppression is that of integration into the dominant culture. Some people consider that separation of different identity groups in society stores up misunderstanding, stereotyped beliefs and prejudice that may lead to conflict. The mechanism we advocate for reducing this risk is for us all to become more knowledgeable about different cultures, beliefs and ways of life, so that we come to respect them and to welcome the diversity they bring to society. In this context, we need to have a broad view of what is acceptable. We often have such strong allegiance to our own culture that the culture of other people can be denigrated and considered inferior.

For example, in Western culture we have fairly standard expectations about the upbringing of children. We expect the focus of child rearing to be the nuclear family, with the child's two parents taking responsibility. We expect children to attend school, or at least be formally educated, from a particular age to a particular school-leaving age, with encouragement for further formal education after that. These things are culturally relative.

Different societies have different views and traditions about child rearing and education, for example (see Dahlberg et al., 1999).

A very wide range of practices can be considered acceptable if we have a broad enough view. In Western culture, babies are generally encouraged to lie on the floor and crawl about on the floor from a very early age. In the culture of the island of Bali in Indonesia it is traditional for children not to touch the floor for the first six months of life. If they are 'late' (in Western eyes) in crawling and exploring the environment, they have the advantage of having been carried, and hence of experiencing a greater amount of physical contact than Western children, during that six-month period.

Children's experiences can contrast greatly. For example, the children of the editor of *The Mother* magazine were still being breast-fed at the age of eight and nine years (www.themothermagazine.co.uk/extraordinarybreast feeding.html), and seemingly enjoying it with no adverse effects. In contrast, many children at the same age throughout the world are working, some-times with exploitation but sometimes with benefit (Hungerland et al., 2007; Liebel, 2004).

Learning about different cultural practices can give us tolerance and respect for the very wide diversity of those practices throughout the world.

- Which cultural practices would it be useful for you to know about?
- What sources of information are there about these practices?

Learning languages

As will have become apparent in various parts of this book, we are very keen on the learning of greetings and other useful words or phrases in different languages, as part of a personal strategy of anti-oppression towards people we may encounter. For health and social care personnel, who are likely to encounter people with a wide range of different first languages (though most, of course, will have English as well), it may be much more useful to learn a few words in many different languages than to know one or two foreign languages in more depth. Indeed, the most useful languages in which to know a few words are not necessarily those conventionally taught, particularly in the school system. Depending on our communities and circumstances, some words may be useful in: Far Eastern languages, such as Japanese, Mandarin, Cantonese, Indonesian or Thai; languages of the Indian subcontinent, such as Bengali, Urdu, Hindi or Gujarati; African languages, such as Kiswahili or Chishona; languages associated with religious identities as well as places, such as Hebrew or Arabic; European languages used also by people of South American origin, such as Spanish and Portuguese; European languages spoken by recent groups of immigrants to Britain, such as Albanian, Polish or Latvian; native languages of Britain and Ireland, such as Welsh, Gaelic or Irish; and so on.

If we take the trouble to learn some greetings in foreign languages, we need to overcome any shyness or fear of embarrassment we may have in actually using those greetings. In our experience, the benefits in terms of conveying respect and welcome far outweigh the occasional problem of using the wrong language or being misunderstood or one's motives being questioned. Use of greetings in other languages can play at least a small role in fostering good relations between different sections of our communities.

- In which languages might it be useful for you to know at least a few words?

Societal agencies

Our knowledge base for the fostering of anti-oppression at a cultural and structural level will be enhanced if we become informed about agencies, laws and policies that operate at a society-wide level in the context of anti-discrimination and anti-oppression.

We can learn about the content and purpose of legislation covering equal opportunities, racial discrimination, disability rights and so on, and the remit, policies and work of bodies that operate at a national as well as local level, such as the Equality and Human Rights Commission.

The media

Culture is largely sustained through the media: books, television, radio, newspapers, magazines, music, art, theatre, films, the Internet and so on. These media can transmit material that is anti-oppressive, or they can create or collude in prejudice, stereotype, oppression and ignorance. It is therefore useful to develop an ability to discern what is helpful and what is unhelpful. We would put it more strongly: as the ability to recognise the truth in what we read, see or hear.

Integrating anti-oppression into lifestyle

Ultimately, what we are arguing for is the development by each of us of a style of behaving and living that becomes naturally anti-oppressive. Welcoming and respecting diversity, and applying the WISE principles and other strategies for anti-oppressive practice, becomes second nature and an expression of our personality and values.

Evaluation and learning

Nevertheless, we must not become complacent. There is a need always to evaluate the effectiveness of our efforts, at all three of the levels of Personal,

Organisational and Cultural. Being anti-oppressive almost certainly requires a commitment to lifelong learning to improve our practice.

Alliance with people or groups at risk

Some of us may decide to express our anti-oppression through an active alliance with particular people or groups who may be at risk of oppression. For example, we may become closely involved in interaction with a local minority ethnic community, or we may join an association representing disabled people, or we may get involved in a campaign for better treatment of prisoners or asylum seekers. Many of our students are involved in voluntary work, for example in supporting people who have experienced domestic violence, or single parents, or children leaving care, or older people. At least one student corresponds with people on Death Row in American prisons.

Political and protest action

Anti-oppression is, of course, a political stance. It is about gaining more influence for, and better treatment of, people at risk of discrimination and oppression. It therefore requires action at a political level. This means clearly stating one's beliefs and standing up for them, arguing for them in public, and actively promoting good practice and protesting at bad practice. We may wish to consider joining political or protest movements for change: Amnesty International, for example. Some of us will have the courage to take to the streets in marches or demonstrations against social injustice and oppression. Others may work in quieter but equally valid ways, for example by contributing to discussion groups or using the media.

Conclusion

There are all sorts of ways in which we can promote and practise anti-discrimination and anti-oppression at all levels. As well as developing personal anti-oppressive actions, we can accumulate knowledge about the organisations we learn or work in, and the communities we live or have activities in. We can use this knowledge to include in our anti-oppressive practice actions that help to ensure better experiences for people in an organisational, community or societal context. We can work to strengthen the anti-oppressive practice of our organisations and communities as a whole. This can become part of the integration of anti-oppression into our whole lifestyle and expression of our personalities and values.

A motto we sometimes try to convey to our students is 'Anti-oppressive practice is fun!' But we should also recognise that anti-oppression is political and requires struggle. There are forces of human nature that militate against anti-oppression, as described in Chapter 1. Anti-oppression can thus be dangerous and arduous, as well as enjoyable and natural.

Chapter 12 will explore some of the complications of pursuing anti-oppressive practice, and the need for constant reflection, review and learning.

Summary

- Anti-oppressive practice can be reviewed through a series of questions at individual, organisational, and community and cultural levels.
- Individuals can develop a personal plan of action for anti-oppressive practice at all these levels.
- Knowledge can be developed of a wide range of cultural practices.
- Knowledge and use of the law and the media is helpful.
- Political alliance with vulnerable people and groups is necessary.

12

Reflecting on Experience

Aim

- To highlight some of the ideological complexities associated with anti-oppression.
- To suggest a strategy for working with and resolving these complexities.

This chapter revisits, highlights and analyses some of the complexities associated with pursuing and achieving the goal of anti-oppression. Reflection is encouraged on contributions that can be made to managing the complexities, thereby freeing up energies for change and better practice.

Differences in ideology

Anti-oppressive practice is closely associated with the concept of equality and yet this concept remains hotly contested due in part to ideological differences leading to varied interpretations of meaning. As discussed in Chapter 3, liberalism and neo-liberalism have different conceptions of equality and both ideologies continue to inform economic and welfare debates about acceptable levels of state intervention to reduce inequality. The debates about welfare provision and reduction of inequalities have shaped ideas about equal opportunities. As Bagilhole says:

> The idea of equal opportunities is at the core of social policy because as a discipline it concerns itself with the relationship between opportunities to access welfare

services and the outcome of particular services on different groups within society. (1997: 17)

State intervention to solve social problems resulting from inequality of opportunities would be seen by some as an appropriate duty of government. Liberalism favours some degree of state regulation without interfering too much in individual freedom and liberty. This line of thinking has informed equality and meritocracy debates, resulting in the development of policies and procedures aimed at removing barriers to equality. Institutionalising fair procedures has exercised the minds of many within the field of equal opportunities who wish to see progress through measurable equality outcomes. Health and social care organisations have followed this line, in order that merit is allowed to inform distribution.

Critics of meritocracy suggest the rejection of equality on the basis that it is the wrong focus. For example, Cavanagh takes a view that:

> if we just want to show that we don't want to see people's chances being affected by other people's prejudices – then we should pursue this idea directly, since equality is too clumsy and expensive a way of achieving it. (2002: 145)

If the focus were to shift away from thinking equality, to pursuing issues around prejudice, then anti-discrimination law enforcement would need to have a much bigger and more robust role to play, because to date it has had limited impact. There is evidence to suggest that certain groups of people, while protected in law, continue to receive less favourable treatment (EOC, 2007; Healthcare Commission, 2005; Commission for Racial Equality, 2000, 2007).

An alternative view of equality is associated with neo-liberalism, as it rejects meritocracy and focuses attention on equality before the law supported by minimal state intervention. In this case the law ought not to be concerned with social and redistributive justice. According to this view, a minimalist state would serve society well as it allows for economic competition and for individuals to be responsible for their welfare needs through economic activity. State welfare dependency is discouraged, because it produces an underclass of welfare claimants. Minimalist state intervention is opposed by social democratic ideology which is based on the belief that the state can be used to alter distribution of resources for economic and social ends, and that inequalities can be tackled within a capitalist system by working towards fairness and justice so as to bring about a more equal society. According to the Equalities Review:

> A more equal society would put scarce resources to better use. The more evenly resources are distributed, the more likely they are to be used where they are most needed and to provide higher returns. In this way, they generate improved well-being, quality of life, social progress and consumption. (2007: 19)

This argument for equality puts the emphasis on tackling social inequalities through social policies, and therefore advocates collective provision of welfare as opposed to the trickle-down effect of individual endeavour.

An important point to note along this equality journey is that, despite the different ideological positions, successive Conservative and Labour governments, post-Second World War, have retained the main infrastructure of the welfare state. In this regard, Powell and Hewitt suggest that:

> a welfare state is a state in which organised power is deliberately used in an effort to modify the play of market forces in at least three directions – first by guaranteeing individuals and families a minimum income irrespective of the market of their work or property; second, by narrowing the extent of insecurity by enabling individuals and families to meet certain contingencies (e.g. sickness, old age and unemployment) which lead otherwise to individual and family crisis; and third, by ensuring that all citizens without distinction of status or class are offered the best standards available in relation to a certain agreed range of social services. (2002: 6)

In this definition of the welfare state, health and social care services are major players holding responsibility for ensuring equal and free access, where appropriate, to their services.

The Third Way/New Labour administration at the time of going to press presents a critique of all the other ideologies by focusing on modernisation and partnerships between government, communities and commercial industry while still maintaining collective provision of welfare (Powell, 2002). Self-reliance, self-promotion and social entrepreneurship are all encouraged. The emphasis is on moderate state intervention playing an enabling function, at societal, group and individual levels, supported by ideas of rights, obligations and responsibilities. Critics of the Third Way from a radical socialist perspective see this ideology as having failed to devise a system of public investment for equality, by being too closely aligned with neo-liberalism (Rojek, 2003).

Ideological differences are likely to be reflected in the devising and application of social and economic policies. The way the subject of equality is dealt with will be complicated because of the diversity of ideas about the best way to reduce unacceptable forms of discrimination and inequalities. Therefore translating such complexities into a workable framework of anti-oppressive practice in health and social care requires imagination and ongoing creativity.

A way forward

Genuine service user involvement and enhanced use of anti-discrimination legislation could offer a possible way forward. In addition to service user involvement in planning and delivering care, students, practitioners and service users can share their perceptions of what is realistic and achievable in an open and honest way. It can be argued that lack of service user involvement, either by design or default, has probably been one of the key factors in slowing progress within the field of equal opportunities in service delivery and in the employment of practitioners committed to working in an anti-oppressive way. Tackling the role culture of professional demarcation that is dominant in health and social care is a topic that students could be encouraged to research with a view to identifying new ways in which service users can be involved as equal partners, creating a new culture of inclusion.

An inclusive culture would enable practitioners and service users to work together in analysing the organisational changes that would need to be implemented to create anti-oppressive service organisations. Using the legal requirement for equality schemes can act as a springboard, and the results of a systematic review of existing organisational policies and analysis of equal opportunities can assist in establishing a baseline for the following questions:

- Where are we now?
- Where do we want to get to?
- When do we want to get there?
- By what means are we going to get there?
- How do we know when we get there?

This approach follows standard strategic management ideas about planning for change. It is argued that if a systematic planning framework is followed, it can help those involved to be clear about what needs to be done (Mintzberg, 1994). The process of analysis can also assist people directly involved to have an overview of the work of the organisation, which they can then share with their immediate team members prior to finalisation of the policy. The new working structures which are likely to emerge as a result of joint working among different professional groups and service users ought to have those who receive care at the centre of operations, thereby creating a user-led service. The current arrangement of a systems-led service has so far failed to embed equal opportunities as an integral part of everyday practice.

Conclusion

This book has clearly illustrated the political nature of anti-oppression. This is a good thing overall because politics is a powerful vehicle for bringing about positive and significant change. The framework for helping students and practitioners to engage in anti-oppression politics is the codes of practice. Applying these is particularly important for health and social care practitioners who work with vulnerable people who need protection from oppression. We have argued that problems have remained unchallenged in health and social care because it has been assumed that caring people would not oppress those in their charge. However, when discrimination has been identified and caring professionals have been asked to change their behaviour, resistance has been stiff, confirming that those within the caring professions are just as capable of being oppressive as those outside. In addition to a lack of vigilance, the organisational cultures dominant in health and social care tend to serve the powerful well and not the vulnerable. Service users have never been fully involved in designing the systems currently in operation. They have been expected to fit in with what's there.

Anti-oppression politics must address this imbalance of power. Targeted use of anti-discrimination laws to inform anti-oppression politics is beneficial and there should be commitment to this. After all, respect for the rule of law is a societal value that has stood the test of time and is incorporated into the professional codes of conduct. Finally, for anti-oppressive practice to become the norm, there needs to be a cultural change and for respect to be afforded to every individual, because to be respectful is to be anti-oppressive.

Summary

- Ideological differences inform the diversity of ideas about anti-oppressive practice in health and social care.
- The complexities resulting from ideological differences can engender creativity to produce positive outcomes.
- The anti-discrimination legal framework can support and complement professional codes of practice in developing anti-oppressive practice.
- The imbalance of power between professionals and service users must be addressed.
- Reflective health and social care practitioners can develop knowledge and skills to assess and evaluate progress and take remedial action as required.
- This book has presented a range of practical approaches to a political stance of anti-oppression.

References

Abberley, P. (1987) The concept of oppression and the development of a social theory of disability. *Disability, Handicap & Society, 2*, 5–19.

Adams, R. (2003) *Social Work and Empowerment*, 3rd edn. Basingstoke: Palgrave Macmillan.

African Rights (1995) *Rwanda: Death, Despair and Defiance*. London: African Rights.

Agnew, T. (1998) Survey finds failure in NHS equality practice. *Health Service Journal, 108*(5621), 2.

Alcock, P. (2003) *Social Policy in Britain: Themes and Issues*, 2nd edn. Basingstoke: Palgrave Macmillan.

Alyson, S. (ed.) (1993) *The Alyson Almanac: The Fact Book of the Lesbian and Gay Community*. New York: Alyson.

Anionwu, E. (2005) Review: the experiences of overseas black and minority ethnic registered nurses in an English hospital – a phenomenological study. *Journal of Research in Nursing, 10*, 473–4.

Anonymous (2005) *A Woman in Berlin*. London: Virago.

Arblaster, A. (1984) *The Rise and Decline of Western Liberalism*. Oxford: Blackwell.

Arredondo, P. (1996) *Successful Diversity Management Initiatives*. London: Sage.

Asamoah, Y. (ed.) (1996) *Innovations in Delivering Culturally Sensitive Social Work Services*. New York: Haworth Press.

Ashrif, S. (2002) Questioning models of anti-oppressive practice. Paper available from Student Youth Work Online (http://youthworkcentral.tripod.com/aopmod.htm).

Auluck, R. (2001) *The Management of Diversity: The UK Civil Service Journey Continues*. London: Civil Service College Directorate.

Ausubel, N. (1984) *Pictorial History of the Jewish People*. London: Robson.

Bagilhole, B. (1997) *Equal Opportunities and Social Policy*. London: Longman.

Barnett, R. (1997) *Higher Education: A Critical Business*. Buckingham: Open University Press.

Barrett, L. (1998) *The Rastafarians*. Boston, MA: Beacon Press.

Barry, B. (2005) *Why Social Justice Matters*. Cambridge: Polity Press.

Bateman, N. (2000) *Advocacy Skills for Health and Social Care Professionals*. London: Jessica Kingsley.

Bauby, J.-D. (1998) *The Diving-Bell and the Butterfly*. London: Fourth Estate.

Baxter, C. (1988) *The Black Nurse: An Endangered Species*. Cambridge: National Extension College Trust.

Baxter, C. (ed.) (2001) *Managing Diversity and Inequality in Health Care*. Edinburgh: Baillière Tindall.

Bell, B. (1997) The performance of immigrants in the United Kingdom. *Economic Journal, 107*, 333–44.

Bennett, J. (2006) Achieving race equality through training: a review of approaches in the UK. *Journal of Mental Health Workforce Development, 1*, 5–11.

Beresford, P. (2006) Service users, social policy and the future of welfare. In: L. Budd, J. Charlesworth and R. Parton (eds), *Making Policy Happen*. London: Routledge.

Betts, T. (2003) Utah State University student ditches rent, lives in tent. *Brigham Young University NewsNet* (www.byu.edu/story.cfm/45896).

Bhattacharyya, S. (1988) *Genocide in East Pakistan/Bangladesh: A Horror Story*. Houston, TX: Ghosh.

Blakemore, K. (2003) *Social Policy: An Introduction*, 2nd edn. Buckingham: Open University Press.

Blakemore, K. and Drake R. (1996) *Understanding Equal Opportunities Policies*. London: Harvester Wheatsheaf.

Boud, D., Anderson, G. and Sampson, J. (1996) *Learning Contracts*. London: Routledge.

Bragg, M. (2006) *12 Books that Changed the World*. London: Hodder and Stoughton.

Brandon, D. (1995) *Advocacy: Power to People with Disabilities*. Birmingham: Venture Press.

Brandon, D. and Brandon, T. (2001) *Advocacy in Social Work*. Birmingham: Venture Press.

Braudel, F. (1994) *A History of Civilisations*. London: Penguin.

Brazier, M. (1991) *Protecting the Vulnerable: Autonomy and Consent in Health Care*. London: Routledge.

Browne, A. (2006) *The Retreat of Reason: Political Correctness and the Corruption of Public Debate in Modern Britain*. London: Civitas.

Burke, P. and Parker, J. (eds) (2006) *Social Work and Disadvantage: Addressing the Roots of Stigma Through Association*. London: Jessica Kingsley.

Butt, J. (1994) *Same Service or Equal Service?* London: NISW/HMSO.

Cabinet Office Strategy Unit (2003) *Ethnic Minorities and the Labour Market*. London: Cabinet Office.

Cahill, T. (1995) *How the Irish Saved Civilization*. London: Hodder and Stoughton.

Cain, P. (1995) The ethical dimension. In: P. Cain, V. Hyde and E. Howkins (eds), *Community Nursing: Dimensions and Dilemmas*. London: Hodder Arnold.

Cain, P. (1997) Using clients. *Nursing Ethics, 4*, 465–71.

Cain, P. (1998) The limits of confidentiality. *Nursing Ethics, 5*, 158–65.

Cain, P. (1999a) Controversial issues: a case for neutrality? *Nurse Education Today, 19*, 159–63.

Cain, P. (1999b) Respecting and breaking confidences: conceptual, ethical and educational issues. *Nurse Education Today, 19*, 175–81.

Cain, P. (2002) Cardiopulmonary resuscitation. In: K. Fulford, D. Dickenson and T. Murray (eds), *Healthcare Ethics and Human Values*. Oxford: Blackwell.

Carretta, V. (1996) *Unchained Voices: An Anthology of Black Authors in the English-Speaking World of the Eighteenth Century*. Lexington, KY: University Press of Kentucky.

Carretta, V. (2007) *Equiano the African: Biography of a Self-made Man*. London: Penguin.

Cassidy, J. (1995) Face values. *Nursing Times, 91*(43), 16.

Cavanagh, M. (2002) *Against Equality of Opportunity*. Oxford: Oxford University Press.

CEMS (2000) *Experiences of Minority Staff in Bromley NHS Trust*. Egham: Centre for Ethnic Minority Studies, Royal Holloway, University of London.

CEMS (2001) *Mental Health Needs of Young Black and Asian People in Slough*. Egham: Centre for Ethnic Minority Studies, Royal Holloway, University of London.

CEMS (2002) *Views of Minority Staff on the Impact of the Berkshire and Battle Trust's Equal Opportunities Policy*. Egham: Centre for Ethnic Minority Studies, Royal Holloway, University of London.

CEMS (2005) *Black and Minority Ethnic Representation in the Built Environment Professions*. London: Commission for Architecture and the Built Environment (CABE).

CEMS (2006) *Birmingham Mental Health Trust Diversity Handbook*. Egham: Centre for Ethnic Minority Studies, Royal Holloway, University of London.

Chu, J. (2004) God's things and Caesar's: Jehovah's Witnesses and political neutrality. *Journal of Genocide Research, 6*, 319–42.

Clark, C. (2000) *Social Work Ethics: Politics, Principles and Practice*. Basingstoke: Palgrave Macmillan.

Clark, T. (2002) New Labour's big idea: joined up government. *Social Policy and Society, 1*, 107–117.

Cohen, G. (1995) *Self-ownership, Freedom and Equality*. Cambridge: Cambridge University Press.

Coker, N. (ed.) (2001) *Racism in Medicine*. London: King's Fund.

Coleman, T. (2000) *The Railway Navvies: A History of the Men who Made the Railways*. London: Pimlico.

Collier, J. (1999) Tackling institutional racism. *British Medical Journal, 318*, 679.

Collier, R. (1994) *Watch Your Language: A Guide to Writing Gender Neutral Terms*. London: City Centre Project.

Collier, R. (1998) *Equality in Managing Service Delivery*. Buckingham: Open University Press.

Commission for Racial Equality (1983) *Ethnic Minority Hospital Staff.* London: CRE.

Commission for Racial Equality (2000) *Racial Equality and NHS Trusts.* London: CRE.

Commission for Racial Equality (2006) *Race Equality Schemes and Policies.* London: CRE.

Commission for Racial Equality (2007) *Report of Formal Investigation into the Department of Health.* London: Equality and Human Rights Commission.

Cook, M., Mills, R., Trumbach, R. and Cocks, H. (2007) *A Gay History of Britain: Love and Sex Between Men Since the Middle Ages.* Oxford: Greenwood World.

Cooke, L., Halford, S. and Leonard, P. (2003) *Racism in the Medical Profession: The Experience of UK Graduates.* London: British Medical Association.

Corber, R. and Valocchi, S. (eds) (2003) *Queer Studies: An Interdisciplinary Reader.* Oxford: Blackwell.

Coulshed, V. and Orme, J. (2006) *Social Work Practice*, 4th edn. Basingstoke: Palgrave Macmillan.

Cowan, T. (1992) *Gay Men and Women who Enriched the World.* Boston, MA: Alyson.

Cowden, S. and Singh, G. (2007) The 'user': friend, foe or fetish? A critical exploration of user involvement in health and social care. *Critical Social Policy, 27,* 5–23.

Cox, C. and Marks, J. (2006) *This Immoral Trade: Slavery in the 21st Century – What Can We Do?* Crowborough: Monarch.

Crisp, Q. (1996) *The Naked Civil Servant.* London: Flamingo.

Dadabhoy, S. (2001) The next generation: the problematic children. In: N. Coker (ed.), *Racism in Medicine.* London: King's Fund.

Dadrian, V. (1995) *The History of the Armenian Genocide.* Providence, RI: Berghahn.

Dahlberg, G., Moss, P. and Pence, A. (1999) *Beyond Quality in Early Childhood Education and Care: Postmodern Perspectives.* London: Routledge Falmer.

Dalrymple, J. and Burke, B. (2006) *Anti-Oppressive Practice*, 2nd edn. London: Open University Press.

Davis, R. (1997) *The Gift of Dyslexia*, 2nd edn. London: Souvenir Press.

De Bary, W. and Bloom, I. (1999) *Sources of Chinese Tradition, Volume 1: From Earliest Times to 1600.* New York: Columbia University Press.

Denman, S. (2001) *Race Discrimination in the Crown Prosecution Service – Final Report.* London: Crown Prosecution Service.

Department for Education and Employment (1998) *A New Contract for Welfare: The Gateway to Work.* London: Stationery Office.

Department of Health (2001) *Valuing People: A New Strategy for Learning Disability for the 21st Century.* White Paper. London: Stationery Office.

Des Forges, A. (1999) *Leave None to Tell the Story: Genocide in Rwanda.* New York: Human Rights Watch.

Disability Rights Commission (2006) *Equal Treatment: Closing the Gap. A Formal Investigation into the Physical Health Inequalities Experienced by*

People with Learning Disabilities and/or Mental Health Problems. London: Disability Rights Commission.

Dominelli, L. (1997) *Anti-Racist Social Work*, 2nd edn. Basingstoke: Macmillan.

Dominelli, L. (2002a) *Anti-Oppressive Social Work Theory and Practice.* Basingstoke: Palgrave Macmillan.

Dominelli, L. (2002b) *Feminist Social Work Theory and Practice.* Basingstoke: Palgrave Macmillan.

Dustmann, C. and Theodoropoulos, N. (2006) Ethnic minority immigrants and their children in Britain. *Discussion Paper No. 10/06.* Centre for Research and Analysis of Migration, University College London.

Ebrey, P. (1996) *The Cambridge Illustrated History of China.* Cambridge: Cambridge University Press.

Economist (2006) Not a black and white question. 15 April.

Eke, C. (2006) New immigration plan criticised for brain draining Africa and the Caribbean. *Weekend Black Britain* (www.blackbritain.co.uk/week end), 9 March.

Elam, D. (1994) *Feminism and Deconstruction.* London: Routledge.

Elsie, R. (1993) *An Elusive Eagle Soars: An Anthology of Modern Albanian Poetry.* London: Forest.

Elsie, R. (1996) *Studies in Modern Albanian Literature and Culture.* New York: Columbia University Press.

Equalities Review (2006) *Interim Report.* London: Cabinet Office.

Equalities Review (2007) *Fairness and Freedom: Final Report of the Equalities Review.* London: Cabinet Office.

EOC (2004) *Britain's Competitive Edge: Women Unlocking the Potential.* Manchester: Equal Opportunities Commission.

EOC (2007) *Moving On Up? The Way Forward: Report on the EOC's Investigation into Bangladeshi, Pakistani and Black Caribbean Women and Work.* Manchester: Equality and Human Rights Commission.

Equiano, O. (2003) *The Interesting Narrative and Other Writings.* London: Penguin.

Esmail, A. and Carnall, D. (1997) Tackling racism in the NHS. *British Medical Journal, 314,* 618–19.

Esmail, A. and Everington, S. (1993) Racial discrimination against doctors from ethnic minorities. *British Medical Journal, 306,* 691–2.

Feinberg, L. (1997) *Transgender Warriors.* Boston, MA: Beacon Press.

Feinberg, L. (1999) *Trans Liberation: Beyond Pink or Blue.* Boston, MA: Beacon Press.

Ferguson, I., Lavalette, M. and Mooney, G. (2002) *Rethinking Welfare: A Critical Perspective.* London: Sage.

Fernando, S. (2005) Multicultural mental health services. *Transcultural Psychiatry, 42,* 420–36.

Field, J. (2002) *Social Capital: Key Ideas.* London: Routledge.

Finkelstein, V. (1981) To deny or not to deny disability. In: A. Brechin, P. Liddiard and J. Swain (eds), *Handicap in a Social World*. London: Hodder and Stoughton.

Finkelstein, V. (1992) Revolution! A fable of turning tables. *New Internationalist*, 233.

Fox, K. (2004) *Watching the English: The Hidden Rules of English Behaviour*. London: Hodder and Stoughton.

Francis, V. (1998) *With Hope in Their Eyes: The Compelling Stories of the Windrush Generation*. London: Nia.

Frye, M. (1998) Oppression. In: M. Andersen and P. Collins (eds), *Race, Class and Gender: An Anthology*. Belmont, CA: Wadsworth.

Fryer, P. (1984) *Staying Power: The History of Black People in Britain*. London: Pluto Press.

Gaine, C. (1995) *Still No Problem Here*. Stoke-on-Trent: Trentham.

Georgiades, N. and Phillimore, L. (1975) The myth of the hero-innovator and alternative strategies for organisational change. In: C. Kiernan and F. Woodford (eds), *Behaviour Modification with the Severely Retarded*. Amsterdam: Associated Scientific Publishers.

Gerrish, K., Husband, C. and Mackenzie, J. (1996) *Nursing for a Multi-Ethnic Society*. Buckingham: Open University Press.

Gillon, R. (1986) *Philosophical Medical Ethics*. Chichester: Wiley.

GMC (2003) *Code of Conduct and Guidance on the Register of Interests for Members of the General Medical Council*. London: General Medical Council.

Goffman, E. (1963) *Stigma: Notes on the Management of Spoilt Identity*. London: Penguin.

Goodwin, N. (2006) *Leadership in Health Care*. London: Routledge.

Gottlieb, K. (2000) *The Mother of Us All: A History of Queen Nanny*. Trenton, NJ: Africa World Press.

Gray, B. and Jackson, R. (2002) *Advocacy and Learning Disability*. London: Jessica Kingsley.

Gray, J. (1989) *Liberalisms: Essays in Political Philosophy*. London: Routledge.

Green, C. and Chee, K. (1997) *Understanding ADHD: Parent's Guide*. London: Vermilion.

Green, G. (forthcoming) *The End of Stigma?* London: Routledge.

GSCC (2002) *Codes of Practice for Social Care Workers*. London: General Social Care Council.

Hall, S. (1997) *Representation: Cultural Representation and Signifying Practices*. London: Sage.

Hall, S. (1998) The Great Moving Nowhere Show. *Marxism Today*, Nov./Dec., 9–14.

Hanson, F. (2003). Diversity's business case doesn't add up. *Workforce Management*, 82, 28–32.

Harrison, S. (2004) Racism and the NHS. *Nursing Standard*, 19(6), 12–13.

Harvey, D. (2007) *A Brief History of Neoliberalism*. Oxford: Oxford University Press.

Hatch, M. (1997) *Organization Theory*. Oxford: Oxford University Press.

Haugaard, M. (ed.) (2002) *Power: A Reader*. Manchester: Manchester University Press.

Hausmann, G. (ed.) (1997) *Kebra Negast: A Book of Rastafarian Wisdom*. New York: St Martin's Press.

Hawkins, M. (1997) *Social Darwinism in European and American Thought, 1860–1945*. Cambridge: Cambridge University Press.

Hawkins, P. and Shohet, R. (2000) *Supervision in the Helping Professions*, 2nd edn. Buckingham: Open University Press.

Hayek, F. (1982) *Law, Legislation and Liberty: A New Statement of the Liberal Principles of Justice and Political Economy*. London: Routledge.

Healthcare Commission (2005) *Count Me In: Results of a National Census of Inpatients in Mental Health Hospitals and Facilities in England and Wales*. London: Healthcare Commission.

Hess, A. (ed.) (1980) *Psychotherapy Supervision: Theory, Research and Practice*. Chichester: Wiley.

Hind, T. (2004) *Being Real: Promoting the Emotional Health and Mental Well-being of Lesbian, Gay, and Bisexual Young People Accessing PACE Youth Work Services*. London: PACE.

Hodge, S. (2005) Participating discourses and power. *Critical Social Policy*, *25*, 164–78.

Honos-Webb, L. (2005) *The Gift of ADHD: How to Transform Your Child's Problems into Strengths*. Oakland, CA: New Harbinger.

Hopkirk, E. (2004) Priceless books ruined by arson at synagogue. *London Evening Standard*, 21 June.

Howe, S. (1866) *On Laying the Cornerstone of the New York State Institution for the Blind*. Batavia, NY: Henry Todd.

Hughes, C. (2002) *Women's Contemporary Lives*. London: Routledge.

Hungerland, B., Liebel, M., Milne, B. and Wihstutz, A. (eds) (2007) *Working to Be Someone: Child-Focused Research and Practice with Working Children*. London: Jessica Kingsley.

Hurley, S. (2005) *Justice, Luck and Knowledge*. Cambridge, MA: Harvard University Press.

Hutson, S. and Liddiard, M. (1994) *Youth Homelessness: The Construction of a Social Issue*. London: Palgrave Macmillan.

Iscoe, I. (1974) Community psychology and the competent community. *American Psychologist*, *29*, 607–613.

Jackson, K. (2007) A history of heroines. *Daily Mirror*, 8th March, p. 22.

Jaggar, A. (1983) *Feminist Politics and Human Nature*. Brighton: Harvester Press.

Jewish Social Work Interest Group (2000) *Jewish Issues in Social Work and Social Care: Resource Pack for Educators and Practitioners*. Newcastle: Faculty of Health, Social Work and Education, University of Northumbria at Newcastle.

Jewson, N. and Mason, D. (1986) The theory and practice of equal opportunities policies. *Sociology Review*, *34*, 307–334.

Johns, N. (2005) Positive action and the problem of merit. *Critical Social Policy*, *25*, 139–63.

Johnson, P. (1987) *A History of the Jews*. London: Weidenfeld and Nicolson.

Johnstone, G. (ed.) (2003) *A Restorative Justice Reader: Texts, Sources and Context*. Uffculme: Willan.

Jones, C. (2004) What I wish I knew: my own goals for anti-racist practice. Available at http://colours.mahost.org/org/whatiwish.html.

Joseph, A. (ed.) (2003) *From the Edge of the World: the Jewish Refugee Experience through Letters and Stories*. London: Vallentine Mitchell.

Joseph Rowntree Foundation (2006) Parenting and children's resilience in disadvantaged communities. Available at www.jrf.org.uk/knowledge/findings/socialpolicy/0096.asp.

Kadushin, A. (1992) *Supervision in Social Work*, 3rd edn. New York: Columbia University Press.

Kandola, R. and Fullerton, J. (1998) *Diversity in Action: Managing the Mosaic*, 2nd edn. London: Chartered Institute of Personnel and Development.

Karenga, M. (1993) *Introduction to Black Studies*, 2nd edn. Los Angeles, CA: University of Sankore Press.

Kemp, E. (2000) Partnership in the provision of education and training. In: R. Pierce and J. Weinstein (eds), *Innovative Education and Training for Care Professionals*. London: Jessica Kingsley.

Kendrick, M. (1994) Some reasons why Social Role Valorization is important. *International Social Role Valorization Journal*, *1*(1), 14–18.

Kiernan, B. (1996) *The Pol Pot Regime*. New Haven, CT: Yale University Press.

King, M. and McKeown, E. (2003) *Mental Health and Social Well-being of Gay Men, Lesbians and Bisexuals in England and Wales: A Summary of Findings*. London: MIND/UCL.

King's Fund Centre (1988) *Ties and Connections: An Ordinary Community Life for People with Learning Difficulties*. London: King's Fund Centre.

Knott, K. (1998) *Hinduism: A Very Short Introduction*. Oxford: Oxford University Press.

Kotter, J. (1990) *A Force for Change: How Leadership Differs from Management*. London: Free Press.

Kretzmann, J. and McKnight, J. (1993) *Building Communities from the Inside Out*. Chicago, IL: ACTA.

Krise, T. (ed.), (1999) *Caribbeana: An Anthology of English Literature of the West Indies, 1657–1777*. Chicago, IL: University of Chicago Press.

Kumar, V. and Kumar, M. (2002) Leadership effectiveness: an analysis. In: S. Bhargava (ed.), *Transformational Leadership: Value-Based Management for Indian Organisations*. New Delhi: Sage.

Kunstreich, T. (2003) Social welfare in Nazi Germany: selection and exclusion. *Journal of Progressive Human Services*, *14*(2), 23–52.

Law, I., Phillips, D. and Turney, L. (eds) (2004) *Institutional Racism in Higher Education*. Stoke-on-Trent: Trentham.

Lawrence, E. (2000) Equal opportunity officers and managing diversity changes. *Personnel Review, 29*, 383–401.

Levitas, R. (2005) *The Inclusive Society? Social Exclusion and New Labour*. London: Palgrave Macmillan.

Liebel, M. (2004) *A Will of Their Own: Cross-cultural Perspectives on Working Children*. London: Zed Books.

Lipsitz, G. (2006) *The Possessive Investment in Whiteness: How White People Profit from Identity Politics*. Philadelphia, PA: Temple University Press.

Lorbiecki, A. and Jack, G. (2000) Critical turns in the evolution of diversity management. *British Journal of Management, 11*(3), 17–31.

Lovaas, K., Elia, J. and Yep, G. (eds) (2007) *LGBT Studies and Queer Theory*. Binghamton, NY: Harrington Park Press.

Lucas, J. (1971) Against equality. In: H. Bedau (ed.), *Justice and Equality*. London: Prentice-Hall.

Lukes, S. (2005) *Power: A Radical View*, 2nd edn. Basingstoke: Palgrave Macmillan.

Mace, J. (1997) Soviet man-made famine in Ukraine. In: S. Totten, W. Parsons and I. Charney (eds), *Century of Genocide: Eyewitness Accounts and Critical Views*. New York: Garland.

Mackay, F. and Bilton, K. (2000) *Learning from Experience: Lessons in Mainstreaming Equal Opportunities*. Edinburgh: Governance of Scotland Forum, University of Edinburgh.

MacPherson, W. (1999) *The Stephen Lawrence Inquiry Report*. London: Stationery Office.

Madood, T. (2007) *Multi-Culturalism: Themes for the 21st Century*. Cambridge: Polity Press.

Mandela, N. (1994) *Long Walk to Freedom*. London: Abacus.

Martin, V. and Henderson, E. (2001) *Managing in Health and Social Care*. London: Routledge.

Mason, T., Carlisle, C., Watkins, C. and Whitehead, E. (eds) (2001) *Stigma and Social Exclusion in Healthcare*. London: Routledge.

Masters, A. (2006) *Stuart: A Life Backwards*. London: Harper Perennial.

McIntosh, M. (1988) White privilege and male privilege: a personal account of coming to see correspondences through work in Women's Studies. *Working Paper 189*. Wellesley Centers for Women, Wellesley College, MA (available from www.wcwonline.org).

Mencap (2004) *Treat Me Right! Better Healthcare for People with a Learning Disability*. London: Mencap.

Mencap (2007) *Death by Indifference*. London: Mencap.

Mental Health Foundation (2000) *All About ADHD*. London: Mental Health Foundation.

Menzies, G. (2002) *1421: The Year China Discovered the World*. London: Bantam Press.

Miller, E. and Gwynne, G. (1972) *A Life Apart*. London: Tavistock.

Miller, N. (1995) *Out of the Past: Gay and Lesbian History from 1869 to the Present*. New York: Vintage.

Mintzberg, H. (1994) *The Rise and Fall of Strategic Planning*. London: Prentice-Hall.

Mirza, M. (2005) Ticking all the boxes. *BBC News Magazine*, 12 December (http://news.bbc.co.uk/1/hi/magazine/4521244.stm).

Mor, C. (2007) *A Blessing and a Curse: Autism and Me*. London: Jessica Kingsley.

Morris, J. (1992) Personal and political: a feminist perspective on researching physical disability. *Disability, Handicap and Society*, 7, 157–66.

Morris, P. (1969) *Put Away: A Sociological Study of Institutions for the Mentally Retarded*. London: Routledge and Kegan Paul.

Mowlam, M. (1999) House of Commons, Written Answers 100810, *Hansard*, 30 November.

NHS Confederation (2005) *Positively Diverse: Quick Guide*. London: NHS Confederation.

NHS Executive (2000) *The Vital Connection: An Equalities Framework for the NHS*. London: Department of Health.

NMC (2002) *Code of Professional Conduct for Nurses and Midwives*. London: Nursing and Midwifery Council.

NMC (2006) *Policy on Valuing Diversity*. London: Nursing and Midwifery Council (www.nmc-uk.org).

NSCSHA (2003) *Independent Inquiry into the Death of David Bennett*. Cambridge: Norfolk, Suffolk and Cambridgeshire Strategic Health Authority.

O'Brien, M. and Penna, S. (1998) *Theorising Welfare: Enlightenment and Modern Society*. London: Sage.

O'Hagan, K. (2001) *Cultural Competence in the Caring Professions*. London: Jessica Kingsley.

Oderberg, D. (2000a) *Applied Ethics*. Oxford: Blackwell.

Oderberg, D. (2000b) *Moral Theory*. Oxford: Blackwell.

ODPM (2003) *More Than a Roof: A Report into Tackling Homelessness*. London: Office of the Deputy Prime Minister.

ODPM (2004) *What Is Supporting People?* London: Office of the Deputy Prime Minister.

Olsen, N. (2000) *Albania: An Oxfam Country Profile*. Oxford: Oxfam.

Orwell, G. (2003/1933) *Down and Out in Paris and London*. London: Penguin.

Owusu, K. (ed.) (2000) *Black British Culture and Society*. London: Routledge.

Pascoe, S. (2004) *Moving Onwards and Moving Upwards: A Study of the Impact of a BME Managers' Development Programme on its Participants*. Unpublished dissertation, Royal Holloway, University of London.

Payne, M. (1997) *Modern Social Work Theory*, 2nd edn. Basingstoke: Macmillan.

Payne, M. (2005) *Modern Social Work Theory*, 3rd edn. Basingstoke: Palgrave Macmillan.

Pearce, N. and Paxton, W. (2005) *Social Justice: Building a Fairer Britain*. London: Politico's.

Perez, J. (2004) *The Spanish Inquisition: A History*. London: Profile.

Philpot, T. (ed.) (2000) *Political Correctness and Social Work*. London: Civitas.

Picardie, R. (1998) *Before I Say Goodbye*. London: Penguin.

Pierson, J. (2002) *Tackling Social Exclusion*. London: Routledge.

Ploeg, J. and Scholte, E. (1997) *Homeless Youth*. London: Sage.

Pollard, V. (1999) *Dread Talk: The Language of Rastafari*. Montreal: McGill-Queen's University Press.

Pope-Davis, D., Coleman, H., Liu, W. and Toporek, R. (eds) (2003) *Handbook of Multicultural Competencies in Counselling and Psychology*. London: Sage.

Powell, M. (1999) *New Labour, New Welfare State?* Bristol: Policy Press.

Powell, M. (ed.) (2002) *Evaluating New Labour's Welfare Reforms*. Bristol: Policy Press.

Powell, M. and Hewitt, M. (eds) (2002) *Welfare State and Welfare Change*. Buckingham: Open University Press.

Proctor, B. (1988) Supervision: a co-operative exercise in accountability. In: M. Marken and M. Payne (eds), *Enabling and Ensuring Supervision Practice*. Leicester: National Youth Bureau.

Race, D. (1999) *Social Role Valorization and the English Experience*. London: Whiting and Birch.

Race, D. (ed.) (2003) *Leadership and Change in Human Services: Selected Readings from Wolf Wolfensberger*. London: Routledge.

Rawls, J. (1971) *A Theory of Justice*. Cambridge, MA: Harvard University Press.

Rawls, J. (2005) *A Theory of Justice*, revised edition. Cambridge, MA: Harvard University Press.

Rees, G. (1993) *Hidden Truths: Young People's Experiences of Running Away*. London: Children's Society.

Reeves, J. (1992) Things are puzzling. In: N. Blishen and E. Blishen (eds), *The Kingfisher Treasury of Stories for Children*. London: Kingfisher.

Restricted Growth Association (2007) Launch of p2bs campaign. *Small Talk*, Spring: 8.

Richardson, C. (2002) The worst of times. *Guardian*, 14 August.

Robert, N. (2005) *From My Sister's Lips*. New York: Bantam.

Roberts, D. (2000) *Kosovo War Poetry*. London: Saxon.

Robertson, J. (2000) *Don't Go to Uncle's Wedding: Voices from the Warsaw Ghetto*. London: Azure.

Robinson, J. (2005) *Mary Seacole: The Charismatic Black Nurse who Became a Heroine of the Crimea*. London: Constable.

Rojek, C. (2003) *Key Contemporary Thinkers: Stuart Hall*. Cambridge: Polity.

Rowden, R. (1990) Colouring attitudes: racism in nursing. *Nursing Times*, 86(24), 47–8.

Ruth, S. (2006) *Leadership and Liberation*. London: Routledge.

Ruthven, M. (1997) *Islam: A Very Short Introduction*. Oxford: Oxford University Press.

Saunders, P. (2000) *Unequal but Fair? A Study of Class Barriers in Britain*. London: Civitas.

Sawley, L. (2001) Perceptions of racism in the health service. *Nursing Standard, 15*(19), 33–5.

Schein, E. (1992) *Organizational Culture and Leadership*. San Francisco, CA: Jossey-Bass.

Schlesinger, A. (1999) *The Disuniting of America: Reflections on a Multicultural Society*. New York: Norton.

Schneider, R. (2001) Diversity now a business imperative. *People Management*, 3 May. (Available at www.schneider-ross.com/resources.press.php.)

Seacole, M. (2005) *Wonderful Adventures of Mrs Seacole in Many Lands*. London: Penguin.

Sewell, T. (1998) *Keep on Moving: The Windrush Legacy – the Black Experience in Britain from 1948*. London: Voice Enterprises.

Shakespeare, T. (ed.) (1996) *Walking Through Leaves: The Memoirs of Sir William Shakespeare*. Privately published by the editor.

Shakespeare, T. (1997) Foolish to feel ashamed. *Disability Now*, March, p. 14.

Shakespeare, T. (2006) *Disability Rights and Wrongs*. London: Routledge.

Singh, V. and Vinnicombe, S. (2003) *The Female FTSE Report*. Bedford: Centre for Developing Women Business Leaders, Cranfield University.

Snow, J. (2007) Giftedness versus disability: a reflection. Paper available at Enfys Acumen (www.enfysacumen.com/white_papers.html).

Society for Human Resource Management (2007) *The Glass Ceiling: Domestic and International Perspectives*. Alexandria, VA: SHRM.

Solomon, N. (1996) *Judaism: A Very Short Introduction*. Oxford: Oxford University Press.

Spencer, S. (2006) *Race and Ethnicity: Identity, Culture and Society*. London: Routledge.

Staines, R. (2006) Is racism a problem in nursing? *Nursing Times, 102*(10), 12–13.

Tackey, N., Tamkin, P. and Sheppard, E. (2001) *The Problem of Minority Performance in Organisations*. Brighton: Institute for Employment Studies.

Taylor, A. (2003) *Responding to Adolescents*. Lyme Regis: Russell House.

Thompson, N. (1993) *Anti-Discriminatory Practice*. Basingstoke: Macmillan.

Thompson, N. (2003a) *Anti-Discriminatory Practice*, 3rd edn. Basingstoke: Palgrave Macmillan.

Thompson, N. (2003b) *Promoting Equality: Challenging Discrimination and Oppression*. Basingstoke: Palgrave Macmillan.

Thompson, N. (2006) *Power and Empowerment*. Lyme Regis: Russell House.

Thompson, S., Shakespeare, T. and Wright, M. (2007) *A Small Matter of Equality: Living with Restricted Growth*. Newcastle-upon-Tyne: Newcastle University and the Restricted Growth Association.

Travis, A. and Rowan, D. (1997) Ethnic equality: a beacon burning darkly. *Guardian*, 2 October, p. 17.

Trevithick, P. (2005) *Social Work Skills: A Practice Handbook*, 2nd edn. Maidenhead: Open University Press.

Turney, B. (1997) *I'm Still Standing*. Winchester: Waterside Press.

UKCC (2001) *Fitness for Practice and Purpose: Report of the UKCC Commission for Nursing and Midwifery Education*. London: United Kingdom Central Council for Nursing, Midwifery and Health Visiting.

University of Reading (2006a) *Community Nursing Course Handbook and Portfolio*. Reading: School of Health and Social Care, University of Reading.

University of Reading (2006b) *Social Work Course Handbook and Portfolio Guide*. Reading: School of Health and Social Care, University of Reading.

University of Reading (2007) *Practice Portfolio Guide for Social Work*. Reading: School of Health and Social Care, University of Reading.

Vanier, J. (1979) *Community and Growth: Our Pilgrimage Together*. Toronto: Griffin House.

Vickers, M. (1999) *The Albanians: A Modern History*. London: Tauris.

Walker, L. (2007) HIV/AIDS: challenging stigma by association. In: P. Burke and J. Parker (eds), *Social Work and Disadvantage*. London: Jessica Kingsley.

West, P. (2005) *The Poverty of Multi-Culturalism*. London: Civitas.

White, T. (1998) *Catch a Fire: The Life of Bob Marley*. London: Omnibus.

Wilkinson, R. (2005) *The Impact of Inequality: How to Make Sick Societies Healthier*. London: Routledge.

Williams, B. (1993) *Morality: An Introduction to Ethics*. Cambridge: Cambridge University Press.

Williams, D. (1998) *Nobody Nowhere*. London: Jessica Kingsley.

Williams, P. (1999) An exploration of the application of Social Role Valorisation in special hospitals. *Journal of Psychiatric and Mental Health Nursing*, 6, 225–32.

Williams, P. (2001) Social Role Valorisation and the concept of 'wounds'. *Clinical Psychology Forum*, 149, 6–8.

Williams, P. (2004) Incorporating Social Role Valorisation into other contexts of needs assessment, anti-oppressive practice and the application of values. *International Journal of Disability, Community and Rehabilitation*, 3(1). www.ijdcr.ca/VOL03_01_CAN/articles/williams.shtml.

Williams, P. (2006) *Social Work with People with Learning Difficulties*. Exeter: Learning Matters.

Williams, P. and Dale, C. (2001) The application of values in working with patients in forensic mental health settings. In: C. Dale, T. Thompson and P. Woods (eds), *Forensic Mental Health: Issues in Practice*. Edinburgh: Baillière Tindall with the Royal College of Nursing.

Wolfensberger, W. (1969) The origin and nature of our institutional models. In R. Kugel and W. Wolfensberger (eds), *Changing Patterns in Residential Services for the Mentally Retarded*. Washington, DC: President's Committee on Mental Retardation.

Wolfensberger, W. (1972) *The Principle of Normalization in Human Services*. Toronto: National Institute on Mental Retardation.

Wolfensberger, W. (1992) *The New Genocide of Handicapped and Afflicted People*. Syracuse, NY: Syracuse University Training Institute.

Wolfensberger, W. (1998) *A Brief Introduction to Social Role Valorization*, 3rd edn. Syracuse, NY: Syracuse University Training Institute.

Wolfensberger, W. and Glenn, L. (1975) *PASS: Program Analysis of Service Systems*. Toronto: National Institute on Mental Retardation.

Wolfensberger, W. and Thomas, S. (1983) *PASSING: Program Analysis of Service Systems' Implementation of Normalisation Goals*. Toronto: National Institute on Mental Retardation.

Wolfensberger, W. and Thomas, S. (2007) *PASSING: A Tool for Analysing Service Quality According to Social Role Valorization Criteria*, 3rd edn. Syracuse, NY: Syracuse University Training Institute.

Women and Work Commission (2007) *Towards a Fairer Future*. London: Department for Communities and Local Government.

Woodward, K. (ed.) (1997) *Identity and Difference*. London: Sage.

Index

transsexual people *see*
    transgendered people
Tubman, Harriet, 141
Turkey, 13
Turney, Bob, 18
Tutu, Archbishop Desmond, 7

Ukraine, 13
United Nations, 120, 145–6
Universal Declaration of Human Rights
    (1948), 75

valuing of culture, language and beliefs,
    120–3
Vanier, Jean, 34
victimhood, 38
voluntary work, 196

welcoming attitudes, 116–17, 122, 131, 133
welfare state provision, 101, 200
West, P., 23
wheelchair users, 17
white privilege, 33–4
Wilberforce, William, 7–8
Wilde, Oscar, 143

Williams, Donna, 18
WISE principles, 116–17, 130–3, 195
Wolfensberger, W., 34, 36
A Woman in Berlin, 17
women
    achievements of, 6–7, 14–16
    attitudes to, 5
    labour market participation by, 96
    as priests, 15
words, use of, 28–9
working-class youth, 153–4
working groups on policies, 188
World Health Organisation, 142, 145

Young, Baroness, 14
young people
    with ADHD, 147–8
    from disadvantaged areas, 153–4
    and homelessness, 151–2
    at risk of offending, 18
Youth Action, 154
Yugoslavia, 132, 137

Zogu, Ahmet, 138

Research Methods Books from SAGE

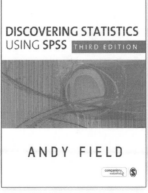
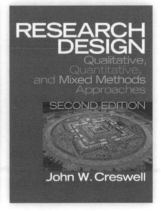

The Qualitative Research Kit

Edited by Uwe Flick

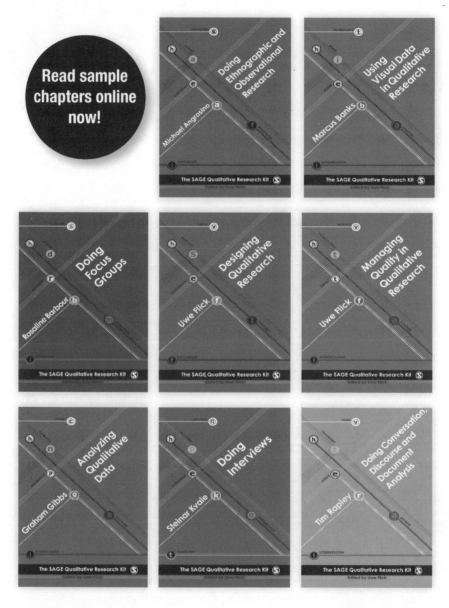

www.sagepub.co.uk